THOUGHT PARALYSIS

The Virtues of Discrimination

Farhad Dalal

KARNAC

First published in 2012 by
Karnac Books Ltd
118 Finchley Road, London NW3 5HT

British Library Cataloguing in Publication Data

A C.I.P. for this book is available from the British Library

ISBN 978 1 78049 052 6

Edited, designed and produced by The Studio Publishing Services Ltd
www.publishingservicesuk.co.uk
e-mail: studio@publishingservicesuk.co.uk

www.karnacbooks.com

THOUGHT PARALYSIS

Exploring Psycho-Social Studies Series

Published and distributed by Karnac Books

Other titles in the Series

Object Relations and Social Relations: The Implications of the Relational Turn in Psychoanalysis
Edited by Simon Clarke, Herbert Hahn, and Paul Hoggett

Researching Beneath the Surface
Edited by Simon Clarke and Paul Hoggett

Social Symptoms: The Role of Identity in Social Problems and Their Solutions
Mark Bracher

Losing the Race: Thinking Psychologically about Racially Motivated Crime
David Gadd and Bill Dixon

Relocation, Gender, and Emotion: A Psycho-social Perspective on the Experience of Military Wives
Sue Jervis

CONTENTS

ACKNOWLEDGEMENTS

I am grateful to a number of people who have read sections of the work, and variously offered encouragement and helpful criticism, which have significantly influenced the shaping of the book. Parizad Bathai, Dick Blackwell, Steven Clark, Simon Clarke, Naaz Coker, Andrew Cooper, Alison Donaldson, Sally Davison, Duncan Cox, Sue Einhorn, Lynda Haddock, Paul Hoggett, Oliver James, Stig Johannessen, Sue Kay, Stefani Kuhn, Liz Mason, Ali Rattansi, Otto Rheinshmiedt, Alison Shaw, and Ray Soper.

In particular, I would like to thank my old friend, John Bayley, and my wife, Angelika Gölz, for their commentaries and close reading of the text.

Some of the material distributed through the book has previously appeared in a number of journal articles: 2005, "Institutions and racism: equality in the workplace" *Soundings* 30, pp. 139–155; 2005, "The hatred of asylum seekers" *Mediactive*, 4; 2008, "Against the celebration of diversity" *British Journal of Psychotherapy*, *24*(1); pp. 4–19; 2008, "Thought paralysis: tolerance, and the fear of Islam", *Psychodynamic Practice*, *14*(1): 77–96; 2009, "The paradox of belonging", *Psychoanalysis, Culture & Society*, *14*: 74–81; 2009, "Skirts, sarees and sarongs: the rhetoric and reality behind the celebration of diversity in organisational life", *International Journal of Learning and Change*, *3*(3): 308–328; 2011, "Tolerating discrimination; discriminating tolerance", in *The Reflective Citizen* (pp.19–41), London: Karnac.

ABOUT THE AUTHOR

Farhad Dalal works as a psychotherapist and group analyst in private practice, and has done so for about twenty-five years. Now living and working in Devon, he is a training group analyst for the Institute of Group Analysis, London. He also works with teams and organizations as a facilitator and consultant. Until recently, he was an Associate Fellow at the University of Hertfordshire's Business School. He has published numerous papers on the subjects of psychoanalysis, group analysis, policy, organizations, and racism. He has also published two books. The first, *Taking the Group Seriously*, argued against individualism and for the relational nature of human life. In the second, *Race, Colour and the Processes of Racialization*, he drew on diverse disciplines to form his understanding of some of the causes of the hatred of others in general and racism in particular.

For Angelika

For whom I have provided many an opportunity
to practise the art of tolerance.

CHAPTER ONE

Introduction: thought paralysis

Over the past few decades there have been many heroic struggles and enormous efforts put into challenging the inequalities and iniquities endemic in our society, specifically in the areas of "race", gender, class, and disability. And, indeed, a great many positive changes have taken place. For one thing, the struggles have brought about a profound change in social conventions in Britain, so that it is no longer acceptable in polite liberal company to say dismissive or hateful things about women, Blacks, or lesbians; changes in the legislature mean that same sex relationships are granted official recognition—something that was unimaginable fifty years ago. Yet, it is also the case that despite these efforts, despite substantial changes in the legislation and so forth, the statistics tell us that racism and sexism continue to flourish; for example, in the 2010 season of the BBC Proms concerts "only 1.6% of the conductors and 4.1% of the composers [were] women" (Thorpe, 2010). But worse, in some cases *the situation has actually deteriorated*: two cases in point being the fact that the pay differentials between men and women have actually *widened* in the last year or two (Hencke, 2009), and the fact that in the five years from 2004–2009 there has been a 70% *increase* in the numbers of Black and Asians stopped and searched on the streets of the UK in comparison to the previous five years (Travis, 2010). At the same time, these very same institutions make proud claims in their Equal Opportunity statements that they subscribe to the values of inclusivity, fairness, non-discriminatory practice, and so on. They back their claims by pointing to the fact that they require all their employees to participate in "equality and diversity" trainings, in order that they develop more tolerant and inclusive attitudes towards others. Despite these efforts and claims, there remains quite a gap between what institutions say they are doing and what is actually happening.

The contrast between the achievements of the Equality Movements and the road yet to be travelled by them is found in two articles that happened to appear on the same day in the *Guardian*. A glimpse of the achievements are found in an article describing the return of the "Freedom Riders" to Mississippi, to mark the fifty-year anniversary of the first struggles against segregation. One returning veteran of the early struggles remarked,

> There are only two kinds of bathrooms now, men and women. The last time I was here there were eight: white men, coloured men, white women, coloured women, white men employees, white women employees, coloured men employees and coloured women employees. [MacAskill, 2011]

It is a testament to the achievements of the struggle that it is so hard in this day and age to even imagine that strict apartheid was the social norm in parts of the USA (and not so very long ago at that). Meanwhile, in the UK at that time, while there was no formal apartheid, virulent racism and sexism were the prevailing norms.

A glimpse of the road yet to be travelled is provided by the headline, "14,000 British professors – but only 50 are black" (Shepherd, 2011), which computes to just 0.34%. The headline speaks for itself.

So, how is it that, regardless of the enormous amounts of money and effort being poured into equality initiatives, inequality continues to flourish to the extraordinary extent that it still does? One explanation favoured by those on the "right" is that these initiatives go against "human nature" and so are bound to fail; they would say that the paucity of Black professors is simply due to their (lack of) ability or their poor work ethic. The book proceeds in a different direction. It attempts to answer this question by critically reflecting on the assumptions that formed the rationales of the equality enterprise.

And, while acknowledging successes of the equality movements, the work focuses on some of the dead ends that the equality project has found itself in, in order to learn from them. One reason for some of the wrong turns taken by some influential streams of the equality movements (particularly by those that "celebrate diversity"), is that they subscribe to a singularly impoverished version of human psychology as well as sociology.

The book will be arguing that the equalities project has floundered to some degree in part because of the machinations of vested interests, and in part because of the ways that the equality movements (particularly the "celebrators of diversity"), have conceptualized the problem (and the solutions that follow from them). At times these "solutions" have worked in the direction of reinforcing the difficulties rather than of dismantling them. For example, it turns out that both the racists and *some* proponents of multi-culturalism and diversity buy into the same essentialist premise, to believe that the "difference" each venerates is real and incontrovertible. The category beloved of the racists is that of "race", while the categories beloved of the multiculturalists and diversity promulgators are those of culture and ethnicity. But, peculiarly, the proponents of diversity utilize their category for the same purposes as the racists: to distance human groupings from each other in order to preserve their "authenticity". The racists do this by denigrating those who are different, and the diversity promulgators manage this by idealizing and fetishizing difference. Caught between the two, the casualty, often enough, is thought itself.

A part of my developing argument will be that racism and the other processes of marginalization (of which racism is but a subset) are, in many ways, analogous to parasites. Parasites mutate and evolve to mimic the functioning of the host in order to fool the host into thinking that that the parasite is a good and healthy part of itself. This results in the parasite dropping "below the radar" of the defence systems of the host in order to sneak into its body. Once ensconced, the parasite leeches on the resources of the host, depleting and weakening it, and often enough killing it off entirely. In some cases, like that of the cuckoo, the host is sufficiently fooled into *actively* feeding and nourishing the parasite to the detriment of itself. With regard to equality, this is the kind of situation we currently find ourselves in. My contention is that *some* of the processes of marginalization have mutated into forms that fool liberalism into fostering them and giving them succour, undermining its own integrity in the process. One of the more successful of the recent forms taken by these processes is the "celebrating diversity" movement. The central belief of the diversity movement, that you *must* respect difference, looks decent and innocent enough, but it is not. It is insidious, because it has fooled the host (democratic liberal society) into switching off its immune system, this being the capacity to think. How the processes of marginalization have managed this feat is, in part, what the book is about.

An anxiety and a caution

The danger in writing a book critical of *aspects* of diversity, multiculturalism, and the like is that it might be construed that I am against the emancipatory project *per se*. Further, the critique could be used to give succour to the racist, or those who cry "political correctness" in order to stifle and undermine challenges to the current order of things. So let me be clear on where I stand: unlike some right-wing pundits, I *do* think that there are many anomalies with regard to equality in our society. To my mind, there is no question that there are serious and very real issues to be thought about as to how and why only some "kinds" of individuals appear to make the grade and other kinds hit "the glass ceiling". All of this is beyond question and dispute. There is evidence aplenty that racism, sexism, and the like continue to flourish. For example, in the four-year period from 2005 to 2009, the Metropolitan Police Territorial Support Group (a specialist police unit) has had over 5000 complaints made against them for "oppressive behaviour". And of these, just 0.18% of the complaints were upheld; the rest were deemed unsubstantiated (by the police themselves). One officer has had thirty-one complaints lodged against him, of which about twenty-six were lodged by Black and Asian men. In other words, not only does racism continue to flourish, there seems to be very little real will to confront it by the authorities, and is, often enough, being perpetrated by the authorities themselves. But it is also an error to talk of the authorities as a "them", as though they were all of one mind. In this instance, the police force's watchdog, the Metropolitan Police Authority, is deeply critical of the Territorial Support Group, saying that "it's time for an ethical audit and thorough overhaul. They desperately need better training" (Lewis & Taylor, 2009).

Why training is not the answer to this sort of situation is something I will address later in the text.

So, while I agree with the equality movements that there are profound issues regarding inequality and injustice that need challenging, I disagree with some of the strategies being proposed as how to solve these problems. Some of my disagreements are at a fundamental level, not just with the solutions proposed, but with the very way in which the problems are being conceptualized in the first place.

I also want to distance this book from the many works emanating from the right of the political spectrum that mock and lampoon some of the suggestions and prescriptions put forward by the equal opportunity movements. Their purpose is destructive, to undermine the entire equalities project and to normalize prejudice, hatred, and bigotry as "natural" phenomena. To this way of thinking, the ones causing difficulties are the equality pundits and their ideologies and the poor victims are beleaguered Whites, embattled in their own land. For example, here is a scaremongering, inflammatory headline in the pages of *The Times*: "Adoption couples blocked by race barrier". The article begins:

> Thousands of families seeking to adopt a child are being turned away at their first inquiry, with hundreds told that they are simply the wrong race. One family in four was turned down, of which 13 per cent were told it was because their ethnicity did not match the children waiting for a home . . . [Bennett, 2011]

A little later in the article, the hint is made explicit: that it is White families who are being blocked from adopting "ethnic" children. I do not want to take up the issue of whether families of one colour ought to be able to adopt children of another colour. Instead, I want to focus on how mischievously the paragraph is crafted and what it invites the reader to think. At first read it seems as though thousands of (White) families are being blocked from adopting babies. But a second read tells us that one in four were turned down for a multitude of reasons, *out of which* thirteen per cent were denied because of their ethnicity. The arithmetic is simple: thirteen per cent of twenty-five per cent comes to just over three per cent. In other words just over three out of every hundred applicants were turned down because of their ethnicity—not as exciting as the "thousands" and "hundreds" announced in the initial sentence. It then also turns out that the "thousands" and "hundreds" referred to are not literal, but *extrapolations* from a research whose "sample is small". Surely the intention of the article is malicious, in that it seeks to foster and inflame the racist way of thinking.

So, although this book is going to be critical of certain lines pursued by the diversity and equality movements, my intention is not to attack in order to dismantle the equalities agenda *per se*. Rather, the intention of this work is to *strengthen* these emancipatory movements by critiquing their weaknesses, anomalies, conceptual confusions, and so forth. To use an arboreal analogy, I consider this work as pruning rather than felling.

To anticipate some of the discussion yet to come, in my view, racism at a systemic level and the like are not caused by "ignorance" or by psychologically malfunctioning individuals, but sustained and produced by power relations. The reasons as to why the situation has not progressed more than it might have are several. The first and foremost reason is, quite simply, that institutions and those in power resist structural change (not necessarily consciously) and find ways of apparently complying with equalities enterprise without actually doing so. The equalities enterprise becomes perverted into a paper exercise, the intention of which is to be seen to be doing good rather than doing actual good; the way that they have managed this is by stripping ethics out of the conversation and replacing it with bureaucratic procedure. Further, the diversity agenda has been hijacked by some corporations who purport to subscribe to the emancipatory project for justice but, in fact, exploit the notion of diversity to further enhance their profit margins. These, I contend, are the main obstacles to real change, but this does not let the equality movements off the hook regarding the ways that they themselves have contributed to this situation. The weaknesses of some of the reasoning from sections of the equality movements have created hostages to fortune that have been opportunistically exploited by vested interests, not only in the service of sustaining the status quo, but also of dismantling the equalities project entirely. Their wish, in contrast to mine, is to fell rather than to prune. For example as the book is going to press, the UK government is "consulting" the general public about whether *The Equalities Act* of 2010 should be scrapped entirely, or, at the very least, seriously curtailed because of the "red tape" it generates. It does create red tape, but that is its function, which is as an inhibitor of certain kinds of unethical activities, one of which is as follows. Ian Duncan

Smith, the Works and Pensions Secretary, wants employers to give priority to British workers over "immigrants" from Eastern Europe. But to do this would be to break the law as found in the Equalities Act. So, it would suit his agenda to have this tiresome bit of red tape removed from the statue books. Once freed of this red tape, companies can get back down to the business of favouring the "us" over the "them", and, astonishingly, being rewarded by the government for doing so. Duncan Smith's proposal is extraordinary for its naked advocacy of a return to a version of racism, with the key term changed from "Whites" to "British workers". It is exactly to prevent this sort of thing that the Equality Act exists. But it is also the case that the real problem is not red tape, but the business mentality that puts profit before any sense of loyalty, commitment, or community.

In sum, the fact that the book consists of a deep critique of aspects of the equality movements is not to suggest that the main difficulties are caused by them. The intention of my critique is to pre-empt the exploitation of conceptual weaknesses for reactionary ends. The argument of this book tries to tread the thin line between the apologists, those who deify otherness and difference (diversity peddlers and liberals of a certain persuasion), and the zealots, those who hate and vilify various kinds of others (racists and right-wing pundits).

Two short (schematic) stories and a moral

When Harry was about thirty years old, his promising life trajectory came to an abrupt halt when he was hit by a series of catastrophes. He became depressed. Unable to sustain an independent life, he moved back into the parental home. He began each day by switching on the television and playing computer games. When Harry's father, Jim, remarked to his wife, Sue, that he thought that their son beginning each day in this way was not helpful to his recovery, she rebuked him. Sue said that Jim had just made *a judgement*; she thought it wrong to make judgements about others because judgements *impose* something on them. In her view, then, the making of judgements about others is unethical and should be avoided at all costs.

Jim was troubled; was it the case that he was wrong to form a judgement about what his son was doing? Ought he instead to stand back and accept Harry on his own terms and rationales? And if so, what was Jim to do with his concerns regarding what he was witnessing? Jim ended up in a state of confusion and paralysis.

* * *

The other day, while taking a walk in the countryside along a river, I passed a woman speaking into her mobile phone. I noticed myself have the fleeting thought: her awareness is not in the present; she is not taking in the beauty of the setting, and instead she is preoccupied with something and someone elsewhere.

* * *

The first episode captures exactly the predicaments generated by the prevailing ethos being promoted by *some* multi-culturalists and celebrators of diversity. According to their pronouncements, it would appear that to make judgements about others is wrong *per se*, and instead one *always* ought to accept and respect what ever it is that "they" are doing because it is their way. This is because one's disapproval of "their" ways is born of a judgement made on the basis of "our" way, and so it has no legitimacy. If we are to judge them, we must do so on their terms, not ours.

Not only has this way of thinking become a taken-for-granted norm in many quarters of the equality movements, it is also the norm in the day-to-day life of many ordinary citizens (as Jim's story shows). Citizens with liberal sympathies learn to live lives that have the appearance of being compliant with the diversity ethos; they learn to silence their inner responses in order to be seen to do the right thing. But, as in Jim's case, they are often left in a state of bewilderment, confusion, and paralysis. The fact that disapproval is ruled out of court means that the question that can never be asked is, what is the basis of the disapproval? Is the disapproval an expression of, say, racism, or does it have some other, more respectable basis?

While the liberal citizen is often silent and silenced, there are untold others who feel no hesitation or guilt, or any shame, in voicing their negative views about various "others". They are not unlike the smug judgemental me on the river bank, who, in a subliminal flash, made a series of unreflected unsubstantiated assumptions, culminating in the condemnation and dismissal of the woman while rendering myself superior. This is an instance of judgementalism, and is indeed to be challenged and reproved.

The moral of the two stories show that there is an important distinction to be made between judgement and judgementalism, a distinction not kept sufficiently in mind by the equality movements. In their haste to challenge the *judgementalism* present in much human interaction, they have ended up vilifying *judgement* itself. This, then, is one of the key tasks of the book; it is an argument for the necessity of holding on to our capacity for judgement, and this is the thing: we need to be able to make judgements in order to counter the forces of judgementalism.

A culture of fear: another short story

It is also the case that a certain kind of fear has come to take hold in public conversations in connection to the marginalized and dispossessed, a fear that paralyses our capacities for discernment. For example, in the UK, the governmental agency called the Health Professionals Council has recently determined that "service users" must be drawn into all aspects of the work of health professionals: sit on interview panels, have a presence on various regulatory committees, and so on. The intention behind the suggestion is a perfectly sensible one: to bring the experience of the "user" to the attention of the "provider" so that the provider might better attune what they provide to the needs of the user. That is the background to the story that follows.

I was facilitating an event at which a team of health professionals were reflecting on their day-to-day practice. In the course of this conversation, it emerged that there was a shared *but unspoken* anxiety about asking the fundamental question: is it a good thing to involve service users at all? To ask the question was taboo; the fear was that to ask the question would be taken to mean that one was against service users *per se*.

A participant then described his recent experience of sharing an interview panel with a service user: the service user's behaviour during the interview had been difficult in various ways. It had been a terrible experience all round. But then, and this is key, in a later review of the interview process he found himself not voicing his actual experience and, instead, found himself saying that the presence of the service user had been productive. Several people identified with this "confession" and the conversation moved on to thinking about why it was that they found themselves "performing" in one kind of way in public while keeping their doubts and questions private. What became clear, then, was that they felt unable to exercise their faculties for discrimination and judgement to discriminate *between* various service users. Something silencing was taking place. In effect, the category "service users" was not only being treated as a single homogenous entity, but as a sacred entity. The result was their range of possible responses became reduced to two: *for* them (they are all good) or *against* them (they are all bad). There was no possibility of a more nuanced response to the differences *within* "them".

Another task of this work, then, is to examine and counter the culture of fear and anxiety of speaking one's mind, as this ends up working to the detriment of all. Interlinked with this task is the further one of understanding how and why "the one" comes to stand for "the all", both in the problem as well as the solution.

I should say that I, too, am not immune from the sort of anxiety just referred to. As I write about the problems with a particular service user, I imagine a wave of disapprobation (somewhere in the ether) rising up against me. It is difficult to hold on to the view that to criticize one service user does not mean that one has dammed all service users. This kind of conceptual collapse is continually to be resisted.

In search of Obamaland

Many people might think that a work on the subject of equality is redundant because the equality movements have completed their work. They see in the extraordinary election of Barack Obama to the presidency of the USA in 2008 the death knell of racism, and take it to mean that we are now in a post-racial world. They take the fact that even in the previous Republican administration, President Bush had already appointed two Black people to senior positions (one of them a woman, to boot), Professor Condoleeza Rice and General Colin Powell, as further evidence of the end of racism and sexism. They point to the fact that over the past forty years, many democracies have had female leaders, something unheard of until relatively recently: Margaret Thatcher in Britain, Indira Gandhi in India, and Angela

Merkel in Germany, to name but three. The new prime minister of Iceland, Johanna Sigurdardottir, is openly lesbian—a world first. A recent President of India, Mr Narayanan, was an "untouchable", something that would have been utterly inconceivable previously. So, when these sorts of facts are put together, we can see why it would seem to many that the equality movements have achieved their goals.

These "successes" are used by some to argue that the entire basis of the equality movements is fundamentally incorrect, in that they have misconstrued the nature of the problem. They reason that as some women, Black people, etc. achieve high positions, this is evidence that there is no "glass ceiling" and anyone can succeed if they just work hard enough. The corollary to this is that others do not succeed because they do not have it in them, or they do not try hard enough, or that it is a "life-style choice". This last is the extraordinary claim made in Anthony Browne's book, *The Retreat of Reason*, that "the cause of the gender pay-gap in the UK is not the result of women suffering sex-discrimination in the work place but because of their lifestyle choices" (Browne, 2006). More recently, Catherine Hakim, a sociologist, has claimed in a report published by the Thatcherite think-tank, the Centre for Policy Studies (2010), that the war for gender equality is over because it has been so successful. She is in agreement with Browne, and thinks that women gravitate towards low-paid jobs through choice. She concludes, "We cannot assume that a low percentage of women in higher-grade jobs is due primarily to sex discrimination". It is a life-style choice born of women having different aspirations from men; "Few women aspire to be engineers or soldiers" (quoted in Gold, 2011). In her opinion, the drive for equality actually harms women's prospects in the workplace. Reason has indeed retreated, but not from the places that the likes of Browne and Hakim have deemed.

The liberal ethos of the freedom to live and let live is under attack from fundamentalists of many different kinds. In consequence, there is a growing chorus of voices defending the principles of the Enlightenment and liberalism—a chorus I would gladly join. But here, too, there is danger. A closer look at some of these "defences" (e.g., Browne, 2006; Phillips, 2006) show us that they are the means of smuggling back in a great many reactionary attitudes which re-legitimate all kinds of injustices like racism and sexism.

For example, a normally sane colleague shouts out angrily: he will not be silenced! He has a right to condemn the Muslim practice of child marriage. I agree he has this right, and agree with his condemnation of the practice, but his self-righteous fervour is such that he has not noticed that a great many Muslims, too, find this practice abhorrent. Neither does he notice that some fundamentalist sects of other faiths (including his, the Judaeo-Christian) are also *for* this practice. What leaks out in his cry for justice is something akin to Islamaphobia.

Clearly, then, it is not the case that we are in a "post-racial" world, neither is it true that there is no racism, sexism, and the like. Untold statistical studies like those just cited show that there is still a great distance to go. There is ample evidence that the processes of marginalization continue to do their work in covert and overt forms, in all sorts of territories: ethnic minority households are almost three times more likely than White households to be in a poor neighbourhood (Institute of Race Relations (a)); the ethnic minorities appear to suffer from more "mental disorders" than Whites (MIND); in higher education the ethnic minorities are better represented than the general population, but then they find it harder to get jobs (Business in the Community); in the workplace unemployment rates for "ethnic minorities" are twice as high as for Whites (Institute of Race Relations (b)). The statistics with regard to women show similar sorts of patterns.

In sum, our societies are still riven by very real problems of marginalization of people perceived to be of a different kind. There is terror and there is horror; there is the destruction of lives and families, not only in war-torn Iraq or Bosnia, but also here, in ordinary everyday Britain, in neighbourhoods and workplaces full of genuinely decent folk (no irony intended). As these and other statistical analyses continually tell us, some "kinds" of people continue to do less well than other "kinds" in all arenas of life. As a character in Woody Allen's film *Whatever Works* says, we might have a Black man for President, but he still cannot get a cab to stop for him in New York. He could also have added that it is inconceivable to imagine that a self-confessed atheist could be elected to the USA Presidency today (although he or she is more likely to be able to get a cab to stop for them). We are a long way yet from Obamaland.

The celebrators of diversity

Increasingly, the solution proposed by some to address these iniquities is the celebration of diversity: let us not hate and fear those who are different; instead, let us celebrate our differences from each other, let us celebrate our diversity. The injunction has become ubiquitous, at least here in the West, and specifically the UK and the USA—the axis of decency. In some arenas, it has become so taken for granted that diversity *per se* is a good thing and that it *ought* to be celebrated that no question remains save *how* best to celebrate it. At least, this is how it seems from even a cursory glance at the goings on within public sector services like health and education on both sides of the Atlantic, and also within private organizations of all sizes—from minnows to megalithic transnational corporations.

On first acquaintance, the celebration of diversity seems a perfectly sensible and decent idea. But then, while reading a book on diversity in organizational life, I found myself hesitating and pausing as I read the following sentence: "Both approaches [to diversity issues] have strengths" (Hays-Thomas, 2004, p. 12). I had "stumbled" because my expectation was to read the more usual phrase: "Both approaches have strengths *and weaknesses*". As I immersed myself further in the literature on diversity, it rapidly became apparent that this was no slip of the pen, but an expression of a growing ethos, the ethos being that one should not criticize any point of view; instead, one should celebrate, understand, and accept all points of view regardless, else one would be being oppressive (recall Jim's story). It seems to me that this strategy is singularly dangerous, as ultimately it seems to be suggesting that the way to stop individuals *unfairly* discriminating, is to stop them discriminating *per se,* with the result that thought itself becomes paralysed.

The book looks at how and why this peculiar one-sided situation has come about (a situation that does more harm than good) to become the norm for those promoting equality and diversity programmes in organizations and society in general.

Two caveats and their consequences

The use of the term "diversity" emerges from the world view known as liberalism. In broadest terms, this world view is taken to be the bedrock of the beliefs and practices of democracy—our way of life in the UK.

Straightaway, I have to apply two caveats. First, that there are many versions and understandings of liberalism, some antithetical to each other; in other words, the notion of liberalism itself is imbued with diversity. Second, there are many inhabitants of the UK (and not just immigrant others) who would not identify with the "our" in the phrase "our way of life". But what I have just revealed, to myself as much as the reader, is that *I do* broadly sign up in some unreflected way to the ethos of liberalism, that *I do* consider myself to be part of this particular "us", despite being one of the immigrant others.

The phrase itself, "our way of life", is contentious and tendentious, because even while it lays claim to something, it manages somehow to exclude and de-legitimate untold others. It becomes immediately clear that my uses of "us", "we", "them", "the West", and so on will inevitably draw on a number of unspoken assumptions, assumptions that might well clash with your, the reader's, assumptions as to the nature of the "we" that is being spoken of. For example, there are some who would question whether I, as an immigrant (despite being in Britain since the age of twelve), can ever legitimately place myself as belonging within the British "us". To the racist, I (and my progeny) will forever be one of "them", and to the cultural essentialist. I could never get away from my true, essential identity, my Indian-ness. On the other hand, if I were to claim a continuing sense of Indian-ness, many would say that this is just nostalgia on my part, and, in the colloquial, they would describe me as a "coconut"—brown on the outside but white on the inside. So where do I belong? Which is the "us" that I may claim as my own? Is it really the case that this is an either/or scenario and that *I have to* choose between being *either* British *or* Indian?

Stepping back from the personal to the more general, we see that even while this self-same "West" is allegedly celebrating diversity, ironically, it finds itself confronted by an increasingly belligerent

"Rest", and particularly by the burgeoning identity called Fundamentalist Islam. Should the notion of "celebration" be extended to them? And if not celebration, then should at least tolerant respect be extended? Some say "yes", others "no", and others again say "it depends". Certainly, the stance taken by the governments appears to be contradictory. On the one hand, their rhetoric is one of encouraging their populations to celebrate diversity *within* their national borders, but, on the international stage, their stance is not one of celebration but of confrontation—war.

Tiptoe through the minefield of taboos

I, as an inhabitant of the West, one with not very well thought out liberal inclinations, find myself increasingly unable to speak and reflect on what is going on. Like Jim and the health professionals, I find myself gripped by a thought paralysis that is due in part to confusion, and in part to fear. This is because to engage *publicly* with the subjects of racism, rights, Islam, and so forth, in this place, day, and age, is to encounter a number of potent taboos. Taboos are Manichean structures, binary structures with no in betweens; things are either good or evil; in or out; good or bad, with nothing allowed between these alternatives.

There is George Bush's Manichaeism: "Either you are with us, or you are with the terrorists". Mr Blair's version was: "You either support the war on Iraq, or you are a lover and supporter of the despot Saddam". There is the Islamist's binaried vision: "You accept the words of Mohammed (as I decree them) or you are an infidel deserving of death". Next to which is the Zionist version: "Say anything about the Israeli attitude towards the Palestinians and you are anti-Semitic". And next to that are untold others: "Say anything against the Palestinian Authority or Arafat and you are a rabid Zionist"; "Say anything about the USA's desire for oil as one of its reasons for launching the war on Iraq and you are a paranoid conspiracy theorist". And let us not forget the multi-culturalist Manichaeism: "Respect all differences, else you are a racist", and its liberal counterpart: "Each *must* be allowed their absolute freedom of conscience, else we will be oppressing them".

So, if I mention the fact that the war on terror has killed and maimed untold more innocents than all the terrorist attacks and suicide bombers put together, then does that make me an apologist for the terrorists? If I do not agree with *some* of the practices espoused by *some* followers of The Prophet, then does that immediately make me an Islamaphobe, a cultural imperialist, and a racist?

The paralysis is further reinforced because any and all number of distinct issues (and, therefore, taboos) are overlaid and linked, so that in addressing one issue, one inevitably falls foul of another. For example, I was taken aback (no doubt naïvely) when I read Moazzam Begg say in the book he wrote on being released from Guantanamo Bay that Palestine was "the best known *Muslim* issue" (Brittain & Begg, 2006, p. 44), and that his concern was for the *Muslims* in Iraq. Now, that is not how I primarily think of those embroiled in either of those contexts—as Muslims; neither do I think that the *sources* of the conflagrations have anything to do with religion (more on this in later chapters). In fact, in being asked by Begg to think about these events in relation to Islam, I find myself alienated from the victims in those contexts. In speaking in this way, Begg has appropriated those struggles for his own Islamic ends. The late, great Palestinian, Edward Said, certainly did not think about the conflict in Palestine in these simplistic terms. So, when Begg frames the Palestinian question in this form, then the only way I am allowed to take a position on Palestine or Iraq is to take a position *vi- à-vis* Islam: I can only be for or against Islam (just as I can only be for or against service users), and in the process (whether I want to or not) end up appearing that I am for or against Judaism or Christianity. Increasingly, I find there is less and less room for manoeuvre, and so I become paralysed and, emotionally, I take a step backwards.

But what is it that I step back into or on to?

Wherever I step, I am bound to fall foul of somebody's sensitivities and taboos, including my own. The territory is literally a minefield of taboos. Confounded by the range of taboos, I find myself paralysed, because to step anywhere is potentially to cause offence and court disapprobation in myself as much as in others. Can I find a place to stand, indeed *is there* a place to stand between the apologists and zealots of all descriptions, be they theistic, Marxist, capitalist, or whatever?

Good guys and bad guys

How am I to think about what is going on? The "real" world is not neatly divided into good guys and bad guys. For example, on coming through immigration at Heathrow Airport a couple of years ago, I was powerfully struck by two events. First, that one of the immigration officers scrutinizing the passports was a female in a headscarf, clearly Muslim. I found the image anomalous: here was "the enemy" at the gate, but this time the alleged enemy, a follower of Islam, was actually guarding the gate at the British frontier! Does this mean that the xenophobes like Melanie Phillips (2006) are right and "they" have taken "us" over?

Anyhow, a few moments later, another similarly dressed woman approached a white Englishman ahead of us in the queue who, despite there being signs saying that for security reasons mobile phones were not to be used, was speaking loudly on his mobile phone. She drew his attention to the notices. He hardly looked at her, waved her off dismissively, and carried on speaking as though she were not there until he had finished. She stood helplessly by, watching him all the while.

None of us said anything.

The situation carried the additional irony that, in this vignette, Britain's security was being potentially undermined by an "indigenous" Englishman, and being defended by a Moslem woman. Presumably, in his eyes she (as one of "them") had no authority to tell him what to do in his "own" country.

Thought impasse

Let me go further into the sources of my own thought impasse. Growing up in London in the 1960s and 1970s, racism was open and commonplace. And, although I had never thought of myself in these terms previously, I found myself increasingly being named (and then naming myself) as "Black". I had a growing sense of notional armchair solidarity (I was by no means an activist) with others who laid claim to this kind of identity. In brief, "Blacks" and other marginalized folk were the good guys. But what has happened to me in the current context is that I find that I have lost my "natural" allies, and so do not quite know *where* to stand or *with whom* to stand (see Cohen's *What's Left*, 2007). It is somewhat embarrassing when some of the people one has defended and identified with (various underdogs), start behaving in ways that are, let us say, problematic. The situation is not unlike that of an intimate, a family member or friend, saying or doing something untoward in public. What is one to do? Tough it out and loyally stand by them come what may? Or pointedly distance oneself from them? Whatever one does, of necessity it reveals and exposes something of oneself to the intimate as well as to the onlookers. Thus, one can easily find oneself paralysed and doing nothing. But, in doing nothing, one is inevitably lending the appearance of condoning what is going on. It becomes clear, then, that one cannot ever *do* nothing. For to do nothing is to agree tacitly with the voice that speaks.

So, while having no sympathy with xenophobic Islamaphobes, I also find myself alienated from some of those speaking *for* the Islamists. For example, when Ken Livingstone publicly embraces the Egyptian theologian, Sheikh Yusuf al-Qaradawi, while praising him as a scholar. This is the same scholarly Qaradawi that said of a Moslem who might decide to leave Islam of his own free will: "He is no more than a traitor to his religion and his people and thus deserves killing" (Cohen, 2005). Similarly, I was somewhat bemused when the then British Prime Minister, Tony Blair, decided to honour the so-called moderate Iqbal Sacranie, Secretary-General of the Muslim Council of Britain, by making him a Knight of the Realm. This is the same Sir Iqbal Sacranie that said of the fatwa on Salman Rushdie, "death perhaps is too easy for him . . . his mind must be tormented for the rest of his life unless he begs forgiveness from the Almighty Allah" (Cohen, 2007). As far as I know, he has not publicly withdrawn this view.

More recently, Salman Rushdie himself was also knighted. This set off another round of strong protests by *some* Muslims, including effigy and book burnings. The claim was that as Rushdie had insulted Islam, to honour Rushdie was to insult Islam. It is worth noting the difference in the responses to the two situations: when Sacranie was knighted, there was some (muted) verbal protest, and when it was Rushdie's turn, there was violence in the streets. This difference points to another of the arguments in this book, which is that as these two responses are of very different kinds, it is, at the very least, foolish to extend them both the same courtesies.

The situation can be encapsulated in this way: the attempt to right the wrong of unfair discrimination has taken the course of suggesting that all processes of discrimination are a bad thing. In trying to defend those that are denigrated on the basis of some difference, what has come to pass is the fetishizing of difference. The result: one's capacities for judgement become frozen and one is unable to think.

The particular kinds of discriminations we sign up to, or find ourselves signed up to, are integral to who we are as individuals; they are the basis of our integrity and constitute our ethical natures. We can say, adapting Descartes, *I discriminate, therefore I am*. If I give up discriminating (that is, thinking) then I cease to be human. In fact, I would go so far as to argue that what the world needs is not less discrimination, but more.

The question is, how do I retain my integrity in the face of something that is profoundly disagreeable to me? Is there a course to be set between annihilating the other and annihilating the self?

Method

This book builds on the theorizations developed in my previous book, *Race, Colour and the Processes of Racialization* (Dalal, 2002), and takes them out "into the world" to reflect on policy and practice today, primarily in the UK. The purpose of the reflections is to try to make sense of things for myself as much as for the reader. To this end, I think of the book as a conversation which enquires not only into what has become taken for granted and unquestioned (by me as much as anyone else), but also into issues that have become taboo and unquestionable (also by me as much as anyone else).

The work is "citation lite", as I deliberately do not engage directly with bodies of literature emanating from cultural studies, sociology, and so forth. Rather, what I try to do is work my own way towards a viewpoint by drawing on experiences and material that the ordinary reader will come across in their everyday, day-to-day life, as it is these which are the basis of our forming attitudes and views about equality, difference, and so forth. This material includes news stories and reports, anecdotes, experiences in the workplace, gossip, public proclamations emerging from multi-nationals and government bodies, as well as claims made in the media by various "experts", politicians, and diversity enthusiasts. I ask, what is it that they are saying? What is the basis on which they are saying it? Does the world actually conform to their presumptions and assertions, or are they distorting it to fit in with their ideology? I do this analysis in as straightforward a way as possible through directly engaging with the material in question, showing up the contradictions, elisions, silences, obfuscations, and so forth, as they arise.

Having said that, my attempts to think things through and work things out are, of course, deeply informed by what others have said and thought. In particular, this book and I owe a profound debt of gratitude to the following works, works that have greatly influenced my thinking, works that have educated me. Most prominent amongst these are Kwame Anthony Appiah's *The Ethics of Identity* (2005) and Seyla Benhabib's *The Claims of Culture* (2002); I am also deeply indebted to Nick Cohen's *What's Left* (2005), A. C. Grayling's *Towards the Light* (2007), Charles Guigon's *On Being Authentic* (2004), and Charles Taylor's *Sources of the Self* (1989).

Overview and outline

Multiculturalism provided several answers to the question of what should one do when faced with something one finds disagreeable. Primarily, its watchword has been tolerance, and for good reason. But taken at its most simplistic, the requirement of me is to tolerate the intolerant, to tolerate the intolerable, to tolerate that which, according to my ethics, ought not to be tolerated.

Multi-culturalism's emphasis on tolerance has its source in the principles of liberalism; specifically, the wish to allow people to live their lives as freely as possible. And so it is here that I begin, with an overview of the philosophy of liberalism (Chapter Two, "The struggle to live and let live: the liberal world view"). We will see that there are, in fact, two versions of liberalism and that they are in conflict with each other: one grounded in the values of the Enlightenment (which blinds itself to difference), and the other in the values of the Romantic Movement (which deifies difference). The equality movements do not keep the distinction between the values of the two sufficiently in mind, which is why they end up in a number of conceptual cul-de-sacs.

Chapter Three ("Equal strokes for different folks: the legislature") takes up the story of how and why the attempts to establish the values of liberalism in the legislature have created a number of contradictions. Each bit of legislation was provoked into reluctant existence by events in the recent history of gender and "race" relations in the UK. In the main, these events consist of disturbances (like riots and protests) of some sort, disturbances that were upsetting the complacent equanimity of the establishment. Each bit of legislation, then, is an attempt to "answer" the questions thrown up by a particular conflagration. I make my points primarily but not entirely through a narrative of "race" relations rather than gender or other "differences", else the argument would get too dispersed. In my view (which I hope to convince you of), the legislation ends up making aspects of the situation worse even while its intention is to make it better. One reason for this is that the legislature begins by taking it for granted that the "kinds" of people just exist as eternal facts of nature; it does not take any account of how and why the "kinds" of people come to be manufactured by the processes of power relations. Most worrying is the way that the legislature has come to legitimate the fiction called race in the statute books, and then made things even worse by also instating the idea of *mixed* race, thus giving succour to the myth that there are such things as *pure* races. Thus, even as the legislature works to dismantle racism, it ends up reinforcing and perpetuating it.

The next two chapters dismantle the naïve understandings of the cultural group and the individual found in the equality movements. These two chapters (Four and Five) are where psychoanalytic and group analytic understandings of the human condition are introduced, critiqued, and developed. As it is with people, so it is with psychoanalysis: neither is a homogeneity. Some "kinds" of psychoanalytic understanding are emancipatory, while other kinds are deeply authoritarian and conservative. I have done my best to reduce the use of technical psychoanalytic language in these cogitations to make them more accessible to those unschooled in these ways of thinking. The ideas developed in these two chapters are key, and form the basis of the critiques that follow. The theoretical schema developed in these chapters is "psycho-social" rather than a reductive psychological or a reductive social. Chapter Four ("Manufacturing kinds of people: processes of inclusion and exclusion") critiques the simplistic acceptance that the "kinds" of people just exist as facts of nature, and then offers a more complex understanding of the human group. As the argument evolves, it becomes clear that the cultural group is not the homogenous consensual unity that it is mostly taken to be, but that it is a conflicted multiplicity. Chapter Five ("The human condition") argues that *the* individual is no more a unit than is the social group. The argument proceeds on the basis that as the social is prior to the individuals that are born into it, the internal worlds of individuals are socialized worlds. And, eventually, this leads to the conclusion that the "I", too, is a conflicted entity, generated by the tensions between the varieties of "we" that one belongs to. In effect, the psyche is a politicized entity.

We now find ourselves faced with two realizations. First, that as human life is so entangled, we have neither the possibility nor the luxury of *not* having an impact on the lives of others. Non-interference is an impossible ideal. Second, that conflict, internal and external, is endemic to the situation. One always has to decide which aspect of "them" one will respect and support, knowing all the while that even one does this, one will necessarily offend many others within the same "them". It also becomes clear that the "kinds" of people are not simply found, but generated by these very conflictual engagements. Such is the complexity of the existential situation that confronts the equality movements. On the whole, the equality movements have based their corrective strategies on a much simplified understanding of the world, which presumes that one can legislate away the existential reality, that human life is forever constituted by conflict, ambiguity, and ambivalence.

If the first half of the book is loosely thought of as having to do with "ideas", the focus of the second half is (equally loosely) on "practice". In what follows, I give a reasoned critique of some of the advice being given by mainstream governmental organizations, as well as of a number of the practical programmes proposed by the equality movements to correct the iniquities within the workplace and social life in general. In various ways, they all turn out to be deeply problematic.

A key component of equality work is the requirement by law for institutions to continually collect statistical evidence to get a picture of the problem, as well to monitor the progress being made by the attempts to rectify wrongs. In Chapter Six ("Counting discriminations"), while agreeing that it is good and necessary to collect statistics, I take issue with the kind of "evidence" that is being collected, as well as the way that it is collected. In particular, I take issue with the "ethnic monitoring form". The espoused reason for collecting this sort of data is to observe the workings of racism, yet the data being collected is not of "race" but "ethnicity". Why? Further, the forms are filled out by people who self-ascribe their ethnicity. This would seem to be a good thing in that we are respecting their right to define themselves. But racism works on the basis of other-ascription, not self-ascription. I argue that this manoeuvre is a sleight of hand, and is made possible because the equality movements have taken these categories to be objective entities and, simultaneously, to be subjective experiences. The chapter also notes, in passing, how the statistical evidence is massaged and manipulated to give the right picture to appease the authorities.

The seventh chapter ("Corrupting the liberal ideal: diversity in organizational life") exposes the reality behind the rhetoric of celebrating diversity in organizational life. It shows that the real motivation is not the espoused one of inclusivity and egalitarianism; rather, it is driven by the ethics of the spreadsheet and in the service of increasing profit. Here, we also get to see that the version of "psychology" called on in this literature is not only deeply impoverished, but also ethically compromised. We also see in this chapter that the nineteenth-century project of scientific racism is found to be alive and well in the theory of cross-cultural psychological types. What we find in the guise of science is the reproduction of the old myths about "their" unreliability, weakness of character, and so on. This is the corrupt and insidious end of multi-culturalism's decent enough wish to promote the understanding of others in order to get on better with them. The fact that this kind of nonsense finds a respectable place in scientific discourse is extremely troubling.

Chapter Eight ("Perverting the liberal ideal: fear and control in the Panopticon) remains with institutional life. The formulations of the equality movements are necessarily fashioned out of the paradigms prevalent in the contexts out of which they emerge. I argue that the modern workplace is akin to the Panopticon, with procedures and protocols used as instruments of surveillance resulting in a culture of fear and timidity. I suggest that the ideals of the equality movements are similarly perverted and also put to use as instruments of fear and control

The equality movements are regularly lampooned for some of the suggestions they make about what it is acceptable to say and what is taboo. Often, the good liberal is anxious about what is the current correct term for a particular "them". Chapter Nine ("The difference that dare not speak its name") questions the thinking behind certain kinds of PC-speak and the rationale for it. It does this through a detailed examination of the kinds of advice being given by various agencies, such as the Equality and Human Rights Commission. The chapter details some of the conceptual confusions that lie behind some of their more questionable suggestions as to what are appropriate terms of speech and what are not.

Chapter Ten ("The vicissitudes of unfair discrimination") begins with a human predicament, this being that the ways we come to view and experience the world are patterned by the milieus we find ourselves in; further, that these patterns are value laden and mostly lie below the threshold of consciousness. This leads to an unhelpful and extreme version of relativism. I use these considerations to critically examine structural attempts to counter individual and structural prejudices, in particular the equal opportunity interview and bureaucratic proceduralization. And, last, I look more closely at how unfair discriminatory processes come to be institutionalized and, thus, rendered invisible.

Having spent the previous ten chapters saying what is wrong about the way that the diversity movement have been proceeding, it is beholden on me to say what ways might be more helpful. The task of the final chapters is to establish the ground between the cultural relativists and the cultural imperialists, and then to think about what the notion of engagement would look like on this sort of ground.

The work of Chapter Eleven, "Islam: the new Black", is to think about the basis of the antipathy towards Islam and Moslems in general. Is the fear of Moslems a prejudicial paranoia or is it justified? I argue that the liberal way of thinking, ever vigilant not to be seen to be racist, is afraid to discriminate between varieties of Moslem, in effect, trying to respect them all, but, in doing so, damming them all. And, finally, the chapter looks briefly at how and why democratic governments in the West, as well as sections of the revolutionary left, have come to support and fête the Islamofascists.

Chapter Twelve ("Tolerating discrimination: discriminating tolerance) begins with a study of the politics and psychology of tolerance, to conclude that tolerance is not the opposite of discrimination. I argue for the rehabilitation of the emotions in the thinking regarding theorizations about the engagement with others. I make a case for the necessity of retaining the tension between the liberal values of being true to yourself (authenticity) and being good to others (fairness). I argue that what is often described as a "culture clash" is better described as racism. I then think about two conundrums; what is one to do when one is faced with the intolerable, and what when faced with the intolerant? In this process, I put forward a position in which I argue how and why it is both necessary and legitimate to hold on to one's particular non-universal ethical viewpoints in these sorts of situations. And, finally, I give my rendition of the process of engagement and recognition. I conclude that there is no point of arrival in equality heaven (as is usually promised), and that the political and psychological work consists of a certain kind of permanent ethical struggle for recognition.

The final chapter ("The road to nowhere: conceptual cul-de-sacs") puts the celebrators of diversity in the dock one last time. This time to show that the connotations of "diversity" (which are to do with mixing, change, creativity, and the emergence of the novel) are in conflict with the service it is being put to when it comes to cultures. I critically examine their rationales for the preservation of cultures, and find them wanting. I follow this with a defence of rationality and the Enlightenment—the villains of the piece for Romantic relativists. The final section consists of a discussion around the complexities of disability. I argue that there are two opposing demands that we constantly make, and that they are both true at the same time: remember that I am different; remember that I am the same. These kinds of issues make the emancipatory project increasingly complex, a complexity we have to hold on to. And what we have to resist are the simplifications being foisted on us by the celebrators of diversity.

CHAPTER TWO

The struggle to live and let live: the liberal world view

To begin with, what is the set of problems that we are concerned with?

1. Gratuitous violence is meted out by *individuals* and gangs on the same subset of people. Violence "in the wild", as it were.
2. Some individuals employed by agencies of the state have been known to *deliberately* use the authority of the state to treat this same subset with violence—in particular, the police, immigration authorities, social services, the psychiatric services, and so on. And when the institutions cover up for these individuals, we can call this deliberately sanctioned violence.
3. Some kinds of people seem to fare less well than other kinds in all manner of settings, from health to housing to the job market. This comes about through depersonalized, institutionalized processes which somehow centrifuge certain "kinds" of people to the periphery: institutionalized but invisible violence.

As we proceed, it will be important to keep the distinctions between the three firmly in mind, else we will end up in a number of conceptual difficulties. Often, the solutions appropriate to one of the above are unhelpfully utilized for another of the above. In what follows, I will not only look at some of explanations being offered for this range of problems, but also what is taken for granted and unrecognized in these explanations. The sources of the taken-for-granted are to be found in the values of liberalism—to live and let live. But these values contain a tension (often unreflected) between two sets of contradictory ideals, these being between "treat everyone the same" and "treat each person/group as special". The tension between these sets of ideals continues to bedevil the Equality discourses to give rise to a number of conceptual confusions. In order to understand the sources of these values and resulting tensions, I begin with a short history of, and an introduction to, the principles of liberalism.

The history that follows is by no means comprehensive. I pick out moments that I take to be pertinent to the subject matter of the book. Because I do not quote much from others in what follows, I need to acknowledge my debt to the following texts that have deeply informed my thinking on these matters: Kwame Anthony Appiah's *The Ethics of Identity* (2005), Seyla Benhabib's *The Claims of Culture* (2002); A. C. Grayling's *Towards the Light* (2007); Charles Guigon's *On Being Authentic* (2004); and Charles Taylor's *Sources of the Self* (1989).

The Enlightenment: blind to difference

We do not live in an apartheid state with signs designating some social spaces exclusively for Blacks and others for Whites. We do not live in a nation that proclaims a world view that says that men are a better kind of human than women.

Instead, we live in a liberal democracy that organizes itself according to several beliefs: that every individual human being is worthy of respect from every other; that all individuals are equal to each other in the eyes of the law; that the state does not interfere in personal matters. This "individual" is universal: it is an every-person and any-person. The individual is made universal by stripping persons of all their particularities: gender, history, ethnicity, status, and so on.

This version of liberalism is grounded in the values of the Enlightenment, which arose as a counter to the inequalities and inequities arising from the divisions between nobles and commoners. In contrast to the idea of one rule for the rich and another for the poor, the liberal creed says that whether one is King or serf, both are equal in the eyes of the law. This Enlightenment liberal creed is *deliberately* blind to these differences precisely in order to actively ensure that no one individual is privileged over another because of some status differential. The Enlightenment challenged the world view of the Dark Ages. Answers regarding human life were no longer to be looked for in the holy texts or the pronouncements of priests and kings, but to be worked out by subjecting them to the light of Reason. The ethos of the Enlightenment is captured in Kant's dictum: *Sapare Aude*! Dare to think for yourself.

The values of the Enlightenment have come under fire on two counts. First, for the fact that it is the universal individual that is considered and the particulars of each individual life are deliberately kept out of view; as we have seen, it has proceeded in this way in order to try to promote fairness by keeping status differentials out of the picture. The charge that is made is that you cannot *start* by treating people equally, because they are not starting on an equal playing field. Some are born more privileged and so have more opportunities than others. Some suggest, then, that the Enlightenment is actually a part of the *problem* of discrimination, even while it portrays itself as a solution. While there is something important in this challenge, it should be remembered that the reason that Enlightenment has proceeded in this way is in order to dismantle the mechanisms of unfair discrimination.

The Enlightenment is also vilified by some for being "Eurocentric", who then proceed to discount it on that basis, as its values are "relative" and not everywhere the same. To this kind of challenge, I would say "so what?" Which set of values is not "centric" in some way, and why should its situatedness undermine its legitimacy? I will come back to take further issue with this kind of thinking a little later.

The Romantics: champions of difference

In any case, some of those who voice these sorts of challenges could be grouped under the banner of the Romantic tradition, which emerged as a reaction to the Enlightenment. In order to contextualize the Romantics, I need to back-track a little. When Kant sought to set the individual free to think for themselves, he did so under the impression that each person's reasoning, if done correctly, was bound to lead them to the same (correct) conclusions regarding the world (objective reality). He was confident that each person would reason their way to the *same* set of ethical values, and so all would be agreed how best to live with others. In effect, he believed in the possibility of objectivity and a universal system of ethics and morals with which all right thinking (rational) people would inevitably concur.

But the Enlightenment project of living in and through the Light of Reason did not deliver the coherent and just world that Kant hoped for. Despite the use of reason, people arrived at very different conclusions as to what was a just and ethical life. This precipitated a moral crisis. The previous moral compasses found in celestial and worldly authorities were no longer available. The Romantics, beginning with Rousseau, came to the rescue. In Rousseau's view, the turn to Reason cut off human beings from their "source" and it was this that led to moral decline. Instead of using the mind, he thought that one should turn to the heart (it is for this reason that they are called the Romantics) and the emotions. He thought that if one turned inwards and connected with one's true feelings, then one would *know* right from wrong, The new moral compass was no longer "out there", but "in here", and not in the mind, but the heart.

In Rousseau's view, individuals were born with a true nature, with their "essence" intact. This essence was unique to each individual. He reasoned that as one took on the attitudes and aspirations of esteemed or feared others, the true self became diluted. The loss of contact with the true self is one of the sources, if not *the* source, of unhappiness. According to him, the mind, as the repository of knowledge taken in from the outside, gets in the way of the heart, the repository of *true* knowledge found on the inside. The ethos of the Romantics is best captured in Pascal's poetic aphorism: "The Heart has its reasons, which Reason does not understand".

It was in this kind of way that the Romantics came to be the champions of difference. They valorized the uniqueness of individuals, the source of which was the true self that one was born with. In their view, anything taken in from the outside could never be authentic; the outside dilutes the true self, and so ought to be resisted. The Romantics also eventually came to think that in order to find fulfilment, each individual not only had the *right*, but also a *duty* to express their unique inner selves. The ethical life for the Romantics consisted of individuals daring to express and live out their true desires and aspirations, which flowed out from the essence of their being.

Born to be free (sort of)

At the heart of liberal democracy is the idea of autonomy, of individuals free to choose and act. But here is the first problem: it would seem that when individuals are left free, then they often choose to behave in ways that others disapprove of and think immoral. Clearly, human beings are not just benign creatures, loving, helpful, and considerate of others. They are also mean, hateful, competitive, nasty, greedy, nepotistic, and only partly conscious of the reasons for their actions, thoughts, and feelings.

This, then, gives rise to a need for legislation that seeks to establish minimal norms of good behaviour between individuals, for example, that one should not kill or steal, that one should be honest and fair in one's dealings with others, and so on. This is the first "layer" of legislation; it speaks to individuals and requires them *not to do* certain sorts of things. Isaiah Berlin famously called this negative liberty.

Now, whatever the activity, clearly some individuals fare better than others. This is perfectly acceptable to the Enlightenment ethos because the "cause" is thought to be something specific to their individual natures—some mix of efforts and talents. But now we hit another problem, which is that when we look at society, we do not see the homogenous society that the liberal creed aims to foster. If it were homogenous, then the social-scape would look broadly similar whichever direction we looked in, in that we would find all kinds of individuals evenly scattered in every which direction. We would find Blacks, women, and so on in numbers that were statistically consistent in all arenas from prisons to senior managers to Oxbridge graduates to athletes, and so on. However, instead of homogeneity, we see patterns and stark differentials. When we look at society, not only do we find that some *individuals* prosper more than others (which is perfectly acceptable to the Enlightenment liberalist ethos), but certain *types* of individuals prosper more than others. In other words, not only do we find people clumped together in certain categories, but some kinds of categories are found more on the periphery and others nearer the centre. The categories here are the usual suspects—gender, colour, class, and so on. This patterning is found across a wide range of arenas: employment prospects, crime statistics, patient populations, and so on. The facts have become tedious by dint of repetition, more and more statistics are gathered, and they all show the same kind of thing. In British hospitals, for example, the cleaning and catering staff tend to be primarily Black. So, too, are British boxers. Why is this?

For some, no explanation is necessary. The world is as it is because it is an expression of the natural order of things. In the same way that it is natural for cream to rise to the top of the milk (because it is its nature), so it is natural for some kinds of people to rise above other kinds. Philosophers call this kind of thinking the naturalistic fallacy, in which the appearance of things is accepted as a fact of nature, rather than as something to be questioned. While there is *some* truth in the analogy at the level of individuals (some individuals are better at performing a certain task than others), there is something wrong with it when it is applied to categories of people. If we were to follow this view in regard to categories of people, then we end up saying that Black people are naturally good at cleaning and boxing; it is in their genes or in their nature (women, on the other hand, are mainly good at just cleaning).

If we are not to go down this naturalistic route, then the question remains: how has this patterning come about? How is it that certain *kinds* of individuals are being more successful than other *kinds*? Remember, Enlightenment liberal ideology deliberately set about blinding itself to categorical differences between *kinds* of individuals (the groups that people belong to) in order not to discriminate between them. The principle being that if one cannot see it, then one cannot be influenced by it; one cannot use it or be used by it. It is evident, then, that the strategy of categorical blindness, despite its intention, has not managed to do its work to produce an equitable social scenario.

Something has gone wrong.

Antidiscriminatory legislation

Anyhow, faced with this sort of situation, liberal democracies turned to a new sort of legislation to try to address these injustices: antidiscriminatory legislation. What is significant about this new variety of legislation is that it is aimed at the "group" that the individual belongs to or is seen to belong to. This kind of legislation falls foul of the values of the Enlightenment because, in speaking to categories of belonging, this legislation goes against the Enlightenment liberal strategy of deliberately blinding itself to social categories and is more in tune with the world view of the Romantics.

But now, even despite the additional pieces of *group* legislation buttressing the *individualistic* principles of liberal democracy, differentials between groups of people continue to be evident. Innumerable statistical analyses, census results, and the like, tell us that, despite the best efforts of liberal democracy, society remains deeply divided, and full of iniquities and inequalities. The social-scape is, at the very least, gendered, colour coded, and there are a whole host of other differentials, if we would only look.

Before we can begin to think more about what is going on, and how we might think about the situation, I need to attend to two further elements that are critical to the ethos of liberal democracy, the first of which is privacy.

Privacy

To the liberal schema, the notion of privacy is intimately linked with that of freedom. Liberalism is at great pains to avoid legislating and regulating the private sphere. As Hobbes famously said: "The liberty of the subject is [to be found in] the silence of the laws". One is free to think, believe, feel, and act according to one's will and desire; but now the caveat: as long as one does not impede another's freedom to do so similarly. Liberalism works really hard at trying *not to tell* individuals what to do, think, or believe.

This *private* space is the territory wherein *freedom* resides in the liberal schema. Implicit in this model is the view that the internal life of individuals is divorced from the world and that it is internally generated in some way. This, then, is a model of encapsulated individuals, each living a psychological life separate from others.

Liberalism attends to two sorts of private spaces, one's mind and one's home. But already, even here, we find that things are not that straightforward. The line between the public and the private is constantly being contested. For example, the likes of Mary Whitehouse would seek to regulate what goes on in the bedroom. What about the issue of how families bring up and treat their children in the privacy of their homes? How are these matters to be negotiated?

There is a further, more critical, problem with the idea of privacy *per se*. For example, although we can say that the transactions between family members take place in the privacy of the "home", they nevertheless take place "in front" of the people in that home. In other words they are *public* to the inhabitants of that home. We can see that "private" is not the straightforward opposite of "public". Depending on where one stands, the same event is both private and public at the same time.

Ownership

The third critical component of liberalism is the principle of ownership. According to this principle, one has *rights* over one's property, to do with as one wills and desires.

Here is the interesting thing: in the very moment that something is decreed to be one's property, it is deemed to have taken up residence in the private realm. Once it is private, then what happens to it is nobody's business but the owner's. Here, too, there are all kinds of claims and disputes as to what constitutes ownership, and on what matters the legislature may or may not speak. It would probably be uncontentious of me to say that the thoughts, feelings, and beliefs taking place in the privacy of *my* mind are *my* property; my claim that my house, my dog, and my back yard are also my property for me to do with as I please might also escape controversy. Key, of course, is the possessive pronoun "my"—I possess these things. Things might start getting more contentious if I were to claim that, as a man, my children and my wife are also my property to do with as I will.

On the whole, society has been operating in exactly this fashion: as though women and children are, in fact, the property of men. It was not so long ago that the police in the UK (and elsewhere for that matter) were extremely reluctant to take any action when husbands were violent to their spouses and children, precisely because of these two liberal principles: first, that it was taking place in the privacy of the home, and second, the tacit assumption that as the wife is the property of the husband, he has "rights" over her.

But the legislature has never, in actuality, given individuals *carte blanche* as to what they might do in the private sphere, even when it does not have an impact directly or straightforwardly on another individual. Neither is the law consistent. For example, the growing and ingesting of marijuana for one's own use, in the *privacy* of one's home, is illegal, whereas marital rape, which clearly impinges on the freedoms of the victim, was not illegal in British law until very recently.

In sum, the ethos of liberal democracy is founded on five components: first, that it blinds itself to differences between individuals and groups of individuals; second, that it values the uniqueness of each individual; third, it tries to keep out of the private arena; fourth, it assumes that individuals have rights over their own property; last but not least, it wishes to leave individuals as free as possible to live their lives as their conscience, wishes, and desires dictate. In an even more compressed form, we can say that one is *free* to do what one wants with one's *property* in the spaces that are also one's property. Another name for the spaces that are one's property is privacy.

As we have seen, none of these notions are unproblematic in themselves. The entire conceptual edifice rests on the presumption that there is a clear-cut boundary between the private sphere and the public sphere, which implies that things can go on in the private sphere without having any impact on the public sphere.

The entry of culture

The focus for both the Enlightenment and the Romantics was *the individual*. While the Enlightenment emphasized the commonality of individuals, the Romantics became the champions of the differences between them. Liberalism came to embody both sets of values, the tension between them being managed by granting these individuals their uniqueness in the private sphere, while in the public sphere they are all considered to be of equal status and value as each other. Different but equal, as the adage goes.

What happened next is that the later Romantics, such as Herder (1968), took this picture of individuals and the rights and duties accruing to them and transposed it wholesale to entities called "cultural groups". Now cultures were deemed to be living things with rights over their property: their beliefs, their customs, and ways of life. It was the duty of cultural groups to live according to their conventions, else they would not be being authentic.

With this move comes a subtle but significant shift with regard to the sources of authenticity. For the earlier individualistically inclined Romantics, authenticity was internally derived, something each individual was born with. For the later culturally inclined Romantics, the individual's authenticity is now supplied by the group they are born into: nation, culture, race, or whatever, and so is externally derived. The two are melded together with the belief that there is a natural congruence between the true self and the group it is born into.

As with the private lives of individuals, the demand is that the legislature ought not to meddle in the private lives of cultures. In effect, internal (cultural) spaces are transformed into sacred spaces, where the impure may not tread. But herein lies a twist: although the practices of these cultures are deemed private (because they "belong" to that culture), they necessarily take place in public. There are any number of such beliefs and practices, such as dietary restrictions, clothing, and so on; although private, in the sense that they are "owned" by a culture, they can only find expression in public spaces, spaces shared with others not of their "kind". As I will argue later, the primary (but covert) task of these beliefs and practices is to manufacture and sustain "us" and "them" differentiations, and the signal can only do its work in public.

The Romantic injunction that *individuals* are obliged to express their inner selves is also appropriated, so that now cultures, too, are duty bound to express "their ways" publicly, or else they would not be existing "authentically". And, finally, only those "within" the culture are deemed to have the authority to say anything about the ways of that culture.

We are now in a position to approach an understanding of the rationale for the multi-culturalist agenda.

Multi-culturalism: a spectator sport

Multi-culturalism arose as a counter to the world view of the Imperialist. In the not-so-distant bad old days of European colonialism and imperialism, the cultures of conquered peoples were mostly discounted as primitive and backward, and what was not discounted was plundered for its exoticism. On that basis, it was thought perfectly reasonable to replace "their" culture with "ours". Multi-culturalism is a form of resistance to this imperialistic tendency. It reminds us that the other's culture has its own legitimacy, its own way of thinking about and ordering the world, and that these other ways should not be dismissed, but should be respected. Multi-culturalism's watchword is "tolerance", and its motto is encapsulated in the adage "Different but equal".

So far, so good. But this defence of the legitimacy of other cultures has, in some circles, come to mean that different cultural bodies may gaze upon each other, but they must not form views about each other, because views grounded in one belief system cannot be legitimately applied to another belief system. To pass comment would be to interfere and that, in itself, is intrinsically disrespectful. In this way, some versions of multi-culturalism have reduced the liberal to the status of a spectator who may look but may not speak. The ethos insists that the integrity of one cultural system is not to be compromised or diluted in any way by those of another system. The stance is one of "repel all boarders". The assertion is that any shift in our way of doing things (which we have been doing since time immemorial) is a desecration of our identity and a dilution of our authenticity.

I will take up the problems with these ways of thinking in later chapters. But for now, all I want to do is flag up the fact that the multi-culturalist injunction to respect *the* culture of another, presumes that cultures are consensual and homogeneous.

Anti-racism: the doer and the done-to

During the 1980s in the UK, the anti-racist movement charged the multi-culturalists for having too benign an analysis of the situation (e.g., Sivanandan, 1983). The more naïve versions of multi-culturalism assume that difficulties between (say) Black and White are simply due to misunderstandings. Therefore (they might continue), if we got to know their culture and their ways, we would be less likely to respond negatively to them. While there is some truth in this viewpoint, it is not the whole story. For example, the females of a society are not strangers to the males of that society; they share lives of intimacy and are part of the same culture. Yet, we find that women are marginalized and do much less well than men in the job market. Whatever the causes of this, it is not to do with "ignorance" about their exotic cultures, as the multi-culturalists would have it.

In contrast, anti-racism claimed that it was not ignorance, but group interests that fuelled the derision of some kinds of people, in order to exclude them from full participation in the socio-economic life of societies. A way of distinguishing these two movements is this: the multi-culturalists supposed that the problems were caused by "cultural differences", while the anti-racists conceptualized the problem in terms of power relations and racism.

Anti-racists sought to distinguish racism from prejudice. It was said that prejudice was something that every human was prone to; however, to be racist, one had to have the power to act and institutionalize one's prejudices. They came up with the formula: racism = power + prejudice. While the anti-racist movement was successful in a great many ways by taking on the issue of power, sections of it oversimplified the situation in saying that only Whites had power, and so only they could be racist. This view of power, although Marxist in its origins, is, in fact, individualistic. It says that one person or group has power and another does not.

But power does not work in this one-dimensional way. It is ubiquitous and multi-faceted. The view that people are *either* victims *or* perpetrators cannot really be sustained. For example, the bullied and intimidated factory worker by day might turn out to be the respected and admired jazz saxophonist by night, and the vicious drunken wife-beater later that very same night. In one context he is to be pitied, in another admired, and in the last, surely condemned. So, the problem with some versions of anti-racism was that it rendered the world too simplistic by dividing it into two: the doers and the done to, perpetrators and victims, Black and White. It did not take a sufficiently nuanced account of the complexity of social arrangements.

Diversity: party time

It is into this mix of things that the notion of diversity makes its entry. In itself, it is an attempt to address the limitations arising within the multi-culturalist and anti-racist discourses, yet it brings with it its own sets of confusions.

Other disfranchised groupings (say, wheelchair users), whose primary identity was not that of "race", gender, or culture, found that their needs were not being spoken for by the feminists, multi-culturalists, or the anti-racists. The diversity agenda seeks to expand the territory to include these and all other *varieties* of difference. But it does this in a peculiar way. As we will see, for many diversity advocates it is a point of pride that their project *avoids engaging in politics.* They make it clear that their work is not going to be about changing power relations and so forth. Instead, their work will be about celebration of culture. This split made by the diversity discourses, between politics and culture, is what is most problematic about it, and the source of most of the difficulties that follow.

Here is their maxim: differences are not problems, but assets and resources to be celebrated. And this gives forth their strap line: Celebrating Diversity.

Having positioned itself as speaking for all differences, the diversity agenda takes yet another step, and this time it really is a step too far, and it does so in the following way. It is true that every individual is unique, physically and psychologically, or else we would not be able to recognize each other. It would also be true that each of us has our own unique way of doing things. We could, then, truthfully say that every individual is different from, and therefore diverse from, every other. When used in this way, the term diversity becomes completely individualistic; groupings of people disappear from view, and we find ourselves back with the original individualistic premises of Enlightenment liberalism—*but this time without its moral basis.*

We can see, then, that while the term diversity captures more of the complexities of social life by attending to a greater range of differences, it can end up not taking account of a critical aspect of social life, which is that we live and work in social groups. Not only can the notion of diversity pave the way back to an unhelpful individualism through the process of extreme fragmentation, it can also avoid engaging with the problematics of the power differentials between social groupings, and of facing the fact that some groups do worse than other groups. The fact that this movement declares itself apolitical is what is most problematic about it. Instead of political struggle, they suggest the celebration of differences. In this way, the diversity project has served to obfuscate and undermine the little ground gained by prior movements of multi-culturalism and anti-racism.

For example, what has celebration to do with the fact that a greater proportion of Black people (when compared to White people) or women (when compared to men) do less well in any number of areas of life? The thorny issues to do with power relations are forgotten in the miasma of celebration. As soon as one brings in the word celebration, then the notion of diversity collapses back into a naïve version of multi-culturalism and suffers from the same problems. In particular, it avoids subjects of oppression and marginalization, the hows and whys of certain groupings doing less well than others (in other words, politics). Neither does it take up the question of what we are to do when confronted with differences that conflict with our moral codes.

Reprise: the two conflictual versions of liberalism

We have seen that there are, in fact, two varieties of liberalism whose values are in conflict with each other. One version of liberalism subscribes to the values of the Enlightenment, and the other to the values of the Romantic tradition. Enlightenment liberalism focuses on individuals that are stripped of all their social categories, which leave us dealing with the *universal* individual, the individual in the abstract. It proceeds in this way to ensure that the poor have the same rights as the rich, and that Royal and commoner are both equally answerable to the laws of the land.

Meanwhile, the Romantics turn away from the Mind and look instead to the Heart. In sharp contrast with the Enlightenment, they valorize the *particular* over the *universal*. Where the Enlightenment assiduously avoids engaging with differences, the Romantics literally romanticize difference.

Here is one way of encapsulating a key difference between them: the values of the Enlightenment decree that one ought to be respectful of another, *despite* their differences from "us"; the values of the

Romantics decree that one ought to be respectful of another *because* of their differences from "us".

However, both agree that individuals have *rights* over their *property* and are *free* to do what they will with it. The *private* sphere is, in effect, also the *property* of the individual, which no other has the right to enter or make comment on. There are issues here enough between these two world views. But things got even more confusing when the multi-culturalists appropriated the Romantic vision that pertained to *individuals,* and transposed it wholesale to the entities called cultures. The legitimacy of this move is questionable.

We also saw that antidiscriminatory legislation which is aimed specifically at the social groups that people belong to is in line with the values of Romantic liberalism, but is in conflict with the values of the Enlightenment.

We have also noted that the "rights" being spoken of are not by any means universal. It is only those humans who are thought to be fully human that are deemed to have these rights. That which is construed as property or object has no rights, save those that are conferred upon them by their owner. To put it another way: subjects have the right to determine the rights of their objects.

Finally, it has also become clear that the private and public spheres are not as separated out as liberalism assumes them to be. This, then, causes complications, as the legislature tries to attend to the public while trying to keep out of the private. So, how well do the legislators fare in their attempts to legislate on matters of discrimination and discriminatory processes in general? How cognizant are they about which version of liberalism they are drawing on to create the laws, and how consistent are they? The next chapter sets about enquiring into these sorts of questions.

CHAPTER THREE

Equal strokes for different folks: the legislature

These are frightening times. As I write this (2009), the global economy is in a state of meltdown, the planet's energy resources are running out, and to make matters even worse, the planet's eco-system is said to be on the brink of a catastrophic change.

A possible intimation of things to come occurred in 2000, when a strike by the drivers of petrol tankers brought Britain to a standstill in a shockingly short time. Without fuel, within just three days quite a lot of "normal" life had become impossible. Cars became rapidly redundant, public transport was hardly functioning, supermarket shelves emptied out, and many people could not get to work. Consequently, many institutions could provide only minimal services, or had to shut down entirely. The apparently solid and seamless workings of my day-to-day life were shown to be extremely precarious; the buffer between a functioning civil society and its collapse were revealed as being frighteningly thin. The dystopia envisaged in the *Mad Max* films no longer seemed too fantastical. The films imagined the world after the oil runs out as anarchic, ruled by mobs and gangs, with the strong ruthlessly overwhelming the weak—a Hobbesian nightmare.

My guess is that, in such a scenario, in a world devoid of Law, I would be unlikely to survive for long. Paradoxically, in a world without rules I would be singularly unfree, subject to the whims of the more powerful. Paradoxically, the Law, which could be described as a series of proscriptions, actually creates and protects spaces in which I am able to be free. The kinds of spaces determine the kinds of freedoms I am able to enjoy: for example, the freedom not to be assaulted by noise from my neighbours, and not be killed for protesting about it.

This, then, is the task for the law: it has to strike a balance between the rights of individuals to live their lives as they would wish, and, at the same time, to create and maintain order in society for individuals to enjoy those rights. Without this order, there would be no freedom—at least, not in a form that I would wish it. In sum, the Law generates structures that both create and protect spaces *within which* individuals are free to wander where they will. But, as the spatial metaphor already shows, these freedoms are never absolute, but always contingent and bounded.

Different strokes for different folks

The "shapes" and "spaces" created by the law are not God given (although many would claim that this is so), but made by humans for humans, and, for much of history, made by men for the benefit of men. The laws of the land are expressions of dominant ideologies. The laws are ideology made concrete. Each ideology has its own conception of what is good and right, and would want to write laws accordingly. Royalists would want to write one kind of law, republicans other kinds. And so, politics could be conceived of as the struggle to be in charge of the pen that writes the laws. It is only relatively recently that secular liberals have had the good fortune to have some influence over the pen. Not that they speak with one voice.

The laws reflect and embody the moral and ethical conventions of a society, which, in turn, are the expression of a mix of contesting ideologies. The result is that very different kinds of freedom spaces are generated for different kinds of people, depending on how ideologies view and conceive them. The most striking instance of this being the freedoms afforded to men in relation to women.

This was the case even in ancient Greece, the idealized source of Western civilization. In Plato's *Republic*, Socrates asserts that it is right and proper that women and children are owned *in common* by society (a view resuscitated in the twentieth century by some Communists). Aristotle disagreed. He thought it wrong that women and children should be owned in common, but only because in his view women (and their children) were actually the property of each *individual* husband (or father). For much of history, and even today, it continues to be the case that woman is the *property* of man (Barnett, 2004, p. 553).

More recently, Aristotle found an improbable ally in Colonel Gaddafi. While on a visit to Italy, Gaddafi, claiming to be a feminist, invited a thousand prominent Italian women to an audience with him. Gaddafi denounced the treatment of women in Arabic and Islamic societies, saying, "Why should these women have to apply to the head of state for the right to drive a car?" He continued, this was a matter for "their husbands or brothers [to] . . . decide" (Apperly, 2009).

In the UK, the Christian doctrine of "one flesh" was taken to mean that, after marriage, husband and wife were a single entity. But agency in this singularity resided in the man; the woman's duty was to comply. Consequently, in law, women were incapable of owning property until 1882. For most of history in British law, if the couple parted ways, then by right the husband had sole custody of their children. This was ameliorated somewhat in 1839, when mothers were granted custody rights over their children, but only until they were seven years old. After this age, custody rights reverted to the father. Further, women were said to have forfeited this limited right if they were thought to have committed adultery. No such caveat existed for the men, of course. And it was as recent as 1991 that the law finally accepted that rape could occur within a marriage. Before then, the law presumed that as the wife was the property of the husband, he could do with her as he desired, and so, by definition, there could be no crime. As late as 1946, an English judge thought it perfectly acceptable for a husband to beat his wife because she refused to obey his orders to visit her relations. The judge said that the husband was within his rights because "while smacking a woman as punishment amounted to cruelty under the old law of divorce, it would not have been cruel if the husband had punished her 'as one would a naughty child'" (Meacher *vs*. Meacher, 1946, cited in Barnett, 2004, pp. 553–554).

Let me underline two points. First, the "right" to own property and to have "rights" over it is not a universal right, but extended to only some of the inhabitants of the land. Second, the "West" is not as far from aspects of Sharia law as we would like to imagine, and it is only very recently that it has evolved sufficiently to be able to be considered a substantive alternative to it.

We could describe the equality movements as seeking to extend these rights to all the inhabitants of the land—*universalizing* them, if you will. In this regard, they are following the values of the Enlightenment. Hearkening back to the spatial metaphor, we could also describe the Equality movement as trying to ensure that each individual's freedom "space" is of a similar size and shape. In the UK, the legislation has specifically tried to redress inequalities pertaining to three specific territories: gender, disability, and "race". In what follows, I will mostly focus on "race", as most of the points of relevance can be made through it.

(Note: Much after this chapter was written, the UK government consolidated the range of antidiscriminatory legislation to do with race, gender, disability, religion, and sexual orientation into the *Equality Act* 2010. Below, I reference the *Race Relations Acts* and not the *Equality Act*, but this does not affect the argument, the language and structure of the *Race Relations Acts* having been migrated into the *Equality Act* with little or no change.)

Race in the legislature

The astonishing thing about the *Race Relations Acts* is that not only do they do not define what they mean by "race", they also do not name any of the "races". Neither do they say anything about how many races there might be. This is curious indeed, given that the purpose of these Acts (as declared in its name), is to lay down principles of how the "*races*" should and should not *relate* to each other. The arcane and convoluted language of law, consisting as it does of sub-clauses within sub-clauses, is convoluted in the service of precision. And, given that before a law arrives in the statute books it is pored over by politicians and lawyers, for whom precision is a point of pride, the omissions must be deliberate. So, why have the legislators assiduously avoided defining "race"?

The short answer is that they have not defined race because they cannot. And they cannot, because there are no such things as *the* races. (For substantive arguments on this matter, see Dalal, 2002, particularly Chapter One.)

The notion of race is itself an invention born of a particularly pernicious history. While it masquerades as objective taxonomy, its primary purpose has always been in the service of marginalization and exclusion; its primary function has always been to *generate* various "others" in order to marginalize them—Irish, Jews, Blacks, and so on. In other words, the term race is generated by, and is an artefact of, the problem we call racism.

This is the terrible thing: by instating the notion of race in the statute books, the legislature has given formal recognition and legitimated the existence of a reification, of a fiction. The effect of proceeding in this way has been to perpetuate and reinforce some of the processes of racism, rather than help to dismantle them.

The legislature has passed the buck and left it up to judges and case law to establish whether or not a grouping is a "race". This has resulted in a number of very peculiar anomalies arising. For example, the law recognizes Gypsies, Sikhs, and Jews to be "races", but not Christians, Muslims, or Hindus. How has this situation come about?

The curious case of the missing definition

The focus of the *Race Relations Acts* is on *racial* discrimination. The legislators were particularly careful to confine their definition of "racial discrimination" to the realm of actions and the effects of actions. In line with the liberal ethos, they did not wish to legislate what takes place in the private sphere (be that actions, beliefs, or thoughts), but to limit itself to the public domain.

The first thing to be said is that the intention of these Acts is to be applauded: to protect those who are unfairly treated. But its intention is to protect those who are unfairly treated because of their "race", and herein lies the difficulty. The *Race Relations Acts* (RRA) cope with the somewhat embarrassing fact that their central subject, "race", does not exist by performing several terminological sleights of hand. And it does so in the following way.

The 1976 Act begins with the statement that it is unlawful for a person to discriminate against another on *racial grounds,* which, in turn, is called *racial discrimination.* The Act reinforces this tautology with its next statement: "to racially discriminate" means to "treat another less favourably" on *racial grounds* (RRA, 1976, **1**(1)(a)). Next, it defines *racial grounds* to be those of "race, colour, nationality or ethnic or national origins" (RRA, 1976, **3**(1)). Curious, is it not, that culture is not on this list?

Like me, the reader might be a little confused by the series of circular assertions: racial discrimination occurs when the discrimination is on racial grounds. And racial grounds are those of race. This is like saying "you know you have eaten an apple, because it is an apple you have eaten". In this confusion, it is easy to miss the fact that the notion of "race" has just been smuggled into the legislature via the definition of "racial grounds". This terminological sleight of hand is reinforced with the Act's definition of *racial group*, which is, "'racial group' means a group of persons defined by reference to colour, race, nationality or ethnic or national origins, and references to a person's racial group refer to any racial group into which he falls" (RRA, 1976, **3**(1)).

And now that "race" is installed in the legislature in all its smug, matter-of-fact glory, then it is answerable to no one. It just exists.

But before being able to draw on the protection of the RRAs, a complainant has to establish that they do indeed belong to a "racial group" as defined by the Act. The case brought to the courts in 1983 (Mandala *vs*. Dowell-Lee) is extremely instructive in this regard.

How the first "race" came to be created

A case of racial discrimination was brought against a school by a Sikh family, the Mandalas. The headmaster of the school refused their son entry to the school because he had long hair and wore a turban; both were against the school rules. Meanwhile, the family refused to allow the boy to comply with the school rules, claiming that not cutting one's hair and the wearing of a turban are integral to the Sikh way of life.

The headmaster was championing the values of the Enlightenment (everyone should be treated the same with no grace or favour), while the Mandalas were championing the values of the Romantics (they have a right and a duty to express their different way of life).

The Mandalas initially lost both the case as well as the appeal, because, in the opinion of the courts, Sikhs were neither a racial nor an ethnic group, but a cultural group. As the Appeal Court judge, Lord Denning, famously said,

> The statute in section 3(1) contains a definition of a 'racial group'. It means a 'group of persons defined by reference to colour, race, nationality or ethnic or national origins.' That definition is very carefully framed. Most interesting is that it does not include religion or politics or culture. You can discriminate for or against Roman Catholics ... Communists ... [or] the 'hippies' as much as you like, without being in breach of the law. But you must not discriminate against a man because of his colour or of his race or of his nationality, or of 'his ethnic or national origins.' You must remember that it is perfectly lawful to discriminate against groups of people to whom you object – so long as they are not a racial group. You can discriminate against the Moonies or the Skinheads or any other group which you dislike or to which you take objection. No matter whether your objection to them is reasonable or unreasonable, you can discriminate against them – without being in breach of the law. [Denning, 1983]

The short version is this: as the Sikhs are not a *racial* group, they cannot be victims of *racial* discrimination.

The Mandalas persevered, and eventually the case ended up in the highest court in the land—the House of Lords. The Law Lords noted in their arguments that Sikhs were not distinguishable from other groups in India or the Punjab by reference to four of the categories cited in the Act: colour, race, nationality, or national origins. This left them with the fifth category, ethnicity. They settled on a definition of ethnicity, this being "having a long shared distinctive history and a distinctive cultural tradition. Further common characteristics included a common geographical origin, common language and religion, common literature, and being a minority within a larger society" (Barnett, 2004, p. 548).

On this basis, the Law Lords eventually answered yes, the Sikhs could be considered a race by virtue of their ethnic origins. But notice the confusion of categories: the Sikhs, a *religious* group, are considered to be a *racial* group, by virtue of their *ethnicity*!

Now, having established that Sikhs were a racial group, the next question was allowed: whether or not the Mandalas had been the victims of racial discrimination. And here, too, the House of Lords ruled yes, that the Mandalas, as Sikhs, were being racially discriminated against by being required to remove their turbans in that context.

From this time on, any Sikh could use the Race Relations Acts with no hindrance. For example, in 1986 another Sikh brought a case of racial discrimination against his employers for requiring him to remove his turban in order to wear protective headgear. This time the courts ruled for the employer, saying that the requirement was justifiable on grounds of safety.

Divide and rule

Through other similar court cases, it has come to be established in British law that Jews, Romany Gypsies, Irish Travellers, and Afro Caribbeans are also formally recognized as races. In 1993, the Rastafarians tried to join this elite squad of formally recognized "races", on similar grounds to the Mandalas. Dawkins, a Rastafarian, was refused a job when he said that he would not be willing to cut off his dreadlocks. The industrial tribunal initially agreed with Dawkins, but a later appeal reversed this decision. The legislators concluded that Rastafarians could not "fall within the meaning of racial group, for their 'shared history' is only of some 60 years duration (compared with that of Gypsies, whose history is of over 700 years duration)" (Barnett, 2004, p. 549).

The point about *the* races is that they are supposed to be fixed, discreet, and immutable. Yet, the law allows "for a person to fall into a particular racial group either by birth *or by adherence*" (*Mandala vs. Dowell-Lee*, 1983, IRLR 209, my italics). This suggests that one can not only *choose* to belong to a particular race, but that one can also move from one race to another. And, as the Rastafarian situation shows, any grouping, after sufficient longevity (something between sixty and 700 years) would eventually mutate into a race and benefit from the protection of this law.

This, then, is how things stand in the eyes of the law: the "races" exist, plain and simple. The belief that one race is superior to another, being a *belief*, is perfectly lawful as it is private to an individual. However, racial *discrimination* occurs when someone is treated less favourably because of their "race", and this *is* unlawful.

The situation is both bizarre as well as insidious. The way that the law is set up, it *encourages* social fragmentation because the law will only offer protection to racialized individuals. The law requires and insists that individuals define themselves as members of racial groups before they may avail themselves of the protection of this law.

Discrimination: without favour

The RRA says that racial discrimination occurs if a person (X) is treated, on "racial grounds", *less favourably* than another person (Y) would have been. This rule applies in all manner of situations, from education, employment, and housing, to the basis on which a bank is willing to make a loan or not.

But the notion of "less favourably" is not at all a straightforward one. The ruling of the House of Lords in the case of the *City of Glasgow vs. Zafar* in 1988 is interesting in this regard. The Law Lords accepted that the dismissal of an employee, Zafar, had been unreasonable, but said that the unreasonableness had not been racially motivated because the City of Glasgow was known for treating all its employees similarly unreasonably! And in this regard the City was being singularly fair; a version of "I don't hate Black people, I hate people". The point in law is that the comparator for whether or not racial discrimination has taken place is not with how a hypothetical ethical employer would have acted in that situation. Rather, the case turns on speculation as to how the *actual employer* might have treated another employee in the same situation.

Unfair discrimination is never easy to prove. Organizations habitually and steadfastly deny the charge. And it is easy enough to play the unfair discrimination card when one's competency is called into question. These possibilities have affected the way the law has come to be shaped. To understand more of why these laws came to be written in these particular ways, it will be helpful to contextualize the legislation in the history of racialized relations in the UK.

A very short history of race legislation in the UK

Post-war Britain found its workforce depleted. In the 1950s and 1960s, it specifically set about drawing labour from its colonies and ex-colonies, primarily from the Indian sub-continent and the West Indies. These newcomers were met with hostility. There was no shame attached to racism; it was openly voiced. The new immigrants were often banned from entering some public houses, clubs, lodgings, restaurants, and so forth. It was not uncommon for many to display notices saying "No Blacks, Irish or Dogs". These were the kinds of issues that the very first *Race Relations Act* (1965) wanted to take up by prohibiting racial discrimination in public places such as restaurants, public transport, and so forth. Even so, it was a half-hearted and somewhat lame affair. The Act did not grant those aggrieved any access to the law courts, but instead to a Race Relations Board, which had no power to initiate investigations.

In time, a new *Race Relations Act* (1976) replaced the previous Acts. It created the Commission for Racial Equality (CRE). Much of the law as it stands today is to be found in this Act. This Act outlawed "race discrimination" in education, housing, employment, and the provision of goods, facilities, and services. Although the Act was directed specifically at governmental authorities, it singularly failed in this primary purpose. The failure was aided and abetted by a ruling of the House of Lords (*Re Amin*, 1983) which pronounced that the *services* offered by local authorities such as education, housing, and so forth, were not "services" at all, and so these authorities were not answerable to this law. As to quite why "services" are not services remains somewhat mysterious to me. Anyhow, one of the consequences of this ruling was that local authorities and many other public bodies such as the police and customs fell outside the scope of the Act and were free to continue their racist practices as before. But even this sorry state of affairs was too much for the aforementioned Lord Denning, who, at one time, likened the powers of the CRE to that of the Inquisition (Denning, 1979).

Brixton 1981: the Scarman Report

Events took a critical turn in April 1981, when (mainly) Black youths rioted in Brixton, South London. Property was damaged, widespread looting took place, and over 250 police officers were injured, as were many members of the public. The government appointed Lord Scarman to hold an inquiry into the causes of this troubling event.

The explanation for the riots being voiced "on the streets" was that it was a reaction provoked by aggressive and racist policing methods. For years there had been complaints that the police had been subjecting the Black population to harsh policing, in particular in the use of their powers to "stop and search". The riots occurred after a week of particularly intense police activity on the street, code-named Swamp 81.

In his report, Scarman defended the police and disagreed with the view from "the street". In his view, the riots were not caused by provocative (racist) policing methods, but by social deprivation and "racial disadvantage". Therefore, the solution to the problem, he suggested, was that the sources of racial disadvantage be urgently attended to, in order to pre-empt the possibilities of similar future riots.

Scarman freed *senior* police officers of the taint of racism. He spoke strongly, saying, "I totally and unequivocally reject the attack made upon the integrity and impartiality of the senior direction of the force". He went on to say that some of their actions which look a lot like racism are better described as "errors of judgment, in a lack of imagination and flexibility, but not in deliberate bias or prejudice" (Scarman Report, 1981, Para 4.62, p. 64). He did, however, grant (though the tone is somewhat reluctant) that some officers of *lower rank* were guilty of "ill considered immature and racially prejudiced actions . . . in their dealings on the streets with young Black people" (Scarman Report, 1981, Para 4.63, p 64). And he did acquiesce that "Racial prejudice does manifest itself occasionally in the behaviour of a few officers on the street" (Scarman Report, 1981, Para 4.63, p. 64). Scarman also made a strong stand against the charge that the police force was institutionally racist. He went on to say that if, "however, the suggestion being made is that practices may be adopted by public bodies as well as private individuals which are *unwittingly* discriminatory against Black people, then this is an allegation which deserves serious consideration, and, where proved, swift remedy" (Scarman Report, 1981, Para 2.22, p. 11).

The conclusions of the Scarman report are that the problem lies "in" the community and that there is no problem of any significance with the way that the police conduct themselves. The problems of social deprivation and racial disadvantage are to be dealt with by putting resources into the community. The police, meanwhile, are provided with "training", because there is obviously a "culture clash" between them and the community; the intention of the training being to make the police more sensitive to the ways of the dark folk living in Brixton.

Some of Scarman's suggestions regarding policing methods were put into law in *The Police and Criminal Evidence Act 1984*. In particular, for the first time, this Act made "racial discrimination" by police officers a specific offence. But the rioting continued. There was yet another inquiry, this time conducted by Lord Gifford QC following a particularly violent riot in 1985, on a housing estate called Broadwater Farm in North London. Gifford voiced much stronger and direct criticism of the Metropolitan Police Service than did Scarman. But the government of the day pretty much ignored this report.

Stephen Lawrence 1993: the Macpherson Report

The next critical moment in this history occurred in 1993: the tragic murder of Stephen Lawrence. This horror was compounded by the *débâcle* that was the Metropolitan Police Service's (MPS) bungled investigation into that murder, which led to the known murderers escaping conviction (who are free still to this day). And that *débâcle* was further compounded by yet another: the internal police inquiry conducted by the Kent Police Force regarding the performance of the Metropolitan Police Service (MPS). The Kent Police Force absolved the MPS of any impropriety, including the charge of being racist in the way they conducted their investigations. After much public protest and campaigning, a major official independent inquiry into the whole affair was eventually and reluctantly instigated by the Home Secretary—the Macpherson Inquiry (1999). Its findings were damning of the authorities generally and the MPS in particular. Some of the recommendations of the Inquiry were put into place in the *Race Relations Amendment Act* of 2000.

In this Act, most significantly, for the very first time there was official recognition and acknowledgement that there existed something called "institutional racism". This was a major step. Up to now, on the occasions that there was recognition that something racist had taken place, it was thought of in very individualistic terms, the "bad apple" theory of racism. In this theory, systems and people are on the whole benign, and it is only the occasional *person* who is racist, one bad apple in an otherwise good and decent basket of apples.

While the emphases of the earliest Acts were to outlaw *individuals* behaving in racist ways, the Amendment Acts speak to *institutions*, and, specifically, to the phenomenon of institutional racism. With this notion, there was now a formal recognition and acceptance of the fact that institutions organized themselves in ways that disadvantaged some kinds of people and privileged other kinds, and that this took place inadvertently, with no conscious intention on anyone's part. The Inquiry defined institutional racism is the following way:

> The collective failure of an organisation to provide an appropriate and professional service to people because of their colour, culture or ethnic origin. It can be seen or detected in processes, attitudes and behaviour which amount to discrimination through unwitting prejudice, ignorance, thoughtlessness and racist stereotyping which disadvantage minority ethnic people. [Macpherson, 1999, 6.34]

In its twelfth recommendation, the Inquiry also set in place a powerful definition of a "racist incident" and obliged all police forces to utilize it. The definition being: "a racist incident is any incident which is *perceived* to be racist by the victim or any other person" (Macpherson, 1999, 47:12).

These two interlinked definitions are in a sense "answers" to certain problems, and it is to these that I turn next.

No racism, no problem

One of the key features of the Metropolitan Police's investigation of Stephen Lawrence's murder was their dogged insistence that the murder itself was not racially motivated. They then denied that racism played any role in the way they conducted their investigation, a denial that was backed by the Kent Police Force's investigation into the MPS.

This, then, was the official line that the Lawrence Inquiry faced as it began its investigations. In its final report, the Lawrence Inquiry overturned all these claims, saying that racism played a part not only in the murder, but also in the investigation into the murder, as well as in the investigation into that investigation. In a powerful paragraph they state:

> 6.21 The failure of the first investigating team to recognise and accept racism and race relations as a central feature of their investigation of the murder of Stephen Lawrence played a part in the deficiencies in policing which we identify in this Report. For example, a substantial number of officers of junior rank would not accept that the murder of Stephen Lawrence was simply and solely "racially motivated". The relevance of the ethnicity and cultural status of the victims, including

> Duwayne Brooks, and Mr & Mrs Lawrence, was not properly recognised. Immediately after the murder Mr Brooks was side-lined, and his vital information was inadequately considered. None of these shortcomings was corrected or overcome.

The situation that the Lawrence Inquiry faced was one in which racism had been air-brushed out of the picture by the simple but powerful strategy of dogged denial. No racism, therefore no problem. It was in order to combat this kind of culture of denial that the Lawrence Inquiry came up with its powerful definition of a "racist incident": "any incident which is perceived to be racist by the victim or any other person". The key word is "perceived". Now, if anyone—even a passer by—thinks that "race" has played a part in whatever has taken place, then the police have no choice but to investigate this possibility.

If the intention of the strategy of denial of racism is to shut the door on the possibility that something untoward had taken place, then the intention of the definition of "racist incident" is to wedge the door permanently open. Extreme situations call for extreme measures.

But with the door permanently wedged open, the protocols designed to protect people from "racial" discrimination are always open to potential abuse. Thus, an incompetent person who has been sacked can always trigger these grievance protocols by claiming that they were dismissed because of their "race". This possibility makes organizations extremely nervous, so much so that they might be extremely reluctant to confront an employee who has the possibility of availing themselves of the definition of racist incident.

Meanwhile, on the other side of the fence, there is the strategy of denial of racism. One reason for this strategy is to avoid being answerable to the requirements of the various *Race Relations Acts*. Recall Lord Denning's comments in which he reminded us that one could insult with impunity all those who did not fall under the protection of the RRAs.

An episode that took place in early 2007 in Britain is instructive in this regard. This involved the Channel 4 television programme *Celebrity Big Brother*, which televised the daily interactions of several "celebrities" living together. Three of the inhabitants were accused of bullying and making "racial" comments about the Bollywood actress, Shilpa Shetty.

Now, the facts, as in the things that were actually said ("Shilpa Poppadom, fuck off home, can't speak English properly", etc., etc.), were not in dispute; the recordings were in the public domain. But how were they to be understood? Channel 4's first line of defence was indeed the denial of racism. They issued a statement saying:

> To date there has been no overt racial abuse or racist behaviour directed against Shilpa Shetty within the Big Brother house. However there has undoubtedly been a cultural and class clash between her and three of the British females in the house. [BBC News, 19 January 2007]

If the insults and injuries are caused by a "culture clash", then, while this is regrettable, it is not against the law, and so Channel 4 can breathe easy. But if they had been obliged to follow Macpherson's definition of "racist incident", then the situation would have been very different. If it turned out that "race" and not culture was the issue, then Channel 4 would have been deemed to have broken the law.

Let me now look at the issues raised by the definition of "institutional racism".

The unconscious and institutional racism

Although Scarman had insisted that there was no institutionalized racism in the police force, he did accept that the actions of well meaning *individual* policemen and women could nevertheless be racist at times, but in ways that were "unwitting" and "unconscious". To these two terms the Macpherson Report makes it a point of adding the notion of "unintentional" racism (Macpherson, 1999, 6.13). While recognizing the significance of each of these three adjectives, in its actual definition of institutional racism, the Macpherson report settled on "unwitting".

> The collective failure of an organisation to provide an appropriate and professional service to people because of their colour, culture, or ethnic origin. It can be seen or detected in processes, attitudes and behaviour which amount to discrimination through *unwitting* prejudice, ignorance, thoughtlessness and racist stereotyping which disadvantage minority ethnic people. [1999, 6.34]

But why does the definition call on the notion of "unwitting" (which is akin to "unintentional") rather than that of "unconscious"? The difference between them is critically important.

To begin with, the Macpherson Report forcefully reprimands the culture of denial among some police officers. It also says that the excuse offered—incompetence—could not account sufficiently for the catalogue of failures and oversights in the investigation, and that the only way that the depth and range of the failures could be understood is via the notion of institutional racism, which their report says, is "pernicious and persistent" (6.46). But, on the other hand, the report is also at pains to say that in stating that the MPS is permeated by institutional racism, it is not suggesting "that in its policies . . . the MPS is racist" (6.47). Neither does the charge of institutional racism "mean or imply that every police officer is guilty of racism. No such sweeping suggestion can be or should be made" (6.24).

They are at pains to emphasize that it is the ways that institutions *function* that is racist. But the use of "unwitting" actually gives absolution to the institution and those that benefit from the ways that it is arranged. Consider: the notions of *unwitting* or *unintentional* allow for the possibility that, although harm has been done to another, there has been no *desire* to do so: while the outcome of some series of events is unfortunate, there has been no deliberate malice.

But if one draws on the notion of the unconscious, then the situation is rendered more complicated. And it is particularly complicated if one draws on a psychoanalytic understanding of the unconscious. To begin with, by definition, we do not and cannot know that which we are not conscious of. The notion of unconscious is potent: we do not even know what it is that we do not know, neither can we know that that there is something we do not know. That which is unconscious is truly beyond our ken.

Having made this clarification, let me ask this question: why are some of our wishes and desires not conscious? Psychoanalysis answers that *some* of our desires are repressed and *made* unconscious because they are taboo in some way. And here comes the first twist; although the desires are unconscious, we nevertheless find ways of expressing and fulfilling them without recognizing that we are doing so. For example: I am angry with you, but I repress this knowledge for some reason (say, because I am afraid that you will leave me). But then I find that events have conspired in such a way that I find that

I "accidentally" step on your foot and hurt you. The way the situation looks to all and sundry is that an unfortunate accident has occurred. No blame can be attributed to me. Although I have injured you, I appear to be innocent of malice. It is in this way that I am able to have my cake and eat it, too. I express my anger and yet maintain a façade of innocence—and here is the rub: to myself as much as to you.

We are now in a position to spell out the distinction between "unwitting" and "unconscious", and it is this: racism that is "unintentional" or "unwitting" can claim to be morally "innocent" as there was no *desire* to harm; the harm was truly an epiphenomenon. However, racism that is unconscious, is not only not innocent, it is duplicitous. In unconscious racism there *is* intention and desire to do down the other in some way, but the intention or desire is unconscious. This is the psychoanalytic theory of unconscious motivation.

And now, the second twist: having made the distinction between an "innocent unwitting racism" and a more problematic "unconscious racism", psychoanalysis would question whether the first of these is ever a possibility. Psychoanalysis would say that unconscious motivation is ever present in all our activities, and that the rationales we provide for our decisions and activities are always to some degree rationalizations that serve our interests in some way.

If we now think of institutional racism as consisting of *interest-serving unconscious* processes rather than as processes that cause harm to others *unwittingly*, then it becomes more insidious. The ways that the world comes to be arranged is not accidental, and its consequences are not "unwitting". Rather, it comes to be so arranged precisely to serve the interests of the already privileged; the way that the institution comes to be organized is "witting". However, these structural arrangements do not arise through deliberate design. This is not a conspiracy of the rulers deliberately setting out to bewilder and exploit numerous others. All are unconscious of what is happening, and all, to some degree, co-operate (albeit unconsciously) in preserving the status quo (more on this later). We can also see here that the political notion of "ideology" is entwined with the psychological notion of "unconscious processes'.

In sum, the use of "unwitting" lets institutions off the moral hook.

Dangerous discretion: proceduralizing decision making

The phrase "institutional racism" invites one to assume that racism is embedded in the institutions we inhabit. This is so. Racism is institutionalized in the structures, conventions, and procedures of organizations. But racism is also institutionalized in the psyches of the individuals who compose those organizations, although not in the same way and to the same degree in each and every individual. If racism, sexism, and so forth are institutionalized, then all are riven by it and to varying degrees all will find themselves perpetuating it, *despite themselves*. And it is not just specific organizations such as the police or housing authorities which are patterned by the processes of racism, but society as a whole.

The point is that even as the law makers and law enforcers are trying to address the sources of social inequity, they nevertheless end up reproducing them to some degree. This is because the "authorities" do not stand outside or above the "system" they are seeking to manage or re-engineer. They are a part of it and, so, informed by it. In doing their work, law makers and enforcers are continually obliged to use their discretion to adjudicate between alternatives. These processes of discretion will be necessarily biased in directions determined by the dominant discourses that they are subject to. They will be unconsciously (and sometimes quite consciously) prone to favour one way of reading things rather than another.

This tendency to be biased has long been recognized in even the hard, "objective" sciences such as physics and medicine—sciences that use instruments to measure and count data. Despite themselves, experimenters tend to read "objective" results in ways that substantiate their assumptions and beliefs (see, for example, Gould, 1984). It is for this reason that experimental protocols such as the double blind and randomized control trials were conceived. These protocols are attempts at minimizing the bias that humans inevitably bring to any and every situation.

This, then, is the dilemma: as soon as there is an opportunity to use one's discretion, one will do so in ways that are patterned by the ideologies that one is constituted by. However dispassionate and objective we think we might be being, our opinions and judgements are always going to be skewed to some degree. This point was noted in the submission of the 1990 Trust to the Macpherson Inquiry (6.29), which said: "Racism within the police can be both covert and overt, racism can be detected in how . . . existing policy is ignored or individual officers' *discretion* results in racist outcomes" (my italics).

If the problem is that the processes of discretion are necessarily biased, then this is the solution: remove or reduce the number of available opportunities in which individuals will be required to use their discretion. Discretion, discernment, discrimination all require individuals to call on their thinking and feeling processes to arrive at a decision, at a judgement. It is for this sort of reason that the individual's capacities to think have come to be replaced by protocols, procedures, and policies to reach conclusions and decide on directions. Procedures seek not only to limit the range of options available to the one making decisions, they also intend to drive the individual to making the "right" decision. Thinking has been replaced with flow-chart-following.

When one looks at the *débâcle* of the investigation into Stephen Lawrence's murder, then one can understand why it is that organizations are being required to proceed in this way. In each and every opportunity afforded the police to *discern* between the possibility that the murder was racist or not, they chose the option that effectively colluded with the murders; with each opportunity to use their discretion, they decided on conclusions that denied the existence of any racist motivations in any of the proceedings. And presumably they did this because at some level their attitudes were not too distant from those of the racists.

It is when one is faced with such situations (and there are many of them) that the rationale for replacing thinking with flow-chart-following becomes understandable. With this definition of "racist incident", even if the policeman genuinely thinks that "race" has not played a part in events, if someone else does raise this possibility, then the policeman is obliged by law to take account of that possibility.

The down side is that this kind of definition allows some criminals the possibility of exploiting this definition of racist incident to cry racial discrimination in regard to their treatment.

I am not against routines and procedures *per se*. What I am against is the mindless application of bureaucratic procedures. Employed in the correct way, routines and procedures are very helpful. One can think of them as the embodiment of lessons learnt from history and experience. Procedures are there to guide how one ought to deal with some future anticipated situation based on experience gleaned from dealing with similar situations in the past. But when procedures are followed mindlessly, when they become bureaucratic absolutes, then the casualty is thought itself.

But there is another, more critical problem with procedures as solutions, which is that the procedures often circumnavigate the problem itself and leave it untouched. It is a "sleeping policeman" solution.

The sleeping policeman solution

One of the ironies of contemporary life has to do with the kinds of solutions we devise for problems thrown up by modernity. For example, manufacturers of cars are designing and selling cars that go faster and faster, resulting in more accidents and deaths. Meanwhile, public authorities try to slow down these increasingly lethal entities by various means including putting humps in the road—sleeping policemen, as they have been called. This strategy works to some degree. Meanwhile, over the decades, the motor industry continues to make cars that go even faster with more efficient shock absorbers, which results in them being able to traverse the humps at greater speeds, and this in turn provokes the local authorities make the humps higher and higher. Not only does the "solution" not address the "problem" (the capacity for speed and acceleration designed into cars), the solution provokes the problem into taking up more extreme forms; the conflict escalates. This is because the values of the solution are in conflict with the values of the problem.

It seems to me that much public policy is of this "sleeping policeman" kind. In the case we have been discussing, the problem is the racism endemic in the police force. The sleeping policeman solution is the definition of "racist incident". The definition "slows down" the police in their anticipated rush to deny racism, and they are now obliged to pause and take account of its possibility. But this policy does nothing to address the problem of racism in the police force, which continues as before, albeit in a more covert form.

The solution allows some "ethnic" criminals who are clearly in the wrong to opportunistically use the racist incident card to claim that they are being unfairly treated. Through this device they turn the tables and it is now the police who stand accused and must justify and defend themselves. These mischievous uses of the definition of "racist incident" feed the resentment of the police towards "those" people, and so will further fuel their racism. The habitual abuse of the definition of "racist incident" by the "bad" people must become tedious, and is likely to lead to the deepening of the culture which dismisses the charge of racism without really looking into it. No doubt many of the previously mentioned 5000 complaints of "oppressive behaviour" made against the Metropolitan Police Territorial Support Group were mischievous (Lewis & Taylor, 2009). But it is also extremely unlikely that there was substance in just 0.18% of the complaints. So, despite the power of the notion of "racist incident", it would seem that it is easy enough to find a way to work around it even while one gives the impression of abiding by it.

The difficulty is that the police (and the authorities generally) are not universally evil and neither are they universally good. Many, I would imagine, are trying to do a very difficult job in the right way, in very difficult circumstances. And yet, as the Macpherson Report has shown, the culture of casual racism is commonplace in the cafeteria. The definition of racist incident, and the procedures surrounding it, leaves this culture untouched, and just drives it underground from where it continues to do its work. This sort of culture is supposed to be being changed by "trainings" that the entire workforce is put through. I will have more to say about training in a later chapter, but what is clear already is that they do not really seem to do the work they were intended for—they leave the problem untouched. For example, here is one not uncommon recent episode, in which one has to assume that all the protagonists (from governmental institutions) will have been put through at least one equal opportunity training, and that these institutions would also have in place numerous procedures to counter racist practices.

In 2008, a diagnosed schizophrenic, Tula Miah, a British citizen of Bangladeshi origin, was picked up in London by the police because he was behaving strangely (Dyer, 2008a). During the interview, Miah gave them a false name and this led to the police deciding that the person they had in custody was, in fact, a Bilal Ahmad, a failed asylum seeker from Pakistan who had absconded. Miah was given a fifteen-minute examination by a doctor who determined that there was no evidence of mental illness. The photograph of Ahmad faxed from the immigration authorities did not match their suspect (and at the time this was acknowledged to be the case by the police themselves); for one thing, Miah was two inches taller than Ahmad. Despite Miah having his bank card upon him, the police did no further checks on his identity. Despite these and other anomalies, they said that they were "90% certain" of who they had in custody and so they deported him to Pakistan. There "he was held in chains and beaten—partly because he angered officials by being unable to communicate with them [in either of the Pakistani languages, Urdu or Punjabi]". Eventually, the Pakistani authorities decided that their prisoner was not Pakistani and put him on a plane back to Britain. Having already tried to cut his wrists, he arrived showing signs of psychosis and severe distress. On arrival, he was detained in a psychiatric hospital for two days and then returned to immigration officials. They, in turn, deposited Miah in Terminal 4 at Heathrow airport, leaving him with a £5 note. It was three days later that this ill, confused, and traumatized individual managed to contact his family.

Unsurprisingly, the Miah family brought a case of racial discrimination against the Home Office whose response was to flatly deny any racist motive, saying that "immigration officers acted in good faith". The Home Office must have an unusual understanding of "faith", given that there is a note on a Home Office file which says "there appears to be some doubt that the person in custody is our subject". They seem to have made no effort to establish which languages Miah spoke; clearly no Pakistani languages (Urdu or Punjabi), but English and also, presumably, he spoke Bengali, Sylheti, or one of the thirty-eight other Bangladeshi languages. Bangladesh and Pakistan are about 3000 km apart (the approximate distance from Paris to Greenland). Despite all this, the police and immigration authorities could only see a brown-skinned "asylum seeker" because presumably, to them, they do in fact all look alike.

Anyhow, just two days after having issued this robust denial, as the case was about to go to the High Court, the Home Office capitulated and settled out of court. But, as a condition of the settlement, the family and lawyers were not only not allowed to discuss the terms of the settlement, but also the fact that a settlement had even been reached. In contrast to the high profile granted the initial story in many newspapers and websites on 8th June, the conclusion of the affair on 10th June got hardly a mention in the press. As none of the aggrieved was allowed to speak, and the guilty ones were not likely to, the result is that the story, starved of content, died a death, not only without a bang but also without a whimper (Dyer, 2008b).

It is hard to absorb the number of ironies contained in this sorry tale. The government of the land puts in place a number of laws that it asks its inhabitants and institutions to abide by. It spends enormous amounts of money and effort putting its employees through "trainings" in fairness, dealing with "others", and so forth. Then, several of the government's own institutions act in ways that blatantly go against both the spirit and the letter of the law. Yet, not only does the government deny that its institutions have transgressed their own guidelines, but also, it is not willing to have its stance tested publicly in the law courts. Instead, it buys off the complainants and in the same moment robs them of their capacity to speak (one of the fundamental freedoms and rights of all human beings).

Why not come clean? Why not put up their hands and say yes, something has gone seriously wrong here, we will try to do something about it. Surely this is the attitude the government wants of its citizens? Instead, a UK Border Agency spokesman obfuscates, saying, "The UK Border Agency carries out all removals with dignity and compassion, and takes very seriously any claim that proper *procedures* have not been followed" (quoted in Dyer, 2008b, my italics). Note the concern for procedure. How far have we actually come from Stephen Lawrence? Despite powerful legislation being put in place, untold episodes like these make governmental agency's claim that they *really* want to tackle the issue of unfair discrimination sound increasingly hollow.

We can see, then, that there are problems aplenty with the way that the legislature has proceeded. But its intention has always been a decent and sensible one: to enable and support the liberal principle of "live and let live". The fact that the legislation is not managing to do the work it was intended for suggests that something critical is missing from the picture.

CHAPTER FOUR

Manufacturing kinds of people: processes of inclusion and exclusion

The legislature, as well as the equality movements, has proceeded on the basis of a particular (problematic) world view, two elements of which are of specific concern to us. First is a simplistic understanding of the social group (whatever name it goes by, race, culture, ethnicity, etc.); second is a one-dimensional rendition of the human condition. If one buys into both of them, then the problem and its solution appear to be relatively straightforward as evidenced by the heroic pronouncements found in the equality statements of innumerable organizations, public and private. According to these, it is a simple enough matter to practise inclusivity, non-interference, tolerance, and respect towards others; it is just a matter of knowledge and will. It seems to me that to try to live one's life according to these principles is a decent and worthy way of proceeding. Problems arise when these values are treated as though they are real achievable ends, rather than aspirations. When this happens, then the values of liberalism come to be distorted and turned into instruments of fear and control. It is for this reason that discussions on these subjects so often have a defensive quality, quickly become heated, and end in an impasse.

This chapter and the one that follows will critique each of these elements. This chapter concerns itself with the rendition of the social group and the next one the rendition of the individual.

Three questions about the kinds of humans

These days, notions of race, culture, and ethnicity are commonplace in casual conversations, newspaper articles, and across dinner tables. A man mentions in passing, "My wife is mixed race," and continues, "she has a Spanish mother and a Black father."

We think we know what we are referring to when we use these terms, but do we? It is conventional to suppose that race concerns physiology, culture relates to behaviour and belief, and ethnicity concerns an internal sense of belonging. This seems reasonable until we ask, what is it that is being mixed in this man's wife? Listening to him, it would appear that she was made by mixing something with a nation with a colour. If you listen (or read) carefully, more often than not, in reportage and everyday speech, the three terms are used interchangeably, often enough in the same sentence. Note the range of categories employed in the recent scandal regarding two *Asian* men found guilty of grooming young girls for sex, and then abusing them. The local MP, Jack Straw, said that it was "a specific problem which involves *Pakistani* heritage men"; the MP Keith Vaz said this was not a "*cultural* problem" (Smith, 2011). A spokesperson from Barnardos used the terms *race, racial background,* and *mixed race* (Davies, 2011). Mohammed Shafique, of the Ramadhan Foundation, said that this was "not a *race* issue or a *Muslim* issue" (Parveen, 2011, my italics); other terms that also featured prominently in the exchanges included, among others, *coloured, White,* and *community*.

Given that the primary task of the equality movements is to address the inequalities between the different *kinds* of people, it is particularly unfortunate that it has taken on a singularly simplistic view of human groupings. In fact, on the whole, the equality movements begin by taking it for granted that the different kinds of people just exist, and that the problems of inequality arise because people of one kind "naturally" tend to have difficulties with people of other kinds. In the UK, race, gender, disability, culture, and ethnicity are given the status of kinds. But how substantial are any of these notions? How real are they? Here are three questions to seed the discussion.

1. The first issue is this: any two individuals (or groups) can be said to be the same as each other on the basis of an infinitely large number of categories—say, colour. And in the same moment, these same two individuals could be said to be different from each other on the basis of any number of other categorizations—say, gender. In other words, *both possibilities are always equally and simultaneously true at the same time*: Mr X is similar to Mrs Y and Mr X is different to Mrs Y. The questions then become, which of the two possible descriptions do we find ourselves settling on, and how and why?
2. Out of this enormous range and number of available categories of similarity and difference, why and how is it that we come to recognize only some of the categories as "kinds" of people? For example, skin colour but not hair colour, religious difference but not vocational difference, and so on.
3. It is also the case (as we will come to see), that some of these differences are presumed to be fundamental and deep, and others are thought to be surface and less significant. On what basis are these claims and distinctions being made, and why is it important?

The problem with race

The problem of race is, simply, that it does not exist. Despite its ubiquity, all attempts to pin down any kind of factual basis for the race concept over the last two hundred years have completely failed. Yet "race" continues to be used as though it actually described something real. The situation is compounded by the fact that the term is instated in law (as we saw in Chapter Three). With the notion of race now established as fact, it comes to be used as the explanation for racism. Why were there riots in Chicago or Bradford? Answer: because of racial difference. And so they are then called "race riots". Faced with this kind of situation, the multi-culturalists ask each of the races to "tolerate" each other. Meanwhile, some sociobiologists think racism to be a natural adaptive trait, and so give succour to the racists. Theirs is a four-step argument, based on the idea of the selfish gene.

Sociobiology

They begin with the assertion that we are programmed by the evolutionary processes to act in ways that will enhance the chances of our genes surviving and multiplying. Next, we are said to share more genes with kin than those not-kin, and this makes us automatically favour kin over others. Third, ethnicity or race is said to be an extension of kinship, and so we are said to naturally favour those of the same race or ethnic group over others. And finally, they complain that when they behave in these "natural" ways, then they are unfairly accused of being racist.

Here are some of the flaws in their argument: any human grouping is found to have approximately 15% of its DNA patterns in common. This means that the other 85% is shared with the rest of humanity. So, why should this 15% seek to favour its kin and not the other 85%? It is also the case that we share 98% of our DNA with chimpanzees, yet we do not treat them too well. And finally, we need go back only 150,000 years to find one of the many common ancestors for all of human kind—thus, we are all kin.

There is no meaningful correlation between genetic makeup and so-called racial groups. The fact that people in geographical regions come to look in particular ways does not make them a "race". As populations move and mix, as they have always done, these so-called "types" also shift and change. Ultimately, the idea of race is an attempt to inject a difference with significance and fix it from the beginnings of time for all of eternity.

The problem with culture (and ethnicity)

As the notion of race is so problematic, we come increasingly to rely on the alternatives called culture and ethnicity. Surely these notions are more substantial? Well, yes, they are, but not in the ways that they are usually thought of.

The question is particularly important because of the status given to culture by the Romantics and the multi-culturalists: they require us to treat cultures as though they were living entities like individual people, and then to confer similar rights on them. The idea of culture that follows out of this is one of it being a bounded entity that has coherence over time. Being bounded, it then automatically owns/possesses an internal space and so what they do within it is a private matter for "them". Being an entity, it is conceived of as a living thing with rights.

There are three critical problems with this conventional use and understanding of the ideas of culture and ethnicity: first, the assumption that they are monoliths; second, that there is a consensus within the group as to its beliefs and practices; third, that each individual belongs to a single group. I take each in turn.

The illusion of unity

To begin with, cultures are not the unitary homogeneous entities that they are taken to be. They are conflictual and riven with differences of opinion. As soon as we try to get a hold of a culture, the illusion of coherence fragments. British culture disintegrates into Northerner, country gent, farm labourer, metropolitan sophisticate, working class, *Guardian* reader, *Sun* reader, Moslem, Catholic, Green, Fascist, and so on; Islam fragments into Sunni, Shia, Wahhabi, Sufi, Black American, and so on. Meanwhile, Hindu culture fragments into entities like Brahmin and Untouchable. And when one probes each of these names in turn, then they, too, fragment into further categories, professor, zealot, drunkard, gay. Neither is there a hierarchy of identities. Some *Guardian* readers are Moslems, others Catholics, and others again vegetarian; some Moslems read the *Guardian* and others the *Sun*. One Egyptian might use the teachings of his Islam to guide his actions, another the profit motive, while another again might insist that it is the love of one's country that ought to be the guiding principle for how one acts; another might think that one's actions should be according to the principles of Communism, and yet another cares not a jot for these values and instead lives a life of hedonism. All are authentically Egyptian, and each of their authentic beliefs is in conflict with those of the others.

The myth of consensual coherence: the Holy Cow

Already we are with the second difficulty with the idea of culture: the illusion of consensus. The bloodshed taking place in Iraq is surely testament to the view that Islam is not a coherent world view; these are bloody differences, with Sunni and Shia each claiming that it is they that have understood the real message of God. But we do not need to go that far to find evidence that so-called ways of life are not consensual. The Klu Klux Klan, Arnold Schwarzenegger, Evangelical Christians, Noam Chomsky, George Bush, Barack Obama, Fox News, Gore Vidal, would all see themselves as defending "*The* American Way". If societies were indeed consensual, then there would be no politics. The UK, too, has had (and continues to have) its share of brutal and bloody revolutions.

While we are more able to be aware of the differences within the "us", we are prone to see "them"—particularly if they are exotic—as a homogeneity. This tendency is reinforced by the more powerful among "them", the elite who pose as traditional authorities, who push a particular line, their line, as the authentic line. There are always competing alternative lines that are silenced by the orthodoxy by branding them as invalid or heretical.

Joallyn Archambault, Director of the American Indian Program and a member of the Sioux Tribe, points out that there is no one origin story for American Indians:

> origin stories . . . vary widely from tribe to tribe . . . Even within the same tribe, traditional beliefs can include multiple creation stories. For example, three different creation stories were accepted in my father's tribe when I was a child. [quoted in Malik, 2008, p. 237]

The point is that all cultures, even the exotic ones in far off aboriginal lands, are political and politicized entities. The diversity advocate's strategy of wanting to make a distinction between cultural practices and politics is unsustainable, because, for one thing, the establishment of one kind of cultural practice over another is itself the outcome of political struggle. Cultural practices that become established as norms, and then taken for granted by "us" as well as "them", are in some senses the emblem of the victorious party. Take, for example, the Hindu taboo with regard to eating beef.

I had taken this to be a universal truth, true of all Hindus for all time, and so was astonished to be recently informed by Lynn Sivanandan (personal communication) that this was not so. It turns out that in at least three Indian states, Kerala, Kashmir, and West Bengal, many Hindu families happily eat beef. It is part of their cultural norm. The South Indian newspaper *The Hindu* even carries a recipe for beef curry on its pages![1] As you might expect, this incenses Hindus of a certain kind—fundamentalist, chauvinistic, right-wing, and fascistic—that go under the banner of the Hindutva (it was a Hindutva ideologue, Nathuram Godse, who murdered Mahatma Gandhi). The chauvinistic Hindutva parties, the BJP, Shiv Sena, VHP, and the like tried (so far unsuccessfully) to have the Indian parliament pass a law banning the killing of cows for food in these states. These spokespeople say that they are defending the authenticity of their culture, that *by definition* Hindus do not eat beef and never have, and that the practice of eating beef is a form of contamination brought into India by Muslim and Christian invaders.

But this is just not so, as the Indian, Hindu, and Brahmin (and, therefore, scoring high in the credibility stakes) historian D. N. Jha (2004) convincingly argues in his scholarly book *The Myth of the Holy Cow*. The accepted myth is that the practice of beef eating was introduced into India by its later Muslim rulers, and then reinforced later again by the by dietary habits of the Imperial British. Jha has infuriated sections of the Hindu orthodoxy by demonstrating that there are no such strictures in the Vedic texts, and, in fact, in some places they actually *advocate* beef as an important dietary item. The law book of Manu "exempts the camel [and dogs] from being killed for food, but does not grant this privilege to the cow". He shows that in ancient times, long before the arrival of the Muslim rulers, not only the practice of *eating* beef but also the *sacrifice* of cows were widespread in what came to be known eventually as India. Jha uncovered convincing evidence of cow slaughter and consumption by Hindus of all classes, including Brahmins, until as late as the nineteenth century. Unsurprisingly, the Hindutva parties have issued their own version of the fatwa on Jha, and even managed to get his book banned in some Indian states. Professor Ram Puniyani summarizes some of Jha's findings:

> Many gods such as Indra and Agni are described as having special preferences for different types of flesh—Indra had weakness for bull's meat and Agni for bull's and cow's. . . . In the Mahabharata there is a mention of a king named Rantideva who achieved great fame by distributing foodgrains and beef to Brahmins. Taittiriya Brahman categorically tells us: 'Verily the cow is food' . . . and Yajnavalkya's insistence on eating the tender (amsala) flesh of the cow is well known. [Puniyani, 2001]

In actual fact, the strictures against eating beef began in Buddhism, from where it migrated into what was to become Hinduism. It was with the advent of the Buddhist philosophy of *ahimsa* (prohibition against killing) that there began to be a shift in regards to the cow. Many "untouchables" took up Buddhism and the practice of *ahimsa* to the displeasure of the beneficiaries of the religio-political system, Brahminism. Brahminism fought back against Buddhism in every which way, one of which was to appropriate elements of Buddhist philosophy that appealed to the populace and make it its own. In effect, the cow was made sacred in order to serve as a political emblem. But it was not until the nineteenth century that this emblem came to full flower, and it did so as a part of the struggle for independence from the British. The "cow-protection movement" became a *political* tool in the service of mobilizing a mass political movement against the British.

Hindus who believe that beef is taboo cannot understand why other Hindus do not think similarly. On a right-wing Hindu website Indiadivine.org (Strap line: "Welcome to the sacred world of Hinduism") some have suggested that Hindus in these states eat beef because of the "Strong political influence of christians and muslims [*sic*]", but others on the website have demurred, saying, "it has something to do with the . . . Communist Party of India . . ." (Indiadivine.org). This is how cultural norms are created and sustained, how one way becomes the right way and the only authentic way. Meanwhile, other sorts of ways that go against the "true way" are denigrated and dismissed as alien and belonging to "outsiders", in this case, Christian, Muslim, and Communist.

The myth called community

The next attempt to salvage the coherence of culture consists of agreeing that there are bloody differences, but beneath that, there is a consensus, a ground of agreements, and that it is this consensus that is the basis of, say, the culture called Englishness. But as we have seen, even as we try to grasp any of these anchors, accent, attitude to food, kinds of food, dress codes, and so on, we cannot, because as we try to grasp it, the one fragments into many.

Ironically, the coherence we call Hinduism has, in a manner of speaking, been created by the very colonial power that dominated it.

It can be (and has been) cogently argued that until relatively recently there was no idea of Hinduism as a coherent, unified body of thought and philosophy. Nussbaum tells us that

> the whole enterprise of codifying the previously informal and regionally various systems of Hindu law was a British enterprise, and Hindu law bears many marks of the English law (including ecclesiastical law) on the model employed by the British legal thinkers of that era [nineteenth century]. [Nussbaum, 2001, p. 215]

Before this time, if asked, a person was more likely to identify themselves as a follower of this or that god, goddess, or cult rather than as Hindu; there were hundreds, if not thousands, of practices and beliefs with allegiances to different entities and values. The British in India set up two different kinds of laws: universal secular laws pertaining to commerce and criminality, and "personal laws" for each of the major religions, Hindus, Muslims, Christians, and Zoarastrians, but not Jews. Personal law included family law, property law, and inheritance law. When it came to these "personal" matters, authority was delegated to courts within these "communities". Unlike the other religions, the problem for the British authorities with codifying Hinduism was that there were no agreed core spiritual texts or beliefs and practices.

Benhabib (2002) takes up Narayan's reflections on one aspect of this process. Narayan asked "how and why [was it that sati] . . . [a] practice marginal to many Hindu communities, let alone Indian ones [in general], came to be regarded as a central Indian tradition" (Narayan, 1997, p. 61). Her answer was that it emerged out of negotiations between the colonial authorities and the elites in India.

The practice of sati, in which a widow throws herself on the funeral pyre of her husband, was abhorrent to the colonialists. It was also undoubtedly abhorrent to many Hindus and Indians generally. The colonial authorities wanted to determine whether this was primarily a religious practice or a social convention. If it were a practice that was sanctioned by the holy books of the faith, then they would be wary of banning it for fear of provoking political unrest. However, "there were few, if any, clear and unambiguous textual endorsements of sati [in the holy books]" (Narayan, 1997, p. 200). The British relied on the pronouncements of the Hindu elite—Brahmin pundits—and took their interpretations to be authentic and authenticating. Benhabib continues,

> A long historical process of cultural interventions and negotiations ironed out the inconsistencies in the accounts of local elites about various myths surrounding the practice of sati. Religious stories in relation to existing practices were codified, and above all, discrepancies in local Hindu traditions that varied not only from region to region but between the various castes as well were homogenized. [Benhabib, 2002, p. 6]

We should remember, too, that although Christianity had by this time its core religious text in the form of the Bible, it was not always the case. Christianity, too, did not arrive into the world fully formed. It was forged over a period of several hundred years in the first millennium in struggles between various beliefs and power struggles between numerous Churches and vested interests. One of the ideological battles for the "soul" of Christianity took place in 325AD at the First Council of Nicaea, which came to play a critical role in the manufacture and shaping of the identity called Christianity. The victors were able to establish several new orthodoxies (note the oxymoron). For example, in the controversy as to whether Christ was created by the Father (which implied that Christ was lesser than the Father), as was believed by the Arians, or whether the Father and Son were of the same substance and co-eternal (and so of equal value), the latter won the day. From this time on, any who did not accept the new orthodoxy were, by definition, heretics to be cast out and punished. Another controversy concerned which day the resurrection of Christ was to be celebrated. According to the Jewish lunar calendar, Easter fell on the fourteenth day of Nisan, and so could fall on any day of the week. It had already previously been ruled that the celebration had to be on a Sunday; this decision established one of the differentiators between Christianity and Judaism. But each Church had its own formula for deciding which particular Sunday. The Council decreed a formula that was to be followed by all. This was another moment in the transformation process through which the federation of Christian Churches became transformed into the Christian empire. Even as the Council was creating a consensual homogeneity called Christianity, it also took the opportunity to cement its identity through the further vilification of the Jews. The Roman Emperor Constantine ratified the decisions of the Council with regard to Easter, saying,

> it appeared an unworthy thing that in the celebration of this most holy feast we should follow the practice of the Jews, who have impiously defiled their hands with enormous sin, and are, therefore, deservedly afflicted with blindness of soul . . . Let us then have nothing in common with the detestable Jewish crowd. [Eusebius of Caesaarea, Volume 3, Chapter Eight]

Once victory is secured, then all are bound to kneel before the new god/king, swearing fealty, and renounce the new false gods. Dress codes, rituals, and dietary practices become emblems of fealty, helping distinguish the righteous from the damned.

There are two further errors we habitually tend to make when thinking about groupings. To begin with, not all identity groups are cultural groups—those located in the category of disability for example. We would not expect *all* wheelchair users to have the same beliefs and values as each other. But what is true of "wheelchair users" is also more generally true of "culture"; as I have been arguing, cultural groups are not really identity groups, either. Those in a cultural group do not all think alike, although the authorities in these groups would like them to do so, and punish those who do not. In this sense, identity is something that is imposed from both within and without the so-called culture.

The second error is to use the fact that Black people are the recipients of prejudice to construe them as being *a community*. To speak of Black people in this way is to assume that they all have the same beliefs and ways of living because of their colour. This kind of attempt to counter racism fails, precisely because it continues to use, and, therefore, reinforce, racialized thinking. Like White people, some Black people are bankers, others are bakers, and others again are criminals and crack addicts. Some speak French as their first language, others English, others Urdu, others Patois, and others Swahili. In no sense can one claim that Black people are a community by virtue of being Black. This way of thinking privileges gross differences between designated groupings, and renders invisible significant and meaningful differences within the designated groupings. It follows that there can be no spokesperson for *the* Black community, as there is no such thing. There are only spokespersons for the interests of particular interest groups, and so they will hold conflictual positions with other spokespersons. Similarly, we cannot simply celebrate the differences of the Muslims from "us" because "they" are not a consensual category, and neither are "we". As soon as one takes account of the differences within the designated us and them, then we are in the territory of politics and power relations, territory which the diversity movement deliberately and assiduously avoids engaging in as it thinks that it just muddies the water. Politics does indeed muddy the water, but that is precisely its virtue; it challenges the simplistic clarity of the diversity promulgators.

The appearance of politics in the foregoing is a prompt for us to turn our attention to the function of cultural practices. My view follows the sociologist of knowledge, Norbert Elias (1976, 1994), to say that the primary purpose of differentials in cultural practices (say, whether to eat pork or not) is not the expression of an inner meaning, but to differentiate an "us" from the "them", as I explain further below.

Differences in the service of differentiation

As we saw in Chapter Two, cultural practices are not designed to be kept private but to be acted out in public. However banal and innocuous, their function lies precisely in creating boundaries by acting as visible markers of differentiation through rituals, dress code, and so on. Although these practices are privately "owned", they are given expression in public spaces, their function being that of differentiating an "us" from a "them".

For example, within the alleged homogeneity called English culture, when making a cup of tea, there are conventions as to whether one is to pour the milk first and the tea second, or *vice versa* (Fox, 2005). The upper classes pour milk in last, as do the working classes. The middle classes stand out; that is, they are differentiated by virtue of pouring the milk in first. These practices are supported by rationales of taste and so forth. I do not say that everyone follows this prescription precisely or even cares about it, but that more often than not, one finds that one's ways of doing things, ways that feel ever so natural, are but aspects of the conventions of the circles one is born into or grew into. There are, of course, many alternative ways of organizing the English social-scape, for or against fox hunting, the Labour party, nuclear weapons, and each way produces its own groupings; allies in one grouping finding themselves foes in another.

Take another example of whether or not men should cover one's head as a sign of respect in a place of worship. Jewish men cover their heads and Christians think it a mark of respect for men to *uncover* their heads. Indulging in unsubstantiated speculation, as Christianity arose out of Judaism, the Judaic convention became reversed as one of the means of distinguishing Christianity from that from which it had emerged. When Islam made its entry, both options were already taken. Indulging in further unsubstantiated anthropological speculation, I would venture the possibility that Islam positioned itself against the faith that it felt most threatened by, Christianity. And it felt so threatened because, like Islam, Christianity was and is also a proselytizing faith seeking to convert the "heathen". So Islam reverses the Christian convention, which then works as a differentiator. Additionally, is this not curious: the neat distribution of the day of the Sabbath between Moslems, Jews, and Christians, this being Friday, Saturday, and Sunday, respectively? I am not, by the way, suggesting that these arrangements have been arrived at through conscious deliberation and calculation.

Cultural practices consist of rules that are the means of policing not only the territory between the "us" and the "them", but are also the means of sustaining and reinforcing the structure of power relations between different groupings *within* the culture. Among other things, *cultural practices are rationales of domination and oppression*. The status quo is then read as an expression of the natural order of things: why the Brahmin should dominate the untouchable, why woman is the property of man, and so on. Cultures are not homogenous, but conflicted and layered. *Cultures are structured by, and structures of, power relations*.

Even so, we tend to experience and treat human groupings as though they were internally consistent, and so tend to praise or condemn them as a whole. For example, Churchill famously saying of the Hindus that they are "the beastliest people in the world next to the Germans" (Lelyveld, 2010), or, more moderately, one might find oneself saying, "the Germans are as different from the Chinese as chalk is from cheese". It is no surprise to us that a piece of chalk is chalk all the way through; whichever bit of the chalk one examines it will be indistinguishable from another piece of the same chalk. The same is true of cheese. But this is exactly what is not true of human groupings; they are not the same all the way through; one "piece" of the human grouping "Chinese" will have a very different experience and viewpoint from another "piece" of the same grouping: the Communist from the Taoist, the man from that of the woman, and so on. And, going further, there are differences of opinion within the body of Communists, and not all women will think alike, and so forth, *ad infinitum*.

One individual, many cultures

The third difficulty with the orthodox view of culture is the tacit assumption that people belong to a single culture, and, indeed, can only belong to one culture at a time. This allows for a great number of dichotomies and oppositions to be asserted, such as Western culture *vs.* Eastern culture, or the West *vs.* Islam, or a male way of doing things *vs.* a female way. In this way of thinking, there is no room for the idea that people inhabit, and are inhabited by, multiple cultural discourses simultaneously, discourses that variously intersect, undercut, reinforce, and so transmute each other. For example, I am sometimes asked, do I think of myself as Indian or as British? The question is in the form of either/or. To answer, I would have to choose one or other belonging. I suspect that on many an occasion the real question behind this one is: Do you think of yourself as one of "them" or one of "us" (and, therefore, prefer "us" or "them")?

In the same way that there can be such a thing as a secular Jew, so can there be a feminist Moslem or a socialist Moslem. To the elite orthodoxy, of course, these terms are oxymorons, contradictions in terms.

Cultures as discriminating moral orders

Let me end this chapter by highlighting the crux of the matter. Cultural mores consist of ways of doing things—the right and wrong way. In other words, *cultures are moral orders*. Moral orders consist of rules, prohibitions, and injunctions as to what is right and wrong, good and bad, and so on. We each inevitably use the conventions and convictions of the moral orders we have imbibed in our ordinary, day-to-day lives, continually discriminating between this and that, and making myriads of unreflected daily decisions on that basis.

Cultures are systems of moral judgement. To put it even more strongly, *the forms of discrimination practised by a culture are what make it what it is; the forms of discrimination are its identity and essence.* We do this (eat beef) and not that (eat pork). *Cultures are discriminatory systems*; indeed, it is the kinds of discrimination one culture practises that make it distinguishable from another culture (and its discriminatory arrangements). If cultures did not discriminate, then they would cease to exist.

Let me revisit the multi-culturalist predicament anew in the terms we have just been discussing. Say the moral codes and sensibilities of culture A are different in certain important matters from those of culture B. What are members of culture A to do? The multi-culturalist solution would have members of A suspend their own moral codes in order to accept and respect those of culture B, but in doing so they would be acting immorally according to their own beliefs, and, further, they would no longer be being "authentic" and in tune with their cultural identity. In other words, the strategy of respecting the other will have achieved the exact opposite of what multi-culturalism wants to do—to preserve cultures in aspic. This version of respect requires the respecter to annihilate their own authenticity in the service of respecting the authenticity of the other.

I will come back to this predicament in the final chapter. But now, having attended to the idea of the group, I want to turn my attention to the idea of the individual that is employed by the equality movements.

Note

1. *The Hindu*, Saturday 3 Jan 2009. "144, TTK Road; (near Music Academy); Tel: 044-28222348; It used to be a hugely popular dish a quarter of a century ago in this unpretentious but excellent Kerala eatery, and it still is. Succulent bite-sized pieces of beef cooked with freshly ground spices and then sautéed dry with slivers of coconut, it goes well with both Kerala parottas and rice; it can also be eaten as a snack on its own. If you're not a big eater, there's enough to go round for two people; excellent value for money. Price: Rs. 40; Bottomline: Tasty, filling and inexpensive to boot". Full recipe can be found at www.hindu.com/mp/2009/01/03/stories/2009010351551100.htm

CHAPTER FIVE

The human condition: psychology

The previous chapter has established that the cultural group is not a singular consensual entity, but an eternally conflicted and conflictual complexity. In what follows, it will become apparent that the individual is also similarly constituted.

In the beginning . . .

In the beginning, there was Man. He was free and lived in peaceful isolation in harmony with Nature. The trouble began with the rise in numbers, when he was forced into contact with other men. Conflicts arose between them as each tried to live according to his authentic (internally derived) desires. The only way they were able to learn to live with each other was by subjugating their natural desires. In this way, they became less free but more socialized. The cost of the accommodation was that their natures became distorted in the effort to live with others—neurosis. This is how Rousseau conceived of the human condition.

In the beginning, there was Man. Free, in his natural state, he was rapacious and greedy, taking, destroying, and devouring whatever he desired with no inhibition: the war of all against all. He cared nothing for consequences; he was all Id. This was Hobbes' view; he thought that the only way this savage being would be able to live with similar others, was by being subject to authority of gigantic proportions and force—the Leviathan. Fear would make them behave decently, but their savage natures would always be present, erupting at the slightest opportunity.

In the beginning, there was Man. He lived in a primal horde that was ruled by a tyrannical despot who indulged all his instinctual passions freely, while the other members of the horde were his slaves. Eventually, the other men overthrew him. Then, knowing that the situation was likely to repeat itself with a new tyrant, they banded together to put constraints on the power of the leader. This banding together was the beginnings of democracy. So thought Freud.

The first thing to be noted is that the "Man" being spoken of by these luminaries and by many others is, indeed, man, the male of the species. In any case, both Rousseau and Hobbes think that man has a primitive, animal-like nature that needs to be socialized, the difference between them being that Rousseau thinks this original nature to be good, that of the noble savage, and Hobbes thinks it bad, just savage. When people come to live together, Rousseau's individual ends up injuring themselves, while Hobbes' individual would injure others. Freud's vision combines elements from both of them.

Readers might recognize their own beliefs about the human condition scattered through the above scenarios. This is how it is mostly with us. We cobble together our view of the human condition, taking a bit from here and another from there. The fact that these bits and pieces often contradict each other does not necessarily trouble us, since we are not always aware of them. And neither do we hold on to these beliefs with any consistency. In one moment and context we think, say, and believe that that deep down humans are good, and in another context we blithely think it is the opposite.

Ask yourself this: do you think that, deep down, humans are the same as each other? Or do you think that, deep down, they are essentially different, unique? I find myself flip-flopping between both these positions. So, if you are anything like me (unfortunate reader), then so must you. In part, I manage this feat because, in some senses, both views are true, and so one or other of the positions will serve my interests better in a particular circumstance. I will say more on this matter as we proceed.

Now, whatever the differences between Freud, Rousseau, and Hobbes, they are all in agreement that it is *the* individual (in the singular) that is primary. They are all in agreement that *the* individual comes into existence first, and it is only later that *the* individual comes to form societies by joining with other individuals. They all also believe that there is conflict between nature and the demands of society. To this way of thinking, culture and the social are optional after-events.

At first glance it would seem that, by privileging the notion of culture and putting it centre stage, multi-culturalism and the celebrators of diversity have advanced in the right direction and moved a considerable distance from the asocial individualism that has blighted much human thought (and continues to be the default mode of thinking for many). In one sense they have, but not in another, and this is because they have replaced asocial essentialism with cultural essentialism. You are what your culture (in the singular) has made you.

I am going to explicate and locate the version of the human condition that is accepted by these movements among a small range of options. I do this in order to shed light on the consequences for the equality agenda that follow out of each version.

Let us take an ordinary enough conflict—"I want to eat beef, but it is prohibited"—and see how different versions of the human condition understand it. I will do this through the device of thinking through how this conflict would be treated by two streams of psychology, the Humanistic and the Psychoanalytic, because the first has its roots in the Romantic tradition and the latter is grounded in the principles of the Enlightenment.

Desire and duty: two readings of a conflict

The Humanistic traditions: conflict between inside and outside

There are two strands in the Humanistic traditions that are of interest to us, the Romantically inclined asocial individualistic strand and the multi-culturalist strand.

Conflict in the individualistic tradition is thought of as arising between internal impulses and external constraints. For example, "I want to drink alcohol, but it is not allowed"; or, "I like beef but there are injunctions against me eating it"; or, "I want to use contraception but the Church thinks it a sin"; or, "I want to marry X, but my parents think that I should marry Y"; or, "my neighbour is annoying me and I want to beat him up but it is not allowed in law". These are conscious conflicts between what "I" want, and what the cultural or authority system says is the good or proper way of behaving.

The work of Romantic psychotherapies (these being those in the Humanistic Tradition—Fritz Perls' gestalt therapy, Carl Rogers' person-centred therapy, etc.) would be to help discern the "real" authentic internal voice from those that have been taken in from others. These sorts of practitioners assume that there is only *one* authentic voice within the client; they take no account of the possibility of the existence of other valid voices within the client. Further, in this individualistic scenario, the desire to eat beef (if true and authentic) has somehow arisen spontaneously from within the individual. It is asocial and internally generated. To this therapist, it is the voiced internal desire (being authentic) that has to be supported to make a stand against other oppressive voices taken in from the external social world.

Meanwhile, the multi-culturalist psychotherapist would also be in favour of supporting the authentic voice within the client. But, unlike the individualistically inclined therapist, the multi-culturalist presumes that the client's authenticity is derived from the culture that the individual inhabits (i.e., authenticity does reside inside, but in the first instance it is taken in from the outside). So, how will the multi-culturalist handle the conflict in "I want to eat beef but it is not allowed (in my culture)"? In the eyes of the multi-culturalist, the client has lost touch with their authentic, culturally informed inner self, and has been seduced and infiltrated by alien cultures and their values and aspirations. They have been corrupted. The task of this therapist would be to help the client get back to their true cultural identity and reclaim it, in whatever sense the therapist understands the term. For example, to reclaim their "Black" identity, or female identity, or Indian identity, and so on.

Because both these strands presume that there is a true, immutable essence (albeit differently derived in each case), this way of thinking is called essentialist. For the individualistically inclined therapist, the entire social world is alien and to be resisted, and for the multi-cultural psychotherapist, resistance is limited to the culture of "others". And neither allow for multiplicity. In the same way that the individualistic therapist does not consider the possibility that there might be more than one sincere voice within the client, the multi-culturalist does not allow for the fact that a person is born into multiple cultures, each authentic, each making their claim on the client.

The psychoanalytic traditions: internalized conflict

The psychoanalytic vision of the human condition is more complex. According to Freud, at some point between the ages of three and five the child takes in the rules of society and makes it part of the self. As is well known, he called this internalized structure the superego. The contents of the superego consist of cultural rules or, as Freud has said, of "all the time resisting judgements of value" (Freud, 1933, p. 67).

In this schema, the resolution of the aforementioned conflict becomes more difficult, because as social rules and mores are internalized, they become a part of the person. These internalized cultural injunctions are not surface phenomena, but an integral part of the psyche. This is the tremendous thing: culture is now inside and part of the person; it has become part of the psychological flesh and tissue, it has become integral to the Self.

The result is that the conflict that was once between the inside and the outside is now between two (authentic) aspects of the inside. In the Freudian vision, when the superego uses these internalized cultural injunctions to successfully inhibit some instinctual urge, then this causes the psychological injury called neurosis.

Thus, within the psychoanalytic frame, the resolution of the earlier conflict of "I want to eat beef but it is prohibited" is now much more problematic. Because now, not only is it a genuine part of myself that wants to eat beef, a genuine part of myself also thinks that it is wrong to eat beef. The Romantics had cast the conflict as between (authentic) *internal* values and (alien) *external* injunctions. But, in the psychoanalytic way of thinking, both elements are internal, and both are "authentic". Thus, I cannot easily dispense with one of the elements without tampering with something integral to me.

The Romantic conception of the conflict can be cast as a conflict between desire and duty (the desire to eat beef, and the duty not to). The individualistically inclined "solution" was to say that it is *one's duty to fulfil one's desire* (go on; eat the beef, you know you really really want to). The multi-culturalist "solution" is to say if you look deep enough you will discover that your true cultural desire is in harmony with your duty (you really, really don't want to eat the beef—truly).

But the Freudian predicament offers us no easy resolution because, with the advent of the superego, we also *desire to do our duty* and, in the same moment, we desire to fulfil our desire. We are in the region of conflict, ambiguity, and ambivalence. So, already there is a diversity of voices within the person, and all this before we even begin to take account of the unconscious.

The psychoanalytic version of the human predicament is tragic in the Nietzschean understanding of tragedy: the conflict is between two "goods", desire and duty, with the tragedy being that one of the goods is bound to lose to the other. If we use the psychoanalytic model of individuals to think about cultures, then it becomes immediately apparent that there is not one voice, but many authentic voices within a culture. We can see, then, that the psychoanalytic schema has already significantly problematized the multi-culturalist solution to "cultural" conflict.

My view accords with the version of events being put up by Freud, but would go much further than him. I follow the group analyst S. H. Foulkes and the sociologist Norbert Elias to take a more radical position in regard to internalization in the following way. Although Freud allows the external sociological to become a part of the internal psychological, he does so only partially by limiting the provenance of the social to the region called the superego. The id, meanwhile, as the provenance of the biological instincts, preserves its autonomy and remains untouched by the social. Thus, in the Freudian model, the two regions remain distinct from each other and in perpetual war with each other. To the radical group analytic understanding (Dalal, 1998, 2002), there is no element of the psyche that is not mediated by the social, not even the id. This makes the whole project of respecting and valuing difference even more problematic and in ways that are not even countenanced by the equality discourses.

Social individuals

Let me begin by noting the obvious: human beings and their ancestors live in groups and have always lived in groups. Arendt says, "the human condition [is that] of plurality ... the fact [is] that men, not Man, live on the earth and inhabit the world" (Arendt, 1998, p. 7). Human life begins and continues in the plural and has never existed in the singular.

Folk psychology (as well as the discipline of psychology) has had a lot to say about how our sociology is infused by our biology (instincts, drives, sublimation, etc.), but has hardly considered the reverse—how our biology is infused with our sociology. Indeed, the very idea sounds bizarre because it appears self-evident that biology precedes sociology in the sense that animals evolved before humans, and before there were civilized humans there were primitive uncivilized humans.

One can come to understand how this counter-intuitive state of affairs comes about in the following way. We are prone to seeing the moment of birth as an absolute beginning, where a primarily biological being (the newborn infant) is confronted with a fully formed society. It appears to us that the moment of birth constitutes the first meeting between these dominions, the biological and the social, and that a bloody battle must inevitably ensue between them.

But if one begins the analysis much earlier in time, then the picture turns out to be very different. Our biology is not a god- or nature-given thing. It has evolved. It is a process that is still ongoing. Let us begin by asking this question: why do things evolve in the direction they do? The answer, simple but not simplistic, is that they are useful to survival. And one of the things clearly visible to all and everywhere is that human beings live in groups, and have always lived in groups. Why do we live in groups? Because to live and work in groups enhances the possibility of survival. In other words, our biology is programmed through the evolutionary processes to make us social beings.[1]

As Elias (1991, pp. 84–85) says: "Humans ... are made by nature for culture and society ... human society is a level of nature". This, then, is the astonishing thing: to realize that we have been and are in the grip of a prodigious all encompassing hallucination—a hallucination that says that our biology is antisocial.

As we go forward further into the discussion, keep these two points in mind: individuals can only exist in the plural, and that the biological imperative is not in conflict with the requirements of social life.

The paradox of belonging

The fact that individuals are intrinsically social beings leads Foulkes to assert that there is a fundamental need in all human beings to belong, to be part of an "us", and that this is a necessary condition for an experience of psychological well-being. But even to put it in this way, to say that there is a need to belong, misrepresents the situation, as it implies that there is the possibility of not belonging. It is the case that we cannot not-belong.

Equal opportunity statements and the like are fond of claiming that their policies are "inclusive". There is much to be said for promoting this attitude, in that it seeks to open boardrooms and so forth to the kinds of people (e.g., women) who have somehow been less able to find their way into positions of power. But the way that inclusivity is spoken of, it would seem that everyone can be and ought to be included, that everyone can belong. But this can never be the case.

The idea of belonging is paradoxical in that, for the experience of belonging to be meaningful, two conditions have to be fulfilled: first, in order to belong to one place, it is necessary for there to be another place *not to belong to*. Second, it has to be the case that only some may belong, and others are excluded. If these two conditions are not fulfilled, then the belonging category becomes infinitely large, encompassing everything and everybody, and so becomes meaningless. In other words, intrinsic to the idea of belonging is the negation of something and someone. There are grounds for this controversial assertion at a psychological level as well as the existential, as I explain next.

The paediatrician and psychoanalyst Winnicott's (1965, p. 149) descriptions of the processes of early infant development are interesting in this regard. Based on his work as a paediatrician and psychoanalyst, he proposed the following scenario. In its earliest days, the infant has yet to gain a sense of itself. In a manner of speaking, the infant's sense of self is dispersed over its environment; it has sensations, but has no location for them; it has no sense of where it begins and ends, what it is and what it is not. At some point, the infant has its first I AM moment, in which it gathers itself together, and so begins to form a rudimentary sense of a "me" that it is progressively able to distinguish from that which is "not-me". Winnicott says that this is also a paranoid moment. This is because as the infant gathers together some elements from the environment to constitute itself, it simultaneously repudiates other elements. In a sense, the infant is saying to the "not-me" elements, "you don't belong". Having made this gesture, the infant now fears attack from the repudiated elements, thus the paranoia. Winnicott then also suggests that "we" groups come about through a very similar mechanism, the repudiation of the elements designated "not-we". Or, to put it another way, a "we" can exist only as a contrast to a "them". Or, to put it another way again, even as one makes a gesture of inclusion in one direction, in the very same moment, one cannot help but make a gesture of exclusion to every other direction.

I will try to make things a bit clearer through two well known jokes that are really parables.

A woman gives her husband two ties. When she sees him wearing one of them, she exclaims, "So you did not like the other." When I was first told this, the moral of the story that I was invited to draw was that in choosing one thing we are not necessarily condemning the other. But, over time, I have come to think that a negation of some sort is in fact taking place, precisely because in that moment one has been chosen over the other. The two ties are different and not equal.

The second joke. A devout orthodox Jew found himself marooned on an uninhabited island. When he was rescued many years later by a passing ship, the rescuers were astonished to see that he had built himself a synagogue to worship in. But then, as they rounded the island, they were further astonished to see yet another synagogue. Mystified, they asked the castaway why he had built two synagogues. He replied that one was the synagogue that he went to, and the other was the synagogue that he did not go to.

Identity

We are now able to see more clearly that identity is not something that simply *is*. There are two problems that the slogans calling for "inclusion" cannot get round. One of these is to do with what identity is not, and the other is to do with what it is. On the one hand, we can see from the parables above that some sort of negation is necessary to the process of identity construction; *the process of inclusion always contains within it a gesture of exclusion*. And, on the other hand, we have also seen that the mere the act of naming a belonging is not only (at some level) always a reification, but it also imposes a homogeneity on the named category. The notion of "vegetarian" generates the "non-vegetarian", and the category "vegetarian" contains communists, fascists, and liberals.

Thus, when one says "I am a vegetarian" (or Christian or whatever), one cannot actually look directly at these terms, or look within them. One cannot probe them. For identity to work, the internal space "knowing who I am" must not be tested. If it is tested, then it disintegrates and is either replaced by another sort of "I am" (say from vegetarian to Conservative), or it leads to complete fragmentation and chaos: in other words, madness. To exist, one has to find a place to belong to, to stand on. The place one stands on, one's identity, is always precarious, and often enough illusory—a reification.

It is precisely because of the impossibility of finding and naming the essence of the "us" that one looks to the margins, to the "not-us". This is the point: the "us" is defined not so much by what it is, as by what it is not.

The structuralist de Saussure (1959) echoes the same theme when he says "concepts are purely differential and defined not by their positive content but negatively by their relations with the other terms of the system. Their most precise characteristic is in being what others are not".

If you are a committed Jehovah's Witness, then all of humanity fits neatly into one of two categories, the saved and the damned. Further, it is the focus on "them", the sinful damned, which lends the pious "us" the impression of unity and oneness, as though "we" are all of one mind.

The "I" and the "we"

The next element reverses the usual arrangement between the individual and social. As we have already seen, the logic of philosophies and psychologies that suppose that individuals are prior to society lead them to think of the social "we" as secondary, as something optional, constituted by the coming together of a number of pre-existing individual "I's".

Radical group analysis reverses this to say that *the "I" is constituted by the varieties of "we" that one is born into*. Each of us, as particular individuals, is born into pre-existing societies constituted by a multiplicity of overlapping and conflicting cultures. The cultures themselves, as well as the relationships between cultures, are constituted by power relationships.

This is the key point: an individual is not born into a single culture, but multiple, sometimes conflicting, cultures. As each of us "grows", we imbibe, of necessity, the range and variety of the pre existing cultural forms, habits, beliefs, and ways of thinking that we are born into. These introjections are not taken into a pre-existing self; rather, they come to actually contribute to the formation the self. Further, because the relationships between the varieties of "we" are, of necessity, power relationships, then we can say that the "I", the "me", is constituted at the deepest of levels by and through the power relationships that are part of the social fabric that one is born into.

The point I want to make through this discussion is that the individual is not a simple unity, or if it is a unity, then it is a conflicted unity always in a state of tension. But I have overstated things in order to counter the Romantic ethos that prevails in folk psychology, which is that the essence of the individual is internal, asocial, and pre-social. I have ended up giving too much emphasis to the social and made it appear that individuals are born *tabula rasa*, and are imprinted by the social. This is not what I think. Individuals bring something of themselves into the mix of things, they are born with rudimentary personalities (but these are not "true" and fixed), they are subject to different kinds of formative emotional and attachment experiences in their infancy and childhood, each "interprets" these experiences in their own way, and so on. It is out of this mix of things that the uniqueness of individuals comes to be constituted. The point I want to make is that the psychological self is constituted by the sociology it inhabits; it is not its opposite. The sense of self, identity, is not only psychological and emotional, but is also profoundly sociopolitical.

Where have we ended up? First, individuals only exist in the plural. Second, identity, who I am, is the same as where I belong. The situation is made more complicated by the third point: that individuals are born into and, so, constituted by a variety of meaningful but sometimes antagonistic belongings, the demands of some being in conflict with the demands of others. The result is that the self, the psyche itself, is constituted by conflictual diversity.

To put it another way, as there are a great many *authentic* voices within the individual, there is no easy "get-out" clause for the Romantic multi-culturalist, as the individual's experience is one of being in a state of perpetual conflict between the demands of a number of authenticities. Each kind of belonging makes its own claim and demand of the person. To be faced with having to decide between these options is to be faced with a series of moral dilemmas. Caught between multiple conflicting demands, depending on the context, one authentic "identity" can be easily replaced by another. To demonstrate what I mean, here is a fictitious example that I have had occasion to use before.

Imagine, in the old South Africa, before the fall of apartheid, a group of Whites at a dinner party. Let us say that there is just one vegetarian among them. To this person, this will be the most critical difference, setting off, perhaps, nausea. To some others, perhaps other differences will be salient. The rogue bachelor will be focused on the availability of single women; to a religious fundamentalist in that gathering, it might be a division between those of his beliefs and those not. In any case, this range of identities would all disappear from view when faced with the intrusion of a rude, drunk, White waiter. Now, the table is united in the guests' outrage at the way that they are spoken to. Perhaps we could say that now the critical identities are organized on class lines: employers and employed. When, a few moments later, an unservile Black person walks into the room, identities would be reshuffled again. The drunk waiter and the diners would come together as "Whites" as they are faced by this belligerent "Black". The changing context calls out a certain "identity", which comes to reside in the forefront of the mind, until it is replaced with another.

I came across another illustration of this same theme some years ago. The Scottish city of Edinburgh has been the home of a number of immigrants from Italy for some generations. Many of them are bilingual, speaking both languages fluently. When a young girl from this community was asked whether she felt herself to be Italian or Scottish, she replied that in Italy she experienced herself as Scottish, and in Scotland she experienced herself as Italian. The fact that there is the constant danger that one's identity can easily shift gives rise to an existential anxiety. And it is in order to defend against this terrifying anxiety that we try to hang on for dear life to a particular identity and try to refuse and fend off all others.

This, then, is the surprising reality: the impression of difference and otherness between the "us" and "them" is as illusory as is the impression of solidity and cohesion within the "us" and "them"; the same is true of "me" and "you". However, the illusions are powerful none the less, and come to have a life as facts in our psyches as well as our engagements with each other. They come to have a particular kind of reality.

Given the fragility of each of these belongings, as well as the fact that there are an infinity of other belongings continually available to each of us, prompts the question: how and why do we come to experience one encounter as taking place across a difference and the other as within a region of similarity? In this moment, do you think of your neighbour as similar or different to you? On what basis? If you experience your neighbour as similar, why are you inclined in that direction at this moment, and what have you done with the differences? And if you are experiencing them as different, what have you done with the similarities? Why? At some level, a decision is continually being made as to whether the experience is one of similarity or of difference. The decision, however, is mostly not a conscious one, nor is it "freely" made. The decision as such is constrained by the discourses one inhabits, discourses that lead one to experience others in particular ways—as one of "us" or one of "them".

Anyhow, it is on this sort of basis that we may conclude that the individual is no more a harmonious "whole" than is the cultural group.

Differences not all in the mind

I should make clear that what I am not arguing is the proposition that all differences are reifications and exist only in the mind. For example, I do not think that gender difference exists only in the eye of the beholder; neither do I think that there are no meaningful differences between someone born and bred in the African Sahara and someone born and bred in the Russian Steppes.

What I am asking, though, is why does one similarity or difference come to prevail over the vast number of alternative possibilities? On first meeting, will *this* African person experience *that* Russian person as similar by virtue of both of them being women, or both being Christian, or vegetarian, or feminists, or will she experience the Russian as different because of skin colour, or language, or political ideology?

So, it is not the case that one simply "finds" a difference, which one then finds oneself responding to. Rather, one finds oneself emphasizing certain differences in order to *create* an experience of sameness or difference. The questions one needs constantly to ask are: given that there are an infinity of differences (and similarities) between two human beings, how and why are we led in a particular moment to experience and construe one difference primary and render the others less meaningful? What, and importantly, whose, purpose is being served by making the differentiation here rather than there?

While it is the case that a difference or similarity is emphasized in order to create a differentiation, it is also the case that some categorizations are indeed reifications having no existence apart from their names, "race" being a case in point. But when it comes to *function*, it matters not whether the differentiation has a basis in material reality; "race" works at least as well as gender or class as a means of creating "others".

Creating types of people

My argument is this: differences are evoked in order to make a differentiation, and, even more specifically, a differentiation between the haves and the must-not-haves.

I have been arguing that cultures are not homogeneities, but structures of power relations that utilize cultural conventions to sustain their own internal divisions between the haves and must-not-haves (men and women, say). Now, it is precisely because of the fluidity of the boundaries there is the ever-present danger of one sort of "us" dissolving and reorganizing into another sort of "us"; therefore, continual work is required to shore up and bolster the "us". This work takes several forms. One bit of the work is done for us silently and automatically by our cognitive mechanisms. Social scientists have demonstrated that when the mind uses an attribute to make groupings out of continuities, there follows a kind of hallucination in which it seems to us that those within each of the groupings appear to be more similar than they actually are, and that the gap between the groupings appears to be greater than it actually is. This cognitive hallucination is necessary for the formation and experience of categories (Brown, 1995; Tajfel, 1981).

But this is not nearly enough, and so the emotions are called into play to help maintain the distance between the "us" and varieties of "them". The primary mechanism is one where the "them" are denigrated and the "us" are idealized. The notions of denigration and idealization, being absolute (good and only good, bad and only bad), create the impression of an antithetical dichotomy between the "us" and the "them". In other words, it has created the illusion of types.

The othering process: dividing, forgetting, splitting

What has taken place is something one might call an *othering process*, wherein a mere "another" becomes transformed into "The Other".

In psychoanalysis, this process is called "splitting", and it occurs in the following way. We can divide the contents of a room according to colour and so create an abstraction, such as all the red things in the room. In doing so, we have also created an apparent opposition, between the things red and things not-red. So far, so good. But then we "forget" that the divided are but abstractions, and that they are both but aspects of the room. We forget this, and grant each of the abstractions a life of its own. We might even then think that the two abstractions are in conflict with each other, because the more one category gains, the less the other gets. To grant the red wall an autonomous life, as though it had the option of leaving the room, is clearly nonsensical. But, in fact, this is exactly how we generate any number of apparently oppositional categories (such as the individual and social, or the internal and external). It is exactly this kind of process that helps generate the different kinds of humankind, in particular the kinds known as the races, cultures, and ethnicities.

Splitting, then, is a kind of forgetting at a profound psychological level, that the divided are aspects of the same process, are necessary to the existence of each other, *and remain so*. "Insides" need "outsides" because without an outside there can be no inside. In the same way, the "us" needs a "them", without which there can be no "us".

Going further, having generated these polarities, then, depending on the ideologies one subscribes to, one or other of the poles will be privileged over the other. For example, the individual over the group, men over women, Whites over Blacks; in one context Catholics over Protestants and in another, the reverse; and so on.

Many other polarities have emerged out of this kind of process, for example, that of objectivity *vs.* subjectivity. Of the two, the Enlightenment championed objectivity, while the Romantics privileged subjectivity. Leaving aside whichever ought to be privileged, what is to be remembered is that both remain abstractions and neither can have an existence independent of the other. The notion of objectivity presumes that a detached observer is outside and removed from what is being observed, and so can neutrally observe and comment from a distance without affecting the observed. Meanwhile, the notion of subjectivity (in its extreme forms) presumes that subjectivity is entirely internally generated. The first of these imagines that one can inhabit an outside without having an impact on the inside, and the second imagines that one can inhabit the inside without being influenced by the outside.

The "physics" of empathy and responsibility

The equality ideals of neutrality and non-judgemental respect for the other is founded on exactly this sort of impossibility: of being able to *not* have a reaction in order to remain neutral and accepting of what is happening. In this sense, metaphorically speaking, these ideals break the laws of physics as they propose that there can be an action without a reaction. Like it or not, I cannot help but be affected by what I see and hear, and I cannot help but affect by what I do or not do.

It is for this sort of reason that the conception of cultures claiming rights over the practices they "own" (because it is no one else's business what they do "within" their culture, as it is private) is also seen to be unsustainable. The multi-culturalist paradigm—equal and different—is an attempt to delimit response and, therefore, responsibility. What is said is that it ought to be no concern of mine as to what takes place in "their" territory. But the only way I can do this is by *feeling* no concern. What is said is that *my* responsibility ends with me and mine, and responsibility for what takes place with and within "them" lies with them. Responsibility—which is a moral emotion—is sequestered and made territorial. But the only way I am able to feel no *responsibility* is by having no *response* to what I witness and experience. And the only way I am able to have no response is by having no feelings, no empathy in regard to what I witness. And the only way I am able to not have an empathetic response is to shut down on their humanity. But this is exactly the dehumanizing process that the equality movements want to redress. We can see, then, that the multi-culturalist paradigm has the potential to create the very problem that it seeks to solve.

But, worse, when I shut down on my response to them, not only am I shutting down on their humanity, but also mine. In the colloquial, we could say that this process is akin to that of "hardening" oneself. But what is being asked of me by the diversity promulgators is not that I should have no response, but that I *must have* a positive and respectful response. This insistence has come about because of the imperialist's tendency to *never* be respectful of the other. The diversity solution, *always* be respectful, is, in itself, at least as big a problem as is the one it is trying to solve. It is at this moment that the principles of live and let live become potential weapons of fear and control.

The metaphor of "no action without reaction" can be further extended to critique the ideal of inclusivity. The existential reality is that "they" can have no existence without an "us" and "we" cannot exist without "them". The ideal of "including everyone" is seen to be meaningless, because the "we" cannot come into being without excluding. If there were no exclusion, the "we" would have no form—we simply would not exist. Sculpting provides a useful analogy; it is that which is removed that gives shape to the sculpture. If nothing is removed, or if everything is added, then, paradoxically, we would end up with nothing, just amorphous lumps. Similarly, the "us" is what remains when the "them" are removed. And this is the thing: they both come into existence in the same moment.

This, then, is the existential situation we find ourselves in. The process of othering is continuous work, because there is always the ever-present danger that we will remember the fact that both "they" and "us" are abstractions, and, if that happens, both will mutate into something else again.

Let me repeat a caution. The fact that our belonging groups are abstractions does not mean that they are devoid of meaning and passion. At the level of pure logic, the abstractions might well be construed as arbitrary. However, the fact that they are abstractions does not mean that they are not real. They have an existence, in the same way as do the "red things in a room". These belongings are critical to us not only emotionally and psychologically, but also sociologically, and so come to inform our dealings with each other. In fact, it is because these categories of belonging are tenuous that we require passion and meaning to sustain them.

Thinking about thinking

Before going any further, I need to say something about thought processes in general. The universe we inhabit is seamless and infinite. Infinity is just too large for our minds to process; we can only digest it in smaller chunks. So, we are obliged to break it up into smaller pieces, words strung together in linear sentences. Our cognitive processes are predicated on the possibility of breaking up this complexity into bits and pieces. *We are obliged to divide in order to be able to think.* This is intrinsic to the human condition. However, the ways we find ourselves dividing and experiencing the world are severely constrained by the cultural systems we are born into. Our thought processes are patterned by the moralities, ideologies, and discourses we inhabit. This leads us to divide and experience the self, the world, and its inhabitants in particular ways—our ways. This is the basis of our particular humanities. In sum, the kind of human being I am is constituted by the kinds of divisions I am subjected to and the kinds of divisions I subject the world to. Misquoting Descartes yet again, we can say, *I divide, therefore I am.*

* * *

We have come a long way from the positivist vision of human groupings (and the individuals that constitute them) as coherent, encapsulated, and differentiated entities. The human condition is otherwise. We are forever embroiled and entangled with each other. As we are interdependent, there is no possibility of doing or saying anything without it having an effect on others and being affected by others. We cannot help but influence and be influenced. We cannot not divide, we cannot not exclude, and we cannot not form views influenced by the norms we inhabit. One consequence of this way of thinking is that it is no longer clear as how one may live according to the liberal principle of live and let live.

In the chapters that follow, I use the models of group and human nature that have been established to critique some of the strategies and solutions being proposed by the equality movements.

Note

1. The idea that our biology is fundamentally transformed by our sociology has support from many directions, for example, from palaeontology. Burkitt (1999, p. 39) describes how, up to the 1960s, the standard view was that the biology of humans evolved up to a certain point, when it became possible for them to develop tools. The advent of tools was then thought to have an impact on the *social organization* of human beings. But then palaeontologists found that tool use was present in creatures not yet human. This gave rise to the surprising notion the presence of tools modified the selection pressures on the evolution of these creatures which eventually became biologically human. Thus, this is an example of something social (tool use) having a deep impact on the biological organization of human beings at the level of DNA. Burkitt concludes: "the development and use of tools was not an outcome of human evolution but perhaps the cause of it" (p. 39). See also Dunbar (1996) who gathers findings that show how the growth of brain size was driven by the increasing levels of complexity of social organization in the pre-human primate world.

CHAPTER SIX

Counting discriminations

Every picture tells a story

While it is true to say that "every picture tells a story", it is also accurate to say that there are many different stories to be told of the same picture, each of them simultaneously (possibly) true. Here is one picture: Jane was made redundant by Abdul, and Harish was not. Let us eavesdrop on their stories.

Jane's story is that the redundancy is the result of unfair sexual discrimination. Her boss, Abdul, tells a different story: that he chose to make Jane redundant rather than Harish because she is a bad time-keeper. Jane says that she is late sometimes (lots of times, says the boss) because of needing to get her children to school. The boss says, but Harish, too, takes his children to school, and although he is ten minutes late on occasion, she tends to be forty-five minutes late as a matter of course. She says that she is a single mum, and Harish has a partner who helps. She claims that the boss Abdul decided to keep Harish on because they were both men and also they are the same race. She also claims racial discrimination. The boss says what nonsense; I am a Muslim and he is a Hindu, if anything, the history of the two faiths would mean that I would take every opportunity to get rid of him; it is you who are racist, not even being able to distinguish between our cultures. She says, yes, but you both come from the same area in Delhi and there was some connection between your families, was there not? This is clear favouritism, if not nepotism.

Many other things that occurred between the protagonists are not even mentioned, and perhaps not even remembered in any conscious way. For example, when Jane joined the company, she had immediately taken a shine to Abdul, who did not reciprocate her interest. On one occasion in an important meeting, Jane had sided with the proposal being put forward by the HR manager rather than with the proposal being put forward by Abdul. Jane tends to talk loudly on the phone and this is annoying to everyone in the office. Jane is bright and tends to speak her mind, while Harish is quiet and compliant. And so on, and so on.

The complexities are legion and even Solomon would be hard put to arrive at a fair conclusion. What this fictitious scenario shows is that, in any particular case, there will always be a number of reasons as to why something has occurred, *and each of the reasons might well have a validity*. Jane's charge of sexual discrimination might be true, but so might be Abdul's counter charge of incompetence. It is never an either/or situation. In any particular individual case of unfair discrimination, there will always be additional reasons as to why things have taken place in the way that they have.

As the judges pronouncing in a case of sexual discrimination once said, "It is very hard to separate out with any conviction which of the range and number of differences played a part in a decision making process" (Barnett, 2004). Ironically, to arrive at some semblance of the truth, one has to discriminate between the alternative narratives, giving more weight to one and less to another. One has to use one's capacity for discernment to sift through the evidence to distinguish the wheat from the chaff to arrive at judgements as to what has actually taken place.

But, as we learnt earlier, the difficulty is that our capacities for discrimination and discernment themselves are inevitably biased. When we find ourselves in the position of having to choose between the different narratives and accounts, then our (unconsciously biased) discriminatory processes tend to work in such a way that we will favour accounts that suit our interests and beliefs.

So, even in blatant cases where the evidence screams out that an injustice has taken place, the general public as well as the police, judges, and juries have all found it possible to claim otherwise. The cases of Stephen Lawrence in the UK and of Rodney King in the USA both bear testament to that. In the first case, a Black man innocently waiting at a bus stop is beaten to death by a group of White men (well known for their racist beliefs), yet many are apparently convinced that the incident has nothing to do with racism. And in the second case, despite there being a video recording of the violence meted out to Rodney King, a twelve-strong jury managed to conclude that the violence was not excessive and that the police were only defending themselves. The same applies to evidence regarding the rape of women. Most recent figures show that, in the UK, just six per cent of cases reported to the police result in a conviction of the rapist.

Statistics: the weapon of choice

Among the many issues confronting the equality movements and governmental agencies is the question of how to demonstrate convincingly that something unfair has taken place when one is faced so many conflicting claims. Well, perhaps counter intuitively, it turns out that the further back one stands, the easier it is to see unfair discriminatory processes at work. In this territory, statistics is the weapon of choice.

But, even when we step back to look at the bigger picture, at the wood rather than a particular tree, we cannot actually *see* the processes of unfair discrimination at work, we can only infer that they might be at work. For example, when Jane's case is put in a collection of similar cases, and then it is found that ninety per cent of those made redundant in this downsizing exercise were women, then we may *infer* that unfair discriminatory processes must be taking place at an institutional level. Similarly, we may infer with some confidence from the statistic that only six per cent of rape cases result in convictions that something problematic must be taking place in the judicial system.

This was the nettle that was finally and firmly grasped by the Stephen Lawrence Inquiry, and it did so in two ways. First, it gave recognition to the existence of institutional racism, and second, it insisted that organizations collect statistical evidence, as this was the only way these sorts of phenomena could be grasped.

Paradigm shift: from innocence to guilt

The suggestions of the Lawrence Inquiry were put into law in 2000 as *Amendments to the Race Relations Act of 1976*. This piece of law making is a watershed. It constitutes a dramatic shift in emphasis, philosophy, and even ideology. The shift is one from a presumption of innocence to one of guilt. The older legislation based itself on the presumption that, on the whole, people as well as the structures of society were generally fair to all its inhabitants, and so one only had to look out for instances of wrong-doing. In contrast, the new legislation begins with the premise that the game is already fixed. Mixing my metaphors, the dice are loaded in such a way that some kinds of folk are prone to do better than other kinds of folk. Institutions, therefore, are obliged to begin with the premise and to take it as a given that their ways *are already unfair*.

What organizations are now required to do by law is to be proactive in gathering statistical data to be used for searching and teasing out the ways in which they are *already* unfair and biased. The ways that organizations are to set about this enquiry are laid out in the legislature in the "general duties" and "specific duties". Organizations have to demonstrate that they are being proactive in the ways specified by these duties, and if they cannot do so, then they are deemed to be breaking the law.

Search and destroy missions: the general and specific duties

The "*general duties*" are "the duty to promote race equality". The word "promote" is important; it means that the status quo is no longer good enough and institutions are legally bound to look for things to do that will improve the situation. There are three components to this duty: eliminating unlawful discrimination, promoting equality of opportunity, and promoting good relations between people of different racial groups. The Act also put in place a number of "*specific duties*", which are the methods and processes through which institutions should fulfil their general duties. One of the special duties is the requirement for organizations to publish a Race Equality Scheme, which, in essence, is the institution's action plan as to how it intends to fulfil its general duties.

In effect, the "duties" oblige institutions to be on a continual search and destroy mission, the mission being the eradication of institutional racism and other forms of unfair discriminatory practice. They are obliged to continually *assess* and *monitor* their procedures for unintended bias of any kind that might disadvantage some groups of people. And when these *adverse impacts* are discovered, then the procedures are to be modified, and those in turn are to be continually assessed and monitored. Organizations are also required to give their employees training with regard to the requirements of the duties. All of this is to be published and available to the general public.

The gathering of data and the generating of statistics is key to the whole mission. Organizations have to keep records of the "ethnicities" of their staff as well as their "users" or "customers". (Other kinds of data are also collected, gender, disability, religious affiliation, and so on. For the purposes of the line of argument being developed here, I do not attend to them.) These statistics are used to look for bias in all kinds of institutional processes: the numbers of each "ethnicity" in different kinds of posts; numbers entering and leaving employment; applying for posts; appointed to posts; offered promotion; given training; being disciplined; activating grievance procedures; and so on. When bias is discovered, then something has to be done to remedy the situation.

Given that I have just spent several pages endorsing the need for statistical evidence, you would think that I would be pleased that the legislature has now made it a statutory requirement for organizations to collect data. I am, but only to a point. My problem is not with the idea of collecting data, but with the *kind* of data that is being collected and the *way* that it is being collected.

The bureaucratization of identity: counting subjectivities

In the UK, one aspect of the process of data gathering is called "ethnic monitoring". When individuals apply for jobs, attend a hospital appointment, are picked up by the police, and so on, they are asked to *self-ascribe* their "ethnicity" by ticking one of sixteen boxes that have been generated by the legislature. In fact there is one more tick box *which does not appear* on the form when presented to people to fill in (more on that in a moment). Crucially, whether or not staff and users provide information about their ethnicity is supposed to be voluntary.

The content of the form is as follows.

What is your ethnic group? Choose ONE section from A to E, then tick the appropriate box to indicate your ethnic group.

A: White:
☐ British;
☐ Irish;
☐ Any other White background (please write in)________________

B: Mixed:
☐ White and Black Caribbean;
☐ White and Black African;
☐ White and Asian;
☐ Any other mixed background (please write in)________________

C: Asian or Asian British:
☐ Indian;
☐ Pakistani;
☐ Bangladeshi;
☐ Any other Asian background (please write in)________________

D: Black or Black British:
☐ Caribbean;
☐ African;
☐ Any other Black background (please write in)________________

E: Chinese or other ethnic group:
☐ Chinese;
☐ Any other (please write in)________________

Not stated: ☐

The last option is not available to the person filling out the form.

Limited freedoms, constrained choices

To begin with, let me take issue with the fact that the "not stated" option is not present on the form being filled out by a member of the general public. There is no legal requirement for people to answer this question—it is voluntary. It is also the case that the entire enterprise is allegedly about respecting a person's right to define themselves; the official guidelines produced by the Departments of Health and Social Care (2005) make a point of saying in paragraph 84 that "self-classification is not a courtesy but a recognition of the fact that a person's ethnic group is an integral part of their identity". It is curious, then, to find, in paragraph 43 of this *same set of guidelines*, this advice to those administering this questionnaire:

> it is not advisable to give patients, service users and staff the opportunity to record 'Not stated' on the forms and questionnaires they might be asked to self-complete. Hence the 'Not stated code' should not be [available to those completing these forms]. [DOHSC, 2005, para. 43]

It transpires that this option is only there as a way to allow computer operators to record that a person has not filled out this form. (This, by the way, is why the data form is called 16+1: sixteen choices offered and one hidden.) But even more troubling is the guidance given by the Commission for Racial Equality (2002, p. 14), which goes so far as to say,

> We recommend that you do not say anything in your explanation to the ethnic background question that might encourage people not to answer it. *For example, do not say 'This question is entirely voluntary'* ... If you are asking for the information electronically, you should not make the ethnic origin field a compulsory one (in other words, people should be able to skip this field). Again, we would recommend that you do not include a 'prefer not to say' option.

This way of proceeding seems to me to be ethically problematic. A particular freedom (of not answering the question) is kept hidden from those presented with the form, with the result that they cannot easily avail themselves of this possibility. Through this means, people are corralled and manipulated in the direction of filling out the form. Even more deceitful is the fact that the entire activity is portrayed as one of respecting the rights of individuals to choose. The overt reason for not letting the public know that the questionnaire is voluntary is to try to get as many people as possible to fill in these forms in order to have as full a picture as possible. While this is true, there is also another reason, which has to do with one of the ways that "organizational performance" is measured.

One of the ways that organizational performance is measured is through something called the data quality indicator (DQI). This, allegedly, is a measure of how successful the organization is at collecting data. The higher the score on this measure, the higher will be the organization's "total performance score". Consequently, the guideline states, "high proportions [of 'not-stated' codes] have an adverse affect on the overall DQI and hence on the organisation's overall performance" (DOHSC, 2005, par. 45).

In other words, people are being tacitly coerced into filling out this form in part for the benefit of the well-being of the organization, so that the organization is seen to be "performing" well. It is, in the true sense of the word, a "performance". But the organization, too, is being tacitly forced to proceed in this way, because it would be penalized in various ways by various governmental watchdogs if its DQI fell below some target.

What we are witnessing here is the needs of the organization trumping the rights of the individuals that it is supposedly serving. Another instance of this is to be found with in the manipulation of statistical evidence.

Hawkeye: the manipulation of statistics

In tennis, despite the presence of a dozen or so officials on court, there are constant disputes as to whether the ball is in or out. A technological solution has been found for this problem. Technology has advanced sufficiently for the advent of Hawkeye, a computerized means of precisely tracking the flight of a tennis ball. In order to prevent abuse of this system, players may only call on the verdict of Hawkeye a limited number of times. But then, on occasions, this "solution" is appropriated and put to a use for which it was never intended. Players who are losing badly have been known to call on "Hawkeye" on occasions when it is clear to all and sundry that there is no doubt as to where the ball landed. They do this in order to try to break their opponent's concentration and so get back into the game. The strategy breaks no rules, instead it uses the rules, but for ends that were never intended. This is called gamesmanship.

Gamesmanship is rife in organizational life, in part because organizational life is set up as a game with the introduction of targets. For example, to help save lives, the ambulance services were given a target of eight minutes for reaching emergency calls. And in order to reduce the extraordinary lengths of time people had to wait to be treated in Accident and Emergency departments in hospitals, the government introduced a target of no more than four hours between registration and treatment. Some beleaguered A&E departments, short of resources, unable to meet the target, resorted to the strategy of delaying registering those coming for treatment by the device of leaving them in the ambulances, thereby delaying starting the clock ticking. This gave rise to situations in which several ambulances were left waiting on the forecourt of hospitals for lengthy periods. While this strategy enabled the A&E department to meet its target, the ambulance service's performance suffered, as the shortage of available ambulances meant that they could not meet their eight-minute target. To solve this situation, the government introduced yet another target: no more than fifteen minutes to transfer the patient from ambulance to registration desk. The way things are set up, each part of the service is actually working against the other; it becomes a competition, it becomes a game, and so inevitably there will be gamesmanship. In some mad way, this actually fits with the market paradigm. What works for the benefit of one is to the detriment of the other. In effect, each of the targets is in conflict with the others.

"Race" statistics are also similarly misused. One of the ways of policing the police with regard to their tendency to racism is to collect statistics on the numbers of the kinds of people they arrest, and so on. The situation, until relatively recently, has been that the police were only allowed to stop and question citizens if there were grounds for doing so (acting suspiciously, driving erratically, etc.). Data collected has consistently shown that the police stop and search proportionately many more Black people than White (say, 70% of those being stopped and searched in the street are Black, in a locality where just 30% of the population are Black).

The situation was exacerbated following 9/11 and 7/7. The British government suspended this safeguard against potential abuses of power in a series of counter-terrorism measures. Today, police no longer have to cite any reasons or give any grounds for stopping anyone in the street. In order not to fall foul of their "race" targets, the police compensated by stopping thousands of White people, in order to ensure that their statistics would look more respectable. The *Guardian* reported,

> Thousands of [White] people are being stopped and searched by the police under their counter-terrorism powers—simply to provide a

> racial balance in official statistics, the government's official anti-terror law watchdog has revealed . . . The latest police figures show that 117,278 people were stopped under section 44 in 2007–08, of whom 73,967 were White, 20,768 were Asian and 15,218 Black. [Travis, 2009, p. 9]

Here, too, the rights and freedoms of innocents are trashed in the service of institutional performance.

But I think that something even more insidious happening. It seems to me that here we are witnessing is not just "Hawkeye" and gamesmanship, but also the "sleeping policeman" scenario, where the solution inflames the problem rather than extinguishing it. Recall that one of the triggers for the Brixton riots was due to the fact that some Black people felt unfairly picked on in the street by the police. They alleged that the police stopped them for little or no reason and asked them to account for themselves in various ways—are they really the owner of the car that they are driving, and so on. The new law allows the police to revert back to this practice with impunity, as they no longer have to give any reason as to why this person has been stopped. The racism (conscious or unconscious) that must be present as the motivation for many of these searches is free to continue, but now it is covered over by the device of stopping many more White people. The gathering of statistical evidence, which was supposed to help reveal the workings of racism, is now perverted to become a cover-up for the problem. It is literally a whitewash. The police are now able to dismiss the charge of racism being present in the stopping of so many thousands of Black people by the device of pointing to the thousands of White people they have also stopped. Of course, it is possible that what the numbers show is that the police are being "colour blind" in their activities and scrupulously fair, but this is not the opinion of the government's own monitoring committee.

So, we can see that there are already many ethical problems to do with the tacit coercion in the way the questionnaire is administered, the way that the data is collected and potentially manipulated, as well as with the conflict between the unspoken and espoused rationales for collecting the data.

But what of the data itself? This is what I turn to next, a close questioning of the actual content of the ethnic monitoring form.

Confusions and conflations: the race–ethnicity fudge

What a strange collection, what a mish-mash of categories this form consists of: two colours (Black and White), a continent (Asia), a nation (China), and, most disturbing of all, the idea of people who are allegedly Mixed. By countenancing a notion of "mixed" as one of the categories of ethnicity, the legislature gives succour to the racists, as it implies that there exist ethnicities that are "unmixed" or pure. The notion of "mixed" might appear innocuous, but it is, in fact, a continuation of one of the more unpleasant ideas in the racist's world view—that of miscegenation. We have to ask: just what is it we think is being "mixed"? The answer appears to be that these people are generated by mixing colour with geography. And in what manner does the mixing take place? This remains somewhat mysterious. We have to ask again, where and when in this world has there ever existed a pure ethnicity?

As we have seen, the legislature not only avoided confronting the fact that races do not exist, but instead it gave "race" credence by instating the notion in law, and then further muddied the waters by incorporating ethnicity into the definition of race, and race into the definition of ethnicity. This fudging then allows a great number of bizarre anomalies pass by without raising any question or comment. There are many strands to be untangled, made more difficult by the fact that they are all a part of each other.

First and foremost, given that the requirement to collect this data has been written into the legislature in a *Race Relations Act*, it is curious, is it not, that the data being collected is called *ethnic* monitoring and not *race* monitoring. In fact, this form completely avoids the use of the term "race". Why is this? The answer, in part, has to do with two interlinked confusions: a confusion as to whether the data being collected is subjective or objective, as well as a confusion regarding the purpose of the questionnaire itself.

Remember, the primary purpose of the questionnaire is to search out processes that marginalize some kinds of people at the expense of other kinds. Its work is in the objective realm, as to what actually takes place between people. At this present time in history, we are prone to "see" people as belonging to certain kinds—Whites, Blacks, and so on. These could be described as categories of "race". Now, although "race" is a category of the racialized imagination, it is, nevertheless, in a peculiar sense objective, in that it has a very real impact on how people are treated "out there" in the world. "Race" is objective in the sense that it is the instrument and means through which people are made Other. If the questionnaire were to be true to its purpose, then it would face up to the fact that what is to be counted are the number of ways that people are "othered". It would be counting the other-ascriptions of the more powerful. Instead, the questionnaire fudges things and turns instead to ethnicity.

The manufacture of objectivity out of subjectivities

So, what exactly is ethnicity? Here we find yet another confusion. On the one hand, we are firmly told in the guidance given to those administering the questionnaire, that "Ethnicity is subjective: a person should self-assign his or her own ethnic group. While other people might view an individual as having a distinct ethnic identity, the individual's view of their own identity takes priority" (DOHSC, 2005, par. 31).

If ethnicity is truly subjective, then any claim made by any individual as to their ethnicity would be incontrovertible and final, and to be respected and accepted on that basis. But this is not what actually occurs. Because, as we saw in a previous chapter, the claim that Rastafarianism constituted an ethnicity was not respected, but overturned by the Law Lords on the basis of objective criteria—that they had not been in existence for a sufficiently long period of time, something longer than sixty years.

Ethnicity is supposedly subjective because it is self-assigned; it is what the person "feels" themselves to be, where they "feel" they belong. And because it is something that they "feel", and feelings are internal to the person, then they are to be taken as true and may not be questioned. Each individual "owns" their feelings, and so, if someone who did not own it questioned it, then it would be a form of disrespect (these are the values of the Romantic). Anyhow, statisticians then count up the various tick boxes, and then present their results in the form of numbers. Once we are in the region of numbers, then it appears that what is being spoken of is objective—that the numbers are numbers of real, concrete things. But this is not true. What has been counted are a number of *feelings*. It is through this methodological sleight of hand that *subjective* impressions are transmuted into *objective* evidence. Further, it is a very peculiar kind of objectivity, one that can never be questioned or interrogated, because, as we are told, a person's own view of their ethnicity has priority. This is the double-bind we are landed with.

But the thing is that self-ascription, although it has its own validity in some contexts, actually misses the point. Racism, sexism, prejudice, and the like are driven not so much what *I* think of myself, but by what *you* take me to be, particularly if *you* are more powerful than *me*. It matters little if a person thinks of themselves primarily as a Cambridge graduate, lawyer, middle class, or British if they are perceived first and foremost by more powerful others as Jew, Black, or Woman, and—this is the point—*treated on that basis*.

We also have to ask: how meaningful is the collection of subjective ethnicities? In my case, I could put up an argument for legitimately entering myself into the "any other" category in A, B, C, D, or E. I could place myself in the "any other" category in B on the basis that we are all "mixed", in C on the basis of being Indian, in D on the basis that I think of myself as Black in the current socio-historic context, in E because I was born a Parsee, and finally in A, because some Parsees think of themselves as being of "Aryan" descent and, therefore, White. And here is the point: the place I would locate myself on this form would very much be context dependent. Given this range of genuine possibilities available to me, how meaningful are the numbers provided by the questionnaire, given that everyone will have the possibility of self-ascribing a number of alternative categories?

Interestingly, the USA census form deals with the question of race differently. It lists fifteen racial categories, but, unlike the British form in which the individual is limited to one choice, the American form allows individuals to choose more than one "racial" category for themselves.

In sum, although the purpose of the questionnaire is to reveal the processes of marginalization at work, all it actually supplies is a picture of the range of ways that people think of themselves in a particular moment (subjectively), and how these are distributed over the social-scape, which has little to do with race and racism.

Over the centuries, the idea of race has been used in two distinct ways—as lineage and as typology (Banton, 1987). If you think of White as a "type", then all Whites belong together (wherever they are "from") by virtue of being White. And if you think of that all White people were spawned by the same source, then that is to use it as a marker of lineage. Whichever way one uses them (lineage or typology), the categories Black and White are categories of race, generated by the processes of racism. They have little to do with shared histories or ways of living. They are only ever communities to the racialized way of thinking. Yet, both are given a prominent place on the *ethnic* monitoring form.

The fudge is that self-ascription is being used instead of other-ascription. In this way, the questionnaire cannot do its real work.

If one were to really grasp the nettle here, one would have a *racial monitoring form,* and it would be filled out through the racialized eyes of the Established. It would draw on the other-ascriptions that we are all so expert at. I look at a room full of people and my eye automatically divides it into White, Black, South Asian, Far Eastern, and so on. These are the ascriptions that drive and feature in the processes of marginalization. One can see why this is notion is disquieting, given the sorry history of scientific racism in Britain, South Africa, and elsewhere.

Reproducing racialized thinking

Although the idea behind the ethnic monitoring form is inclusivity and the recognition of the diversity of the population, in a critical way it actually comes to reinforce the processes of racism as it dooms certain kinds of persons to eternal otherness. Say that there exists a person, Jayanti (and surely there are many such persons), whose progenitors ended up in Britain from India some generations ago. If Jayanti thinks of herself as British, then she has just three possibilities on this form: White British, Asian British, or Black British. As she is unable to avail herself of the first of these, then she is manacled forever to one of the other two categories—Asian British or Black British—and so must remain eternally in the antechamber, never, ever quite really British. I am not, by the way, asserting that such persons *ought to* experience themselves as simply "British". I am saying that if they did, then the questionnaire gives them no opportunity to claim this identity.

Perversely, in its present form, the ethnic monitoring system pushes people into further racializing themselves as well as others. In the current situation, it becomes imperative to be known and be recognized by the legislature by a particular name, as a category, as a kind of people, as a race. This is because once a category comes to be officially recognized as such, then not only does it gain a legitimacy in public discourse, but now, as an entity, it also is deemed to have certain "rights" in relation to other similar entities. You are only counted (and, therefore, you only count) when you are a certain kind of human being.

Although much has been made of the fact that the categories used in the ethnic monitoring form were arrived at after consultation with "communities", it is, nevertheless, written from the perspective of what Elias would call "The Established", the norm of the majority. It is no exaggeration to say that the ethnic monitoring process as conceived actually reflects, reproduces, and furthers the norms born of the racialized thinking of the legislators. The first of two illustrations to back my claim begins with this piece of advice on collecting data on religious affiliation, which is found in the aforementioned *Practical Guide To Ethnic Monitoring In The NHS* (DOHSC, 2005). It states,

> 47. Questions about religion can be asked by using the question and codes from the ONS Census of 2001:
>
> **Religion**
>
> What is your religion? *Tick one box only.*
>
> ☐ None
>
> ☐ Christian (Including Church of England, Catholic, Protestant and all other Christian denominations)
>
> ☐ Buddhist
>
> ☐ Hindu
>
> ☐ Jewish
>
> ☐ Muslim
>
> ☐ Sikh
>
> ☐ Any other religion (please write in)
>
> ☐ Not stated
>
> [DOHSC, 2005, par. 47]

As before, the final tick box is not present on the sheet given out to the public.

Why has the Office of National Statistics (ONS) bothered to spell out some of the subgroups of "Christian", but has not done the same for the other religions cited,[1] and made no mention whatsoever of the Chinese "faiths", Taoism and Confucianism. The answer to the question is that the structure of the questionnaire reveals something about the relative power of each of the groupings. First, you have to have sufficient power to just feature on the list as a category in your own right (for example, all African religions are missing, as are Zoroastrianism and Taoism, among many others); second, the category with the most power is able to further differentiate itself into some of its subcategories (in this case, it is Christianity). Taxonomies are never just objective, as the positivists would have us believe. The point I am continually trying to make is that these questionnaires are reflections of the dynamics of the power relations that are being played out. No doubt if those inhabiting China Town (literal and notional) were to make more of a nuisance of themselves and became a more powerful, argumentative, organized voice speaking out during election time, then it would not be long before Taoism and Confucianism also came to feature on this list of religions.

One of the rationales given for collecting data on religion is that it would help institutions take account of the dietary needs of its customers and staff. This is patently absurd. I know of many people born into the Muslim and Jewish settings who enjoy bacon, and I know of many born into Christian settings who abhor it. And, as we saw earlier, many "kinds" of Hindus eat beef and do not think it taboo. So, if one wants to know about dietary requirements, why not just ask about them directly?

If this example has illustrated how power patterns the questionnaire, the next example shows up the racialized thinking of the legislators.

This time we begin with a piece of advice (from the same guide from the Department of Health) to those administering the questionnaire on how to use the "any other" category:

> 38. This is how it works. If a Trust or council used the 16 codes only, people who say that they belong to the 'Greek Cypriot' ethnic group would be coded to the 'Any other White background' group. If there is a large Greek Cypriot community in a Trust's . . . area, the Trust or council should . . . include a Greek Cypriot code under the 'White'

> heading. In this way, the Trust and council can explore issues for that community while at the same time being able to re-aggregate the Greek Cypriot code back into the 'Any other White background' code for comparison with local or national population data or with data from other places.

Here are two simple enough questions to ask of the Department of Health: first, where would they suggest that one locates Turkish Cypriots? My guess is that they would not suggest that they be coded under the "any other White" section because Turks are not "White" in the racialized imagination. So, here is their second question: could they tell the difference between a Turkish Cypriot and a Greek Cypriot walking down the street? My guess is that they (like me) mostly could not tell the difference. It becomes glaringly obvious that what we are witnessing here is the racialized thinking of the legislators, *which we are being invited to reproduce.*

Interestingly, the Islington Carer's Centre (the London Borough of Islington has a large Cypriot population) did not follow this advice from the government to colour-code Greek Cypriots as White. Islington chose instead to create an entirely new category (on a par with that of White, Mixed, etc.) called Turkish/Greek. They broke this down into five sub-categories, "Turkish/Turkish Cypriot", "Greek/Greek Cypriot", "Turkish", "Greek", and "Any other". I presume that Islington has followed this particular course precisely in order not to reproduce a racialized division between Greek and Turkish Cypriots. This course followed by Islington seems eminently sensible to me. But, if that is the case, then why not extend this strategy to other groupings, too?

In sum: as it is *other-ascriptions* that drives the processes of marginalization, it is these we should be counting, not the *self-ascriptions* of ethnicity. It seems to me that if we want to "measure" racism, then we are obliged to use the reification "race", because the category has been generated by the processes of racism and it is utilized in its work. Confusions abound when racialized categories (like Black and White) are given a respectable gloss of ethnicity. All these confusions have arisen because of not facing up to the fact that not only do the races not exist, but that even culture and ethnicity are ephemeral, always fluid, never natural, always contingent, political and politicized, and generated as well as structured by the processes of power relations.

Note

1. The form could have fleshed out each of the religions in this way: Muslims (Sunni, Shia, Wahhabi, Sufi, etc.); Jews (Reformist, Conservative, Ashkenazi, Haredi, Hasidim, Misnagdim, Modern Orthodox, Sephardic, etc.); Hindus (Brahmins, Kshatriyas, Vaishyas, Shudras, Parjanyas, etc.); Bhuddists (Therevada, Zen, Mahayana, Korean Zen, Nicherian, Tibetan, etc.).

CHAPTER SEVEN

Corrupting the liberal ideal: diversity in organizational life

Spreadsheet ethics

Increasingly, organizations are putting in place a number of diversity initiatives which aim to make organizational life more open and more accessible to people from backgrounds and groupings different from those in the mainstream. The intention is to make the workforce more diverse through employing different *kinds* of people. The focus of diversity initiatives is to set up processes that will allow more women, "ethnic" minorities, those with disabilities, gays, lesbians, and so on, into the structures of higher management. The wish is to make the organizational culture more inclusive. To this end, organizations employ diversity experts—consultants—to help the organization "celebrate diversity" instead of fearing and shunning it.

Rather surprisingly, it turns out that the theme of "diversity" has become almost a universal feature in the "strategic plans" of organizations large and small, public and private. Diversity has also become an integral feature of most contemporary "organizational development" initiatives. It is surprising because previously corporations had been very reluctant to engage with the prior emancipatory movements of multi-culturalism and anti-racism. So, why is it that the idea of diversity is being so readily embraced by them?

The first, and perhaps most pragmatic, reason is that now it is *required by the law* that CEOs and governing boards of organizations demonstrate that they are actively addressing the sources of inequality in their particular workplace.

Second, the rhetoric of diversity is much more up-beat than that of the previous movements: "The 'diversity" approach seeks to tackle discrimination by presenting differences as positives to be benefited from, rather than the basis of negative, unfair discrimination" (Thompson, 2001, p. 35). Confrontation is replaced with celebration.

The third reason is this: the antiracist agenda called for a *redistribution* of resources. If the cake is finite, then the more it is shared out, the less each will necessarily get. Unsurprisingly, this ethos did not find favour with those in the boardroom. In contrast, diversity theology claims that if its doctrine were embraced, then the cake itself would get bigger and everyone, including the already well-to-do, would get more—this is the mythical "trickle down" theory that has been promoted by neo-liberals. They say that the diversity process is going to be a good thing for *the already privileged* as much as anyone else. It is primarily on this basis that diversity has been taken up by profit-making institutions. In the literature, one finds many references to ideas of diversity being "lucrative", a "commodity", an "asset" to be exploited in the service of increasing profit; this is the basis on which it is sold to the boardroom, that the share holders will "do well" out of it. Meanwhile, it is sold to the public on the basis of "doing good", of inclusivity, of acceptance, of respect.

It is the ones in powerful positions (leaders) that control the chequebooks, and so it is they that have to be initially convinced in order for any diversity experts/consultants to be employed at all. It is by this means that the diversity expert enters the portals of the profit-making corporation. It has convinced those in charge of the chequebooks that they, too, will be beneficiaries of a diversity change process. In this world, there are no losers; everybody will win!

But it is not all plain sailing; many organizations continue to drag their feet. Why are they "resisting"? The diversity experts cannot imagine that the "resistance" has anything to do with the self-interest of the already privileged. Instead, they put it down to ignorance: "If Americans were to become more educated . . . they might come to embrace the policy with vigor, but many of them appear to have *resisted education* . . . which is why scholars have found a strong association between prejudice and resistance to affirmative action among the privileged" (Stockdale & Cao, 2004, p. 306–307; my italics).

The diversity experts claim that not only are these people ignorant, they are also resisting education, and, in doing so, they are being irrational. But it seems to me that the "resisters" are, in fact, supremely rational, because they are pursuing the logic of the "bottom line"—that is, they are pursuing the value of maximizing their profits. This blindness on the part of diversity experts is doubly curious because, as we have already seen, they are not shy of citing self-interest as the critical driver for increasing diversity in organizations.

The fourth reason arises from the current fashionable status of complexity thinking in management literature, and in the simplistic way it is often taken up. The idea that novelty emerges unpredictably from a mix of things makes the notion of diversity appealing. In fact, it becomes an idealization: the more organizations diversify, the more novelty they will produce and the more profit they will make. The more novelty they produce, the better they will fare in relation to their competitors.

The fifth reason we have already touched on in Chapter Two, this being that the notion of diversity is easily misused to promote amoral individualism. When used in this sense, then the notion of diversity feeds and fits in well with the ethos of the individual heroic leader that abounds in much organizational discourse and fits well with the philosophical beliefs of economic libertarians. This version of individualism is a "me" philosophy, and without the moral basis of the individualism of Enlightenment liberalism.

The sixth possibility has to do with public image. In the current social climate, companies are increasingly being judged not only by how much profit they make, but also by how socially responsible they are. Reputation becomes an asset, and so many companies are keen to be seen as doing "good works" for the underprivileged. To be seen to be taking diversity seriously is good PR and a part of this trend (to say nothing of the tax breaks that accrue from it).

The final reason has to do with globalization, the growth of the "free" market, the burgeoning of the multi-national corporation, and the reduction of barriers to the free flow of capital. Although multi-nationals voice a rhetoric about "stakeholders", they make no secret of the fact that their primary allegiance is to "the bottom line" and their shareholders. As these companies expand, moving from country to country to reduce their outgoings, they are forced to deal with other kinds of people from other lands. Diversity experts abound in this territory, to help reduce "cultural conflict" and foster the values of diversity. Or so it would seem. Their real work (I contend) is to help the company make a bigger and quicker buck with as little trouble as possible. In the rhetoric aimed at the public, notions of diversity and the celebration of diversity are linked to social conscience. And, indeed, this is what we find when we look at the public declarations of multi-nationals. For example, the diveristy statement on the website of the clothing company GAP:

> At Gap Inc., we value diversity and inclusion. We celebrate it. It's at the core of what we do. Diversity is essential to our culture and business success. That's why we embrace a diversity of styles, ideas and people. ... It means doing what's right by treating every customer, supplier and employee with respect—and delivering results by striving to create an environment where employees thrive and generate top performance. [GAP]

Their equal opportunities statement is as follows:

> Gap Inc. is an equal opportunity employer. All employment decisions are made without regard to race, color, age, gender, gender identity, sexual orientation, religion, marital status, pregnancy, national origin/ancestry, citizenship, physical/mental disabilities, military status or any other basis prohibited by law. Every employee is responsible for helping prevent discrimination and harassment in the workplace. [GAP]

These laudable claims are hard to marry up with the other side of GAP—sweatshops and child labour (McDougall, 2007). Modern corporations pay little or no regard to the communities they destroy when they decide to shut down factories in one place and rebuild in another—cost saving exercises, as they are euphemistically called. Here, at least, they are indiscriminate in whether they are devastating communities in their home towns or in the far away East. For example, there was considerable protest in 2007 when GAP laid off

900 garment workers in the city where their headquarters are located—Los Angeles—and out-sourced the work to distant lands where they are able to pay workers less. Of course it is not just GAP that proceeds in this way. As the Delhi lawyer and activist for the Global March Against Child Labour, Bhuwan Ribhu, says, "The reality is that most major retail firms are in the same game, cutting costs and not considering the consequences. They should know by now what outsourcing to India means . . . a basement or an attic crammed with small children to make a healthy profit" (McDougall, 2007).

This is no secret: in fact, it is promoted as a virtue, as James Worrell, the chief executive of Pharma Services Network (a firm organizing tours of Indian factories for Western pharmaceutical companies), says, "There is a lot of good talent at a much lower price in India" (Timmons, 2010). This is what diversity really means in corporation land—more bang for less buck/rupee/yen.

This, then, is where we stand. The notion of diversity has been made more palatable to the establishment by neutering it; the diversity literature makes it a point of pride to claim that, unlike its predecessors, its agenda is apolitical. Politics just gets in the way of celebration and making money. It is no coincidence, then, that these forms of the diversity movement have been embraced and fostered by the corporate world. The rationale for their beliefs and actions is the same for the libertarians as well as the advocates of diversity—the cake itself will get bigger, and everyone will benefit. As is well known by now, although the cake has indeed become bigger, the promised "trickle down" of wealth never took place and instead the rich got much richer and the gap between them and the poor widened dramatically. Instead of the wealth trickling down, what we got was a "sucking up" of wealth.

To my mind, this sort of version of diversity is a perversion of the emancipatory ideal.

In what follows, I look at some of the literature in the USA and UK on the subject. Three are by diversity consultants (Henry, 2003; Loden, 1996; Thiederman, 2003), two are edited collections of papers, one from academia (Stockdale & Crosby, 2004) and the other from the business environment (Harvard Business Review on Managing Diversity, 2001), and there are two handbooks of practice (Clements & Spinks, 2006; Thompson, 2001).

Diversity peddlers

The literature on diversity is curiously non-diverse. Each paper/book tends to follow the following formula. First, they list four rationales for why organizations *should* embrace diversity change programmes, these being: it is a legal requirement, litigation by the disenfranchised, attracting and retaining "diverse talent", and creating new ethnic market niches. Then, ironically, they almost all bemoan the fact that, despite years of change programmes, there has been little real shift in the demographics of the kinds of people in positions of power. The diversity consultants then, nevertheless, go on to claim that they themselves do have a diversity programme that *does really work*, for example, Loden (1996) says "despite three decades of affirmative action, glass ceilings were still firmly in place for women and people of color above middle management levels" (p. 23). She continues that this is because "sadly, few organizations have applied *proven* change adoption principles to diversity implementation" (*ibid.*, p. 37, my italics).

Each expert proposes their own taxonomy of the different "types" of organizations, and go on to delineate a number of stages that organizations will be led through before getting to equality heaven. For example, Thomas, Mack, and Montagliani claim that their "full integration theory" will lead organizations through a three-stage process to arrive in diversity heaven. They then make the astonishingly confident claim that their "model proposes that each organization *will follow the same path* to integration" (2004, p. 68, my italics). No diversity here, then.

One of the things we are witnessing here is consultants in the marketplace wanting to differentiate themselves from others providing a similar service. For example, Thiederman (2003) insists that the culprit is "bias" rather than prejudice; she has trademarked the term *guerrilla bias*, to prevent others making use of it. Trademarking is a curious move for someone whose espoused ethos is one of openness and inclusivity.

The rhetoric in these works is one of inclusivity, compensating for past wrongs, compassion, non-judgemental acceptance of otherness, and so on. However, just behind the rhetoric, we find the ethics of the spreadsheet. In much of the literature, the main rationale proposed for organizations going through some diversity change process is that of enhancing opportunities to make money, and even more money.

Thiederman (2003) speaks of "lucrative virtue" and Haq (2004) of the "diversity dividend". *Ultimately the diversity movement (in its present form) is an appeal to the self-interest of the already privileged.*

It is a moot point as to whether this is bottom-line thinking, or whether it is bottom-of-the-barrel thinking.

Henry: new taxonomies of human kind generated by the bottom line

The tone of the works written by consultants tends to be "inspirational".

> Few countries are as diverse as America. Throughout our history, peoples from different lands and regions of the world have headed for our shores. They brought with them their cultures, traditions, languages and religions. As we have grappled with the challenges that a multicultural society presents, it has sometimes felt as if the rest of the world has been an observer, taking side bets as to how our grand experiments in social justice, fairness and equal opportunity would turn out. [Henry, 2003, p. 2]

> For several centuries, individuals of European (e.g. Anglo-Saxon) ancestry have made up the overwhelming majority of individuals in the US workforce. [Stone & Stone-Romero, 2004, p. 78]

In this alternative universe inhabited by some diversity experts, the minor details of slavery, land grab, and genocide are happily absent. Henry says, it "is no longer good enough to tolerate differences; we must look for differences" (Henry, 2003, p. 5). And one ought to do this because "difference" is a commodity: "[it] is pure pragmatism to treat diversity as an asset" (*ibid.*, p. 4).

Humanity is now divided into a new taxonomy of just two: those that are multi-cultural or diverse, and those that are not: "Multicultural groups comprise over 30% of the US population". It also happens that these diverse, multi-cultural people are mostly extremely poor. Nevertheless, Henry tells us that there is "a market opportunity *serving* the 'bottom of the economic pyramid' namely the four billion people with incomes less than $1500 a year" (Henry, 2003, p. 6).

It follows, then, that it really is worth the effort of making a little bit of money from each of them, because (thankfully) there are so many of them. Henry tells us, "In the U.S., Latinos, African-Americans and Asian-Americans control more than $1.3 trillion dollars in purchasing power. Older Americans, people with disabilities and gays and lesbians control another $1.6 trillion" (Henry, 2003, p. 6). And looking further afield, we are told that globally, "99% of the population growth is occurring in three regions: Africa, Asia and Latin America, all three comprised of *diverse peoples*. (Henry, 2003, p. 6, my italics).

It is becoming apparent who is being alluded to when the terms multi-cultural and diverse are being used: the dark people.

It also seems to me that it is exactly this kind of thinking that drove the sub-prime fiasco, which has resulted in the catastrophic economic meltdown that we are all drowning in. The banks have tried to make a little bit of money from "serving" those at the "bottom of the economic pyramid"; unfortunately, the pyramids have collapsed.

Ethnic marketing: instrumentalizing the "ethnics"

There are two parts to the task of "ethnic marketing". First, the company needs to find out about *them* and *their* ways of life so that *we* can cater to *their* needs and desires. Second, the company needs to give itself a makeover in order to look more ethnic friendly.

Happily, both these birds can be killed with the same stone: by employing some of *them*. Not only will *they* be able to tell *us* what kinds of things *their* people like, it will also make *us* look good in the eyes of the world (recall the points about reputation made earlier): "A well thought out marketing plan targeting the ethnic market [begins with] . . . the company having diversity represented in its ranks that will better relate, better understand, better serve these customers" (Henry, 2003, p. 58).

Lest we get too dewy-eyed, it is as well to remember that "serve" in this context is doublespeak for "sell to" and "make a profit from".

> Several corporations conclude that because lesbians and gay men have been neglected for so long, even modest attempts at marketing to the community in a positive light could generate sales and secure brand loyalty. [Lubensky, Holland, Wiethof, & Crosby, 2004, p. 213]

Thus, employing ethnics is a means to reaching the ethnics out there. Their presence is instrumentalized, a means to the end of increased profit. The ethnics are *needed* because "Executives, especially those who are not diverse, continue to be relatively unaware of the potential purchasing power of ethnic markets" (Henry, 2003, p. 42).

Recruitment and retention: worshipping the "ethnics"

The next issue concerns the processes of recruitment and retention of "multi-cultural candidates". Not only does it take more effort and costs more money than usual to recruit those at the margins, but it also turns out that even when one makes the effort to reach out to them, they are slow in coming forward as they are quite a demanding lot. Not only do they "look for companies that are already diverse . . . [they] are sensitive to the makeup of the interviewing team"; they also "look for a company where there is *zero tolerance for anything less than absolute trust, unconditional acceptance and respect*" (Henry, 2003, pp. 83–84, my italics).

Absolute trust, unconditional acceptance and respect: if true, these are quite incredible demands. Let us get this clear: here is a consultant telling companies that they should deliver something to the "ethnics" which no other kind of employee would or could be offered, because absolutes and unconditionalities are existential impossibilities. An idiocy is being portrayed as a "right". If this is true, then no wonder "they" find it difficult to get jobs; if only "they" were more realistic in their demands.

The other reason often put up for trying to include "those with diversity" in the workforce is that not only do some of them possess talent, they possess something called "*diverse* talent" (as Henry calls it). But having recruited "those with diversity", companies have difficulties retaining them. This costs money. "Conservative estimates of replacing one experienced engineer range between $50,000 and $100,000 . . . [but if] that engineer is diverse, it will likely be more" (Henry, 2003, p. 90). The issue of retention requires serious consideration. However, the solution suggested by Henry is a strange one. She says that in order to retain these "diverse employees", the company needs to "develop a *reverence* for work experiences, habits and processes of diverse employees" (Henry, 2003, p. 7).

To revere something is not to question it or engage with it, but to stand back in awe, and worship it. This then leads her to her "platinum rule": "Treat others as they *want to be* treated" (Henry, 2003,

p. 171). This injunction to worship at the altar of difference requires the sacrifice of the possibility of thought itself. What an extraordinary idea, that we should treat others as they *want to be treated*. To follow this maxim one would have to completely abdicate one's own sensibilities and ethics: what if "they" want me to behave in a way that I abhor? The proposition beggars belief.

But now, having asked us to revere difference, she also tells us the opposite, that differences are irrelevant:

> In a truly inclusive environment, no one really cares how old you are, where you grew up, what academic degrees you've earned, where you've worked or what style clothes you wear. What counts is the quality of your thinking [and] . . . competence. [Henry, 2003, p. 110]

It is no wonder that so many diversity initiatives come to naught. On the one hand, we are being invited to deify the differences between us and others, and, on the other hand, we are told that these differences do not matter at all, what matters are the individual's talents and capacities. No thought is given to how the "we" might be actively excluding and making life difficult for certain kinds of others. Instead, the problem and the solution are couched in terms of appreciation.

Thiederman: "natural" attractions and repulsions

Several ideas get repeated as "obvious" truths in the diversity literature. One of these is the idea that "It is part of our human nature to gravitate toward and have more positive regard for someone who 'looks like us'" (Henry, 2003, p. 171). It follows (but it is never actually voiced) that it must also be natural to have feelings of antipathy towards others who do not look like us. We can see then that although these diversity promulgators proclaim themselves inclusivists, they are actually in complete agreement with the racists: they both agree that it is natural to have hostile feelings towards those who look different to us. Their difference from the racists lies in their view that one should rise above one's nature rather than give into it.

This is also Thiederman's view, as illustrated by a vignette that she provides. Before attending to the vignette itself, I will contextualize it by giving an outline of her diversity change programme as described in her book, *Making Diversity Work*. This will also serve the purpose of giving us a glimpse of the kind of thing that is being purchased by organizations from diversity experts.

Thiederman would like to help rid companies of "bias". According to her, biases are virus like. She says, "what bias does is interfere with our ability to see people accurately, hence the need to renew our vision" (Thiederman, 2003, p. 7). She has discovered a particularly nasty variety of this virus and has trademarked it: "guerrilla bias"™. She offers organizations the service of virus removal through her "vision renewal programme" (VRP) which "begins with strategies for becoming aware of our biases and moves systematically toward learning to shove our biases aside, and, finally, immunize ourselves from the relapse that so often accompanies personal growth" (*ibid.*). She says that "what the VRP does is freeze-dry each target bias by taking the emotional juice out of it, thus reducing it to an inert lump that can be grabbed and tossed out of your thinking and out of your life" (p. 46). Bias is "an acquired habit of thought rooted in fear and fuelled by conditioning, and as such, can be unacquired and deconditioned" (*ibid.*).

Keep this in mind, as she describes a situation at a conference at which she could not decide where to sit.

> At one table, everyone was White . . . at the other . . . Black . . . my impulse as a White person was to go to the White table; a little more familiarity, a little more comfort. In the end, I gave into that impulse and took a seat at the table with the folks who looked most like me. [Thiederman, 2003, p. 21]

In her analysis of the situation, she says that this was not an instance of bias on her part, because:

> We assume that the clustering of kinship groups is a sure sign that something is wrong. Do these groups feel uncomfortable with each other? It is time we bring balance to this issue of being drawn to people like ourselves. We must learn when it is bias and when it is simple human comfort. It is *this desire for comfort* and the wish *to be with people with whom we identify* that draws us to members *of our own kinship group*. [Thiederman, 2003, p. 22, my italics]

There are several points to be noticed here: first, she feels a kinship because of skin colour. Second, she says that she sat with the White group because "it is simple human comfort"; by implication, she was uncomfortable with the Black group. If this is not bias, then it is certainly racism. Through the device of describing her response as one of "simple human comfort" she need not enquire into the sources of her discomfort because it is "natural". This is exactly the rationalization that was used to justify apartheid, bolstered by the support given it by a number of sociobiologists.

Thiederman is right in saying that our desire for solidarity is "natural", but wrong because the question that she has avoided asking herself is: why is it that she felt a kinship, a *solidarity,* no less, through skin colour? The table could be full of some mix of paedophiles, White supremacists, capitalists, communists, and so on; some of these groups she (presumably) would find no solidarity with. Or is she actually saying that kinship based on skin colour is deeper than all these other differences? If she is saying this, as she seems to be, then, in this regard, this diversity expert would appear to be in agreement with the Klu Klux Klan, and others of that ilk.

Among the many erroneous claims made regarding the human condition is the following: those with a "strong sense of kinship identity tend to be the very people who are most receptive to the ideas and input of other groups" (Thiederman, 2003, p. 22). But in this, too, she and others (e.g., Branden, 1994, Ponterotti & Pedersen, 1993) are severely mistaken. Fundamentalists of all descriptions have very strong kinship identities, yet they cannot countenance the legitimacy of alternative views.

Close encounters with diversity of the second kind

Much of the literature portrays itself as scientific and as dealing in hard facts. One of the ways this illusion is achieved is by continually referring to research. The number of times the phrase "research shows" appears in this literature is extraordinary; pages are peppered with it. But there is never any critical engagement with the research, its methodology, or the robustness of its conclusions. This is the diversity way of proceeding—just accept what is said, because to question and criticize is in bad taste.

A consequence is that claims get repeated time and time again in paper after paper in a version of Chinese Whispers, and through this process gets transmuted into taken for granted truths. One of these unquestioned "truths" is that *there are* two different "kinds" of diversity. The first kind is made up of visible markers like colour; it is called surface diversity, or secondary differences. The other kind of diversity is made up of deeper things like thoughts and attitudes. In a paper, Haq tells us that Loden and Rosener (1991) tell us that diversity is categorized into

> six primary dimensions and several secondary dimensions. The primary dimensions are those that human beings cannot change: gender, age, ethnicity, physical abilities, race and sexual orientation. The secondary dimensions are those which can be changed, such as education, geographic location, social status, income, marital status, parental status, religious beliefs, work experience, and so on. [Haq, 2004, p. 278]

We never find out what the ontological status of these claims are, or anything regarding their epistemological basis, or what the distinctions add to the understanding of organizational life. Notice the pattern: repetition, appreciation, no disputation.

Thus, Haq appears blind to the bizarre nature of the claims that she repeats. Surely, the so-called primary categories are not immutable and *do change:* age changes continually, ethnicity (as something self- and other-ascribed) mutates from context to context, physical abilities can be honed, people's sexual orientation have been known to change over a lifetime, and so on. The list of changeables can also be deconstructed similarly. Here, ideological list-making is masquerading as research and fact finding.

To talk of differences being either surface or deep (the deep ones being fixed and the surface ones mutable) completely misses the point. For one thing, the "lists" are extraordinarily impoverished. As we have previously noted, the number of differences between any two human beings is uncountable, as are the number of similarities between them. The real question is: how is it that out of this range of infinite possibilities one or other similarity or difference comes to be so dominant that all others appear to be of no consequence?

Bizarrely, the course advocated by the diversity experts is for organizations to avoid getting too caught up with surface diversity (colour, gender, etc.) as this leads to strife, and instead one ought to focus on the deeper variety of diversity—the differing ways people feel and think. Further, "organizations [ought to] ... use surface-level diversity as an opportunity to learn about and form deeper-level diversity, [as this leads to] ... many financial and productivity benefits" (Thomas, Mack, & Montagliani, 2004, p. 37).

The problem, though, is that "ethnics", women, and others find themselves marginalized *because of* surface diversity (to use their term). The diversity experts are suggesting that one should not look too closely at, or talk too much about, the actual causes of the problem (say sexism), because that aggravates people; instead, look elsewhere (into the deep) and all will be well.

The portrait of the other

The diversity discourses bolster the illusion that their understanding of human relations is scientific through "research" into the psychology of "cultural types". There are serious issues regarding how the Diversity experts set about this process, both in their methodology and in the worryingly peculiar results which follow out of them. The first problem is to do with their version of psychology itself. Much of what passes for psychology in the volume called *The Psychology and Management of Workplace Diversity* consists of statements such as: "*Research shows* that members of group A are more likely to think/believe/feel X about members of group B", or "X% of group A do such and such and Y% do the other". To my mind, this is not psychology but arithmetic, and an arithmetic that is problematic, as there are serious questions to be raised about how real are the things that they think they are counting or measuring.

The problems arising from this way of proceeding are best explicated by a detailed read of a paper in this volume, written by two professors, Stone and Stone-Romero (2004). The reason for underlining the fact that they are professors is to make the point that the academic community thought sufficiently highly of their work to grace them with professorships. In other words, their views are not eccentric, but (in their context at least) mainstream.

Stone and Stone-Romero's paper sets out to describe the traits of a number of cultures in the North American context; they are named as Anglo-American/European, Hispanic-American, African-American, Asian-American, and Native-American. But soon this set of five rapidly condenses down to two: the Anglo-American and the rest. And the rest, although American, it seems that their strange ways are those from other places and times.

They begin by saying that Anglo-American culture is such that

> there is a limited dependence of subordinates on supervisors, and there is a preference for consultation or participation in decision making. . . . [meanwhile for] Hispanic-Americans [and] Asian Americans there is often a great deal of dependence of subordinates on supervisors. [Stone & Stone-Romero, 2004, p. 85]

It is worth spelling out what they are saying in plain English: Anglo-Americans are able to think for themselves and so are less reliant on their supervisors, while the Hispanics and Asians are reliant on their leaders to tell them what to do, presumably because they are not so able to think for themselves. They claim that this (lack of) capacity is the case for all "collective" cultures.

But then they also say that some of these Asian-Americans, specifically people in Japanese-style organizations (although from collective cultures), will nevertheless be "less likely to need close supervision in order to behave in ways that are consistent with role expectations" (*ibid.*, p. 92).

How can we marry up these assertions? On the one hand the Japanese are reliant on their superiors for instruction, yet they need less supervision. One explanation might be this. Anglos are less reliant on their superiors *and* need less supervision because they are autonomous and think for themselves, but the Japanese need less supervision because once they have received their instruction from their superiors (which they *need* before they can begin their task), then they are diligent about following them precisely. The implication is that they are like efficient automatons or robots. They are sheep on autopilot.

Cultures are also distinguished through their attitudes to status. In *achievement orientated* cultures people gain status on the basis of their actual achievements. Meanwhile, people in *ascriptive cultures* have status given to them (ascribed) on the basis of some mix of their "gender, family connections, and inherited wealth [age, etc.]" (*ibid.*, p. 85).

As you might expect by now, there is but one achievement orientated culture, and it is the Anglo-American. "In contrast", they say,

> research shows that members of other US subcultures (e.g. African Americans, Hispanic Americans, Asian Americans, Native Americans) are much less likely than Anglo-Americans to base their identities on achievement. . . . many African Americans base their identities on such factors as style, expression, spontaneity, and spirituality (Kochman 1974, 1981). [*ibid.*, p.85]

Having just said that achievements play no role in the construction of Native Americans' identity and status, they immediately contradict themselves and tell us that: "Native Americans often base their identities on the extent to which they have worked in the interest of other tribal members" (*ibid.*). "Research shows" one thing and "research shows" its opposite; to the diversity way of thinking, there is no problem accepting both.

These notions are also a recapitulation of the myth that it is only "the West" that operates on meritocratic principles and the rest of the world operates on principles of greed, ignorance, and nepotism. Stone and Stone-Romero seem to be unaware that the meritocratic principle took root in China some two thousand years before the founding fathers gave voice to the American Constitution. In ancient China, candidates were obliged to pass an Imperial examination in order to prove their capacities before they could become a government officer (Twitchett, 1974). This is in contrast to systems to which one may gain entry through virtue of a right inherited through accident of birth (say, the House of Lords in the UK) or by rights accrued through inherited or accumulated riches. I am not, by the way, suggesting that the Chinese are in some way immune to greed, ignorance, and nepotism.

Moving on: cultures are also said to differ according to whether they have a "universalistic" orientation or a "particularistic" one:

> Cultures that subscribe to a universalistic orientation (e.g. European Americans) tend to follow a set [of] . . . rules that are uniformly applied to all people . . . they value literal adherence to contracts, and favour rational decision making. In contrast, cultures that subscribe to a particularistic orientation (e.g. Hispanic, African Americans, Asian Americans) place emphasis on relationships, and are willing to 'bend the rules' to accommodate particular circumstances and individual needs. [Stone & Stone-Romero, p. 86]

European Americans (i.e. Whites) treat *all others* equally, they stick to their word, and make rational decisions. In contrast, those of *all* other cultures are not only nepotistic, they bend the rules as and when it suits them. Well, let us call a spade a spade—they cheat.

It is evident by now that, despite the pretence of many, there are in fact only two cultures in this taxonomy, the Anglo-American and the rest. The two cultures also have different attitudes to time.

> Some cultures (e.g. Anglo-Americans) view time as linear and place a great deal of emphasis on efficiency and punctuality . . . However, other US subcultures (e.g. Hispanic Americans, African Americans, Native Americans) have relatively flexible views about time, and use fairly large intervals in judging lateness. [*ibid.*, p. 86]

They also tell us that "Research shows that Anglo-Americans often place a great deal of emphasis on planning for the future and being able to delay gratification". Perhaps the reader, like me, is bemused as to which alternative universe Stone and Stone-Romero's Anglo-American is residing in. Is the withdrawal of the USA from the Kyoto agreement an example of delaying gratification? But having said this, just a few sentences later they once again blithely say its opposite: "Anglo-Americans . . . expect to produce short term payoffs quickly. As a result, researchers have argued that Anglo-Americans have a short-term, 'bottom-line' perspective" (*ibid.*, p. 87).

How is it that so many blatant contradictions appear to be invisible, not only to these two professors (no less) of psychology, but also invisible to the other academics who took part in the peer review process that the paper presumably went through?

Notice also the not-so-subtle slip in the extract above: Anglo-American is a "culture" and the rest are "subcultures". The slip reveals something about the status that each of these cultures has in the writers' minds.

The final differentiator of cultures is that of *communication styles*, which gets broken down into four subordinate elements: *goal, directness, emotionality, and believability*. Beginning with *goals*, Stone and Stone-Romero assert that, for non-Anglo cultures, "maintaining harmony and saving face are important *goals of communication*. In contrast, members of individualistic cultures (e.g. Anglo-Americans) are more concerned with communicating the truth [*sic*] and with basing their arguments on facts and rational arguments" (*ibid.*, p. 88).

In other words, Anglos are tough enough to speak the truth based on the ability to look reality in the eye and think clearly, while the non-Anglos lie to save face and keep the peace, and (by implication) they rely on fantasy and wishful thinking rather than fact and rationality.

As for *directness*, we are told that people in collective cultures

> beat around the bush rather than getting directly to the point . . . people in individualistic cultures (e.g. Anglo-Americans) . . . are direct in their communication . . . [Further], members of collective cultures often consider individuals from individualistic cultures to be rude . . . because of their direct communication and disregard of social courtesy (e.g. saying 'good morning'). [*ibid.*]

The image here is one of Anglos "staying focused on task" and not concerning themselves overly with social niceties. It would appear that Anglos would not think it rude if a colleague did not greet them with a good morning because there are more important things to think about.

As for *emotionality*, they say that "People from individualistic cultures (e.g. Anglo-Americans) often emphasize calm, unemotional forms of communication, even when there are disagreements about issues" (*ibid.*, p. 89).

It would seem that in this alternative universe, an *Anglo* bullying boss who shouts and threatens his or her subordinates is unknown.

And finally, with regard to *believability*, the non-Anglos give credibility to those who have high status in their cultures—elders and family members. Meanwhile, "[m]embers of individualistic cultures value achievement and accomplishment . . . they are more likely to impute creditability to sources that are expert, intelligent, and have a record of high achievement" (*ibid.*).

Let me sum up the "findings" about "diverse" cultures as presented in this paper.

First, there is only ever one individualistic culture, the Anglo-American. *All* the other cultures are collective.

The portrait provided of the Anglo-Americans is that of free-standing individuals, who think for themselves and are not dependent on supervisors. They have a preference for consultation or participation in decision making (although this seems suspiciously like something collective), and are not affected by hierarchy and status differentials. They treat other people on their own merits as people. Well, that is not quite so. People are valued on the basis of what they achieve. The

Anglo also stays true to his beliefs and procedures—everyone is treated the same. They think rationally about any decisions that are to be made. They tend to be punctual. They also have the capacity to think about the future and so they are able to delay gratification. However, they are also short-sighted and go for short-term, bottom-line gains. The Anglo is direct in his communication; he calmly speaks the truth, a truth which has its basis in facts and rational argument. He is, therefore, brave, no matter what the consequences. He is listened to by others because of his established track record and the fact that he is intelligent and an expert.

Meanwhile, the non-Anglos tend to accept their lot in life. They are heavily reliant on their superiors and like to be told what to do because they have trouble thinking for themselves. They do not gain status by earning it through achieving things; rather, their status is inherited via their social roles. They tend to bend the rules for their own kind: that is, they are nepotistic and they cheat. They are also inevitably late for meetings. They are locked into the past or the present—they cannot look too far into the future. And when they speak, although they beat around the bush, they are courteous and say good morning before they do so. But, alas, they are highly emotional, unless they happen to be Asian or Native, in which case they are not. And, finally, they respect, follow, and listen to people not because of their track record, or because of their knowledge base, or because of their intelligence, but simply because of their attributes, such as being an elder or/and a family member.

Consider, if it is indeed the case that the "the Anglo" is as described: naturally fair, task focused and treating all people on the basis of their merits, then there would be no need for the equal opportunities or diversity movements. If they were indeed so good and true, then there would be no need for legislation *forcing* them to change their attitudes and behaviours. One wonders, where is the rapacious capitalist in these "research" findings?

And I have to admit that I would not want a person such as the non-Anglo is described to be to come into my employment. To employ such a person would be a disaster for any organization: someone who cannot be trusted, who cheats when it suits them, is inevitably late, cannot be relied on, is nepotistic, and cannot think for themselves. Surely what this paper has established are good reasons why organizations should avoid employing the "ethnics".

What we are seeing here in Stone and Stone-Romero's vision of things is the modern version of nineteenth-century scientific racism. The philosophy it puts forward is presumably not unusual, because if it were, then there might have been an outcry.

It is terrifying to me to find this kind of racism masquerading as cross-cultural scientific research in a book that is supposed to contain serious academic studies. But more terrifying than the presence of this paper is the fact that in this volume there is not a single voice raised in argument against it, presumably because to disagree or take an antagonistic stance is anathema. Perhaps it is the case that those who do disagree with Stone and Stone-Romero feel duty bound to remain silent on the matter, because in so doing they would be being respectful of the other point of view: strengths and only strengths, never any weaknesses.

Making allowances

Let me conclude this chapter by supposing that the extraordinary taxonomy supplied by Stone and Stone-Romero is true. If this were the case, then what is the "culturally competent" Anglo manager to do? Indeed, what can he or she do when faced with such an employee—someone who cannot be trusted, is stupid, lies, is tardy and nepotistic. Diversity ideology would ask the manger to *celebrate* these differences. But if they were unable to manage the feat of celebration (and who could blame them?), then, at the very least, they would have to be tolerant and respectful of these differences.

There are several things here. First, one of the charges made by Stone and Stone-Romero against non-Anglo cultures is that they are ascriptive cultures, in that they tend to ascribe respect to others on the basis of who they are rather than what they do and achieve. But this is exactly what is now being asked of the Anglo manager, to respect the employee on the basis of what they are (of a different culture) rather than on the basis of how well they do (not very). I suspect that here we have a classic example of what psychoanalysis calls projection, wherein one denies some attribute of oneself by splitting it off from one's consciousness and projecting it to another.

It seems to me that Stone and Stone-Romero's vision of things leaves open just one option: fundamentally, it is an injunction to the manager to make allowances for "them" and their lackadaisical ways. It says that the Anglo will have to lower their standards in order to accommodate and include the non-Anglo in the work place. They are just not up to it, but the Anglo will have to learn (with the help of training) to accept, respect, and tolerate their inadequacies.

And what if there were indeed such an employee who was being tolerated by the manager? What would be the impact on the rest of the workforce? One of the things it is bound to do is feed the racist way of thinking: here is more evidence that they (in general) are not much good. In other words, the problem of racism is exacerbated by the whole process. It seems to me that here we are witnessing the diversity movement helping racism shape-shift to take on the guise of tolerance, from whence it can continue its work, but now helped by the well meaning. (Recall the analogy with parasites from the early paragraphs of the book.) This is tolerance made perverse, and is of no use to anyone but the racist.

CHAPTER EIGHT

Perverting the liberal ideal: fear and control in the Panopticon

Conversations about equality, diversity, and so on, do not exist in a vacuum. They are bound to draw their forms and rationales from the norms and paradigms of the milieus that they take place in, and so they reflect and reproduce them to some degree. The driving force for the equalities agenda comes from many directions. Crudely, there are three sorts of milieus (not mutually exclusive): perhaps the first impulse comes from "the street" (protestors and activists), then there is the academy (the intellectuals), and finally there are the bureaucrats. Informed by the first two, it is the last of these that produce legislation, draw up protocols and procedures, and give formal advice on how one is best to fulfil the legal requirements. The ruling paradigms of the bureaucrat are the ones that prevail in the modern organization, that of the marketplace.

The worker as castrated Kantian being

The paradigm of the marketplace has become the ruling organizing principle for most, if not all, kinds of institutions. Whatever the project, be it the education of young children, the nation's health care, utilities, and railways, it has become the norm for every kind of institution—public, charitable, voluntary, and private—to produce a "business model" about how they intend to set about their "business". A language of efficiencies, profit and loss, proliferates; so does the idea that all institutions should be "independent" and pay their way. Within this paradigm, the model of the human being that finds favour in mainstream organizational literature is also individualistic and mechanistic; in this view humans can be, and should be, controlled and directed by procedure and protocol. This is compounded by the belief that human beings are selfish and cannot be trusted. This situation has come about in the following way.

It is no surprise that people are reluctant and resentful when others use them for their own ends, when others exploit their efforts and profit from them. In this sort of situation, workers drag their feet and work as slowly as possible. When this happens in the colonial situation, the colonizer calls the colonized constitutionally lazy, but Frantz Fanon saw this laziness for what it was—a form of protest. The same is true of the factory and other institutions generally. As the guru of "scientific management" theory, Frederick Taylor, once said, "hardly a competent workman can be found in a large establishment . . . who does not devote a considerable part of his time to studying just how slowly he can work and still convince his employer that he is going at a good pace" (Taylor, 1911, p. 30). Henry Ford knew about this and tried to pre-empt the resentment by paying his assembly line workers a wage significantly higher than the going rate. Despite the fiscal compensation, the alienated worker had little motivation for giving his all to the task at hand.

Layers of management became necessary to systematically watch over the workforce, to monitor and scrutinize their performance with regard to efficiency. The scrutiny of the worker is the beginnings of a version of Jeremy Bentham's Panopticon in the workplace—a situation in which everyone is somehow watched and monitored to ensure that they are complying with whatever is being required of them. The virtue of the Panopticon is that it is supremely efficient; it works in such a way that the watched never know quite when and if they are being watched, *and so they come to watch themselves*.

This, then, is how a culture of scrutiny and surveillance arose in the modern workplace. *At its heart is the idea that the worker is not to be trusted.* The belief is that at every opportunity he will shirk, steal, or bungle something. So, to control and motivate him, he is given targets, which, if he achieves, gain him praise (employee of the month) and perhaps monetary reward, but if he fails, he faces some retribution. We can see then how the three elements, targets, incentives, and scrutiny, interlock.

This way of thinking came to be increasingly formalized in the latter part of the twentieth century. In the 1950s, James Lincoln (CEO of the Lincoln Electric Company), author of the influential work *Incentive Management* (1951), formed the "Council for Profit Sharing Industries". More instructive than the conclusions that Lincoln and the Council arrive at is how they arrive there and where they begin their analysis. As Fromm (2010) points out, Lincoln's initial premises have the appearance of a humanistic critique of capitalism: "The industrialist concentrates on machines and neglects man ... the goal of profit [for the stockholders] will engender no enthusiasm in the workers". Lincoln recognizes that the worker is alienated and resentful and wants to remedy this. But then, Fromm points out that, unlike the humanists, Lincoln also believes that "Selfishness is the driving force that makes the human race what it is ... it is the force that we must depend on, and *properly guide*, if the human race is to progress". The solution for the Council and Lincoln was that of carrot and stick—to provide the worker with incentives. Through bonuses and the like, the worker comes to be more motivated to work harder. But then, unlike Ford, Lincoln also recognizes that money is not enough to motivate people and that the most potent of incentives "is *recognition* of our abilities by our contemporaries and ourselves". This *recognition* occurs through the worker being *rated* by his peers and bosses, "by all those who have accurate knowledge of some phase of his work. On this rating he is rewarded or penalized" (Lincoln, 1951, quoted in Fromm 2010, pp. 233–239).

Although Lincoln and the Council comprehend the importance of "recognition" with regard to the psychological well-being of individuals, they pervert this psychological need, instrumentalize it, and put it in the service of manipulation. They use the "rating system" to trigger feelings of jealousy and rivalry between the workers, and so amplify the need for "recognition"; these processes are used to manipulate the worker into acting in ways that will benefit the shareholder.

This is what they really mean when they say that they wish to "properly guide" individuals.

This kind of carrot and stick management culture will be familiar to readers, as it is alive and well in the modern organization (including in the public services, such as health, housing, transport, and education) where it has become an unquestioned and unquestionable norm. Not withstanding the rhetoric of autonomy and creativity found in "organizational development" programmes, workers in the contemporary workplace (be they blue or white collared), are increasingly obliged to work according to previously laid down protocols and procedures. But then, despite individuals being put through "trainings" to ensure that they have learnt the party line, they repeatedly fail to do as they are told; they fail to follow procedure as instructed, make mistakes, forget, and, often enough, deliberately do something different from the official line. Why? The cognitivist answer is because either they did so wilfully, or did not understand, or the procdures were ambiguous. This then provokes a new layer of procedure to come into being, the purpose of which is to ensure that the original procedures are carried out as intended, and on and on. Rules are written about the use of rules, and then more rules are written about those. On top of this comes a monitoring process to ensure that the workers have followed instructions. This is a version of what Lincoln calls "rating" and finds its current form in institutions in the idea of "annual appraisals". The rhetoric behind these appraisals is always one of taking the time to reflect on the needs of the worker, and to enable and foster the individual. But, as many will testify, often it comes to be used as a means of policing the workforce. There is a contradiction in the middle of all this. On the one hand, humans are viewed as cognitive thinking machines, but on the other hand, they are not trusted to be in charge of themselves and their thinking processes. This kind of individual is a sort of castrated Kantian being, rational but devoid of autonomy, and, given the individual's propensity to do other than required, expected, or instructed, it would seem not very rational at that. This is the world view that the bureaucrats who write equal opportunity protocols are embedded in and formed by. In many institutions, these bureaucrats go by the name of the Human Resources Department.

Equal opportunities as control mechanism

So far in this chapter, I have been arguing that institutions use their policies, procedures, and protocols to control and police the workforce. What I am now going to argue, more controversially, is that equal opportunity protocols have been similarly appropriated; they, too, are put in the service of controlling the workforce through the evocation of fear. I suggest that, in many circumstances, the emancipatory ideal of the equal opportunity movements have been perverted and put in the service of the Panopticon.

How far-fetched is this? After all, vision statements and equal opportunity statements of institutions are full of ethical claims that they are for fairness, that they desire to foster the needs of their workforce, that they are for inclusivity, against unfair discrimination, for equality of opportunity, and so on. But so, too, are the formal principles of the aforementioned Lincoln's Council, whose unashamed primary agenda is to increase profit; their principles are also full of similar sentiments in which they aspire to "fairness", "development", and "dignity". They say,

> A *free* company must be based on *freedom of opportunity* for each to achieve his *maximum personal development* ... The Council maintains that stabilized prosperity can be maintained only under a *fair relationship* between prices, pay and profits. It believes that if our free economy is to survive, *management must accept the responsibility of trusteeship* to see that this relationship prevails ... the Council holds of paramount importance *the true spirit of partnership* which sound profit sharing engenders ... No policy ... in the industrial relation field can succeed unless it is well adapted and unless it has behind it *the sincere desire of management to be fair* and the faith of management in *the importance, dignity and response of the human individual.* [quoted in Fromm, 2010, p. 238, my italics]

It is striking to me that the language and aspirations found in Lincoln's capitalist Council for Profit Sharing Industries (the purpose of which is to make money) are hardly any different from the sentiments being expressed in equal opportunity statements of modern organizations (the purpose of which is to enhance the well being of the employees). I suggest that, in many institutions, the rosy cosy words of equal opportunity statements are often similarly hollow, their function being that of being seen to do good rather than of doing actual good. The situation is aided and abetted by the positivist belief system that pervades the thinking in modern institutions in general. In this world, things can be controlled; things are right or wrong, black or white. After all, the intention of bureaucratic procedures is precisely to remove the "grey". Procedures are used to drive people towards the correct decision. And they are required to do this by following the cold calculus of "if-then" statements. If X, then do M. There is very little or no room for manoeuvre, little or no room for discretion. In this world, things are very clear-cut. If X and you do N, then you are wrong and penalized.

I think that it is by subscribing to and perpetuating the myth that the *ideals* of the equality movements are readily achievable realities (achievable through the application of will and the technology of following) that these emancipatory movements have created hostages to fortune. If one proceeds on the basis that perfection is possible, and that people, with the help of training, are able to achieve perfection, then we have fashioned a ready-made instrument for control by engendering fear, because one is bound to fail and fall short of perfection. In this case, it is truly as Voltaire once said: the best is the enemy of the good.[1] Let me explain what I mean.

The ideals of the equality movements are exactly that, Platonic ideals; they can never be realized in actuality. For example, we saw earlier that "inclusivity" is not an absolute, and so, if we try to achieve full inclusivity, we are bound to fail because even as we include one thing we necessarily exclude another. We are bound to fail, too, if we try to practise non-discrimination, because without discrimination we would be unable to think. And even when we try to practise anti unfair discrimination, here, too, despite our best efforts, we are likely to perpetuate our biases in ways that we do not even recognize. We also saw that it was impossible to take on a stance of universal respect for all and sundry, because in respecting one we would inevitably find ourselves disrespecting another. The same is also true of absolute tolerance; one is bound to fail.

In this black and white world, faced with these Platonic ideals, one has failed before one has even begun in a version of original sin. Because of this, one is inherently and eternally vulnerable to some charge or other. The inspirational rhetoric becomes a draconian monster, to be utilized as a weapon when needed, to strike fear into the heart of the liberal, to make them more compliant. Although the rhetoric has the appearance of being in the service of furthering the needs of the dispossessed, it does no such thing and actually does the opposite. The rosy glow given off by the rhetoric serves two insidious functions: for one thing, it comes to mask the processes of marginalization that continue to flourish and do their toxic work, and second, the impossibility of measuring up to the rhetoric becomes the means of control. In this black and white world, it is always possible to accuse *all and anyone* of falling short of these ideals, of making mistakes.

The thing is, not only are the individual employees caught by this false reality, so are the institutions that they work in. Organizational rhetoric emanating from HR departments often claims that not only are the goals readily achievable, but that they have already been achieved. But, as the cases of Tula Miah and GAP (among many others) show, there is considerable disparity between the inspirational rhetoric being spouted by organizations and actual lived practice. The terrible thing is that even as the actual situation becomes harder and harder to speak about in any meaningful way, inequality and inequity continue to flourish in the midst of the confusions. We find ourselves immured in the Manichaean land of "either you are with the angels or with the devil" that we met in the first chapter. The situation is further muddied by right-wing bigots, who have a field day denying that there is any inequality in the first place, and point the finger of blame at the equality discourses themselves.

Errors and misdemeanours

So, what is one to do when faced with this kind of situation? What is one to do when faced with the fact that one cannot live up to the Platonic ideals of unconditional respect and acceptance, or of fully eradicating unfair discriminatory practices, or of the fact that we cannot help but divide and discriminate between them, and so forth? One impulse, surely, is not to bother doing anything, because one is bound to fail, and perhaps even make things worse.[2] If we are bound to fail, why even bother to make laws, draw up procedures, and set up protocols?

The difficulties are compounded by a norm established in organizational life, which is twofold: the avoidance of responsibility going hand-in-hand with a blame culture. For example, the unashamed advice provided on my car insurance certificate is that if involved in an accident, I should under no circumstances admit to any liability whatsoever (i.e., even if I were the cause of it). The first port of call, as in the Lawrence, Miah, and Rodney King cases, is invariably denial. And then every opportunity is taken to shift the blame for errors and misdemeanours on to someone or something else. What is avoided is real conversation, real engagement about causes and responsibilities. There is a fear of honest conversation because of the punitive culture of intolerance towards anything that deviates from the letter of the law. There is little place for reason and reasoning. Hawkeye's verdict is final and it stops all conversation, and, indeed, that is its virtue. But now the analogy with Hawkeye begins to be less useful: all the game of tennis needs to work out is whether the ball was in or out; it does not need to figure out whether the player intended to put the ball in or out; the *intention* of the player is always the same—to get the ball in and win the point. But in other areas of human life, not only what happens but also intention is important; there are critical ethical differences between misdemeanours and errors, between those who deliberately do wrong and those who do wrong through error or failing. To this *a*-ethical, either/or way of thinking, wrong is wrong whatever the cause or intention. There are untold examples of institutional procedures chewing up employees who, having made innocent errors, have been treated as though they had perpetrated a wilful misdemeanour. One of many examples that I have come across in my work with organizations is that of a senior health worker being suspended and sacked because of purchasing a computer without following procedure correctly. Although the computer resided in plain view in his office at work, he was treated as though he had stolen from the institution, and was sacked immediately. His life, professional and personal, was shattered.

The resultant culture of fear is a norm in many institutions, and it is no surprise that anti unfair, discriminatory, and equal opportunity protocols come to be appropriated and used in exactly this kind of way. Employees become extremely vigilant about toeing the official line. They become cautious; they become afraid of exercising their faculties of judgement; they are made afraid.

So it is that procedures and protocols that were primarily created to deal with misdemeanours come also to be applied indiscriminately to those who are incompetent, to those who are irresponsible, as well as to those who make errors of judgement. To the lazy, indifferent, mechanistic, bureaucratic way of thinking, wrong is wrong. But readers will also know of many instances in which one does not even have to have done wrong in order to be caught up in complaint and grievance procedures. I know of several instances in the NHS in which a subordinate has maliciously accused the manager, or a patient accused a psychiatrist, of some misdemeanour, and the accusation immediately (and mindlessly) triggers a set of draconian procedures. Often it is the case that the accused is immediately suspended, and then, quite unbelievably, there is an embargo on any communication between the accused and their colleagues, even outside the workplace. The situation is often Kafkaesque, with the accused not even allowed to know the nature of the charges against them. The investigation, as such, is mostly not about ethical questions, but about whether or not procedure has been followed. The accused, profoundly isolated from colleagues and friends at work, inevitably become emotionally distressed and paranoid. Often, by the time the "investigation" has been completed (six months to over a year), even if found innocent the person is unable to return to work, because in the meantime they have suffered a mental and emotional breakdown.

The reason why institutions act in these sorts of draconian ways is that they, too, are afraid of being punished and penalized. When charged, they protect themselves in one of two ways. The first is the familiar strategy of denial. Bureaucracies are well versed in the satanic arts of spin. They are practised at gamesmanship, at covering up wrong-doing with obfuscation, and to this end they are expert at using official criteria and regulation as justification when accused of wrongdoing. Recall the various instances we have already come across: the Home Office's defence of its employees, the police, Tracy McNeill, and so on.

But if denial does not work, then institutions protect themselves by sacrificing some of their own—the innocent being sacrificed along with the guilty. The ferocity with which institutions turn on their employees is driven by the wish to appease and convince the authorities that the institution has no case to answer. The primary aim is to ensure that there is no legal comeback.

The fact that procedures and protocols are perverted through different Hawkeye scenarios does not necessarily lead to the conclusion that we should abandon making procedures. After all, procedures and legislation were called into existence in the first place *because there was a need for them,* a need that continues. Without them, the situation is likely to be a lot worse.

The problems that I have been highlighting are as follows: first, that ethical protocols regarding fairness and justice come to be used as instruments of fear and control. Second, that protocols tend to be activated in a mindless fashion, making no distinctions between errors and misdemeanours. And finally, I think the aims of the equality movements could do with being a bit more modest and not feed the myth that equality heaven is readily achievable, because these myths and absolutist claims lend themselves to being used in the service of intimidation and control. All these things work towards generating thought and action paralyses.

What I have also been arguing in this chapter is that many of the difficulties within the equality discourses are there because they are a reflection of the difficulties that already exist at a fundamental level in contemporary ways of thinking about human beings in organizational life. At the heart of these difficulties is the capitalist belief that the human being is a commodity, and the cognitivist belief that the human being is a machine that can be trained to think, feel, and act in specific ways for certain ends.

There is no clear, straightforward solution to this situation. When things go awry, instead of resorting to the mindless operation of punitive procedure, something akin to the activity of ethical engagement is called for. I say more about this a little later, but for now let me just say that this engagement is likely to be conflictual and unequal because of power relations and the offices held by the protagonists. And even though the engagement might be taking place between individuals, it is not individualistic. The situation is ever-complex, and what we have to resist is the simplifications being foisted on us by the celebrators of diversity.

Notes

1. Voltaire's poem "La Bégueule". "Dans ses écrits, un sàge Italien / Dit que le mieux est l'ennemi du bien" (In his writings, a wise Italian says that the best is the enemy of the good).

2. I am reminded of the advice emanating from some quarters (Institution of Occupational Safety and Health, as well as some predatory lawyers) during the snowfalls of the winter of 2010. People and organizations were being advised *not to clear* a path through the snow because then, if anyone slipped, they would be liable to litigation because it could be claimed that the job had not been done properly. On the other hand, government advice made it clear that this was not the case, but this sensible advice did not receive too many column inches in the newspapers (www.direct.gov.uk/en/Nl1/Newsroom/DG_191868).

CHAPTER NINE

The difference that dare not speak its name: the lexicon police

Training the mind

How is one to reside in the space between the extremes of annihilating the other and annihilating the self? One answer given by equality discourses is, by being very, very careful with the language one uses. And the way this is to be achieved is through training. Training is big business. Organizations spend a lot of money purchasing trainers and trainings of all kinds: health and safety, customer relations, equality, and so on. In part, organizations do this in order to fulfil the legal obligations placed on them by the legislature. To this end, it has become compulsory for employees to go through a "training" in equality and diversity. Mostly, these trainings are computer based (because it is cheaper). On completion, employees are deemed to have mastered the skills of empathy and sensitivity to others. The e-based equal opportunity trainings I have had sight of are, in my view, moronic, patronizing, and tokenistic, with their primary purpose being to demonstrate that the institution has fulfilled its legal obligations. In other words, they are in the service of being seen to do good, rather than actually doing good.

One e-based equality training (in the South West of England) begins with a letter written by Lord Herman Ouseley, Chair of the Commission for Racial Equality in which he sets out the rationale behind the training:

> Inequalities, unfair treatment and exclusion thrive in situations where we lack knowledge about cultural differences and the confidence necessary to relate to people from other backgrounds. If we know so little about other people who are unlike ourselves, we may be more naturally inclined to remain close only to those people who we feel most comfortable with and avoid those about whom we are ignorant. [Devon Partnership Trust, Equality and Diversity Training]

This is the multi-culturalist ethos in its purest form, an ethos that I have been critiquing variously over the previous pages. Although we are told the intention of the training is "not to instil political correctness or tell people what to think", at the conclusion of the training one is given a multiple choice test, which, if one does not pass, then one has to repeat until one does reproduce the correct answers. The employee is reassured: "If you don't pass on the first attempt—don't worry—you can have another go". The test consists of questions such as:

> What is diversity? Is it
>
> (a) Promoting equal opportunities
>
> (b) Recognising that we are all different
>
> (c) Accepting people of different races
>
> (d) Valuing difference, rather than being afraid of it

If you do not produce the correct answer (d) then you will have to repeat the test until you do. A colleague tells me that a member of the team she works for keeps failing this test because, in her view, Gypsies and Travellers are not a distinct ethnicity. Whether one agrees with her or not is not the point. She will only pass this test when her thinking conforms to the party line. It is important to note that she chooses a different answer from the decreed correct one not because of stupidity, or because she does not understand the arguments, but because she disagrees with their conclusions. What has happened to the ideal of including and respecting all differences? If and when she does eventually capitulate and tick the "correct" answer, it will be out of exhaustion and compliance. There is no possibility that this kind of "training" can lead to real changes in attitude or practice.

Diversity management as an exercise in etiquette

When the diversity experts are not telling organizations how to make more money out of the marginalized, they are giving them lessons in sensitivity and etiquette and how not to cause offence to others. For example, the e-training just referred to provides this (infantile) advice on how to greet others:

> It is advisable to:
>
> Ask for people's first names
>
> Check with a person how he or she wishes to be addressed
>
> Check that a person's full name has been given
>
> Ask which name is the personal name; which name (if any) is the family name; and which name is used as a surname
>
> Check how a person's name should be pronounced; and if appropriate, how it should be spelt. [Devon Partnership Trust, Equality and Diversity Training]

Clements and Spinks say in their volume, *The Equal Opportunities Handbook*, "by the time you have considered the issues in this book you will have developed greater sensitivity to what might be offensive" (Clements & Spinks, 2006, p. 27). Their aim is to enable the reader to "behave towards everyone . . . with fairness, courtesy, and sensitivity" (*ibid.*, p. 2). They inform the reader that they need not learn about the contents of specific cultures, because they will be taught a set of six "skills" that they will be able to "transfer" into each new situation. These "skills" are those of empathy, understanding, raised awareness, sensitivity, thinking about the consequences, and a desire to be fair. But in what sense can these be considered to be "skills"? The "desire to be fair" is not a skill, but a moral attitude. In my view, the diversity experts are obliged to use this kind of language in order to give the impression that they have a "real" product to deliver, *a thing*, an outcome that can be transferred and "owned".

I am not against fairness or courtesy. However, they completely miss the point with regard to processes of exclusion and marginalization. The question we have to ask is how is it that most *kinds* of people get stripped out of the hierarchy the further "up" one goes, so that eventually, at the highest levels, there remains primarily just one *kind* of person and one kind of colour? Let us accept Clements and Spinks's thesis, that the privileged are prejudiced with regard to some of their employees, and that this prejudice is due to ignorance. The authors' invitation is for people to turn *inwards*: "we would encourage you, if you feel up to it, to examine your beliefs, attitudes and values regarding others who are different from you . . . [to] dig underneath layers of defence and justification built up over the years" (*ibid.*, pp. 14–15). Let us now suppose that a greater sensitivity to others is achieved. The authors' belief is that now the more powerful will be less prejudiced and will be able to recognize the virtues of others. Thus, they will be more likely to encourage and promote "others" into more responsible positions. This is, of course, a possibility. However, the statistical evidence is against it. Despite the "personal growth" model having been used in organizations for some decades, there has been little real change—*as all the diversity experts agree*. It seems to me that while the more powerful are now more sensitive and courteous to their employees, the status quo remains the same. For example, the organization might put aside a room for the purposes of prayer by devout Muslims in their employ. In such a case, courtesy and sensitivity would have been used in the service of assuaging the resentments of the marginalized, in order to preserve and perpetuate the traditional structure of power relations. In my view, this kind of cultural courtesy is no more than patronage by another name. If institutions were really serious about attending to the needs of their marginalized employees, one of the things that would make the biggest impact would be the provision of a crèche. And this, it has to be pointed out, has nothing exotic or mysterious about it.

The tacit expectation in the literature tends to be that the leaders in the brave new world will continue to be male and White, but with one difference: the multi-culturally "competent" leader will manage to command and control his charges with the "skills" of empathy, courtesy, and dignity, and so get more co-operation out of them. The result? More bang for less buck, as the saying goes.

The first slip: from unfair discrimination to discrimination

A key component of these trainings is a concern with language and its usages, but the way it proceeds ends up creating more problems than it solves. And it is exactly these problems that are opportunistically seized by those who would like to undermine the entire equalities agenda. Given the concern about language, it is particularly unfortunate that Equality-speak continues to use, support, and perpetuate fictions like "race". But most unfortunate is a fundamental slippage which eventually leads the entire enterprise into a conceptual quagmire. This slippage has to do with the term that is at the heart of the endeavour: *discrimination* itself.

In a key text employed in the training of social workers in the UK, Thompson defines "discrimination" to be: "unfair or unequal treatment of individuals or groups" (Thompson, 2001, p. 33). The definition has collapsed the distinction between "discrimination" and "unfair discrimination".

So, although the project is really about "*unfair* discrimination", it has become foreshortened to that of "discrimination", with the result that the discourse comes to speak of "anti-discrimination", rather than "anti unfair discrimination". The issue is not just of relevance to pedants, because it is yet another nail in the coffin of the thinking process itself. As we have previously noted, it we were to stop the discriminatory processes, then this would entail the cessation of thought itself. Of course, this not at all what Thompson intends, but this conceptual cul-de-sac is where the definition leads.

It is also the case that what Thompson is actually inviting us to do is *to discriminate* between that which is fair and that which is not, and to choose the former over the latter. In other words, antidiscriminatory practice is itself discriminatory—as indeed it should be. The project is, after all, a moral one in that it says (as it should) that some ways of being are preferable to others. All decisions that result in the distinguishing of right from wrong are necessarily acts of discrimination.

Unthinking categories and differentials

The injunctions about language use emanating from Thompson and others of like mind are not so much about not-thinking, but unthinking, in the following way. We are advised to avoid using certain categories, for example, "the elderly". "Terms such as 'the elderly', 'the old', 'EMI' are commonly used but are, none the less, very dehumanising—they depersonalize the people to whom they refer" (Thompson, 1995, pp. 11–12). We are told that "diversity and difference are the roots of discrimination in the sense that it is through the identification of differences that discrimination . . . take place" (Thompson 2001, p. 35). Let me spell out what is being suggested, as it is so astonishing:

- because some categories are mobilized in the processes of discrimination, then we ought not to use those categories;
- if we ceased using the category, then the differentiation would disappear and so there would be no "object" for the discriminatory processes.

On this basis we are told, "We should avoid grouping people together according to age . . . abandon the 'us–them" mentality" (Thompson, 2001, p 102). I agree that the elderly are often treated in shabby ways and pushed to the margins of mainstream society; they are the "them" to the mainstream "us". This is true, but to then suggest that, therefore, one should not utilize the categories "the elderly" or "old people" is, to my mind, nonsensical.

It seems obvious to me that the categorization "old" *is* useful. They (and I know that all too soon I, too, will become a part of this "they") *do* have very particular needs and requirements, which ought to be catered for. To treat the elderly and infirm like everyone else would surely be an exercise in negligence. Society ought to be discriminating in favour of them receiving more resources of a certain kind than the rest of us. I want to stress that I do not dispute the view that "the elderly" are in many ways treated as second-class citizens. But not using the categorization is not likely to change that particular situation.

Surely, rather than stopping utilizing the category "the old", what is required is for the activities of marginalization and denigration of "the old" to be addressed. In fact, Thompson does say on many occasions that, ultimately, this is the purpose of antidiscriminatory practice, to challenge and confront the instruments of marginalization. But how are we to fight for the old without mentioning their name? Thompson does not guide us on this matter. What is even worse is that we are being led into a 1984 land. If we did not name the elderly, then it would merely serve the purpose of rendering invisible the injustices meted out to them.

This kind of suggestion regarding language use, although mistaken, is not, however, completely facile. It has its roots in a serious point about the nature of language.

The nature of language

The "common sense" understanding of language is that language is passive, in that it is merely the means of capturing and representing an unproblematic objective reality. To this way of thinking, things in the world are already differentiated, and language merely gives these things names and describes the relations between them.

This positivist view has been convincingly challenged and critiqued from many perspectives. The alternative proposal is that language is not a passive means of apprehending a pre-existing reality, but that it is critically active in informing and forming the way that reality comes to be apprehended.

To this way of thinking, one's experience of the world is always mediated through language, and the *kind* of language one is embedded in informs the *kind* of world one comes to actually see and experience. Sedimented in language are the taken for granted assumptions, norms, and values that are outside the scope of consciousness, which lead to the world and self being perceived and experienced in particular ways. What we are speaking of here is ideology. The point about ideology is that it is deeply *unconscious*; it is a part of the deep structure of experience itself. So, language does not just represent pre-existing differentiations, *it actually generates these differentiations even as it names them*. But even more, because languages are value laden and words are cathected with emotions, one ends up unknowingly *discriminating* between the differentiated. We experience and react, often automatically, for reasons that we do not really know but rationalize and justify none the less. The key point is that language structures experience.

This far, I am in agreement, but this far only. It is with the next steps that problems arise. Because language and one's experience of the world are linked in this way, the following assumption is made: changes in the way language is used will not only modify the way an individual experiences the world, but also lead to shifting the iniquities in the structure of power relations to some degree. Thompson says that it works towards "undermining the continuance of a discriminatory discourse" (2001, p. 33).

This line of reasoning is the one that is generally held within the mainstream of the equality movements. For example, it is precisely reproduced in a recent discussion paper, *The Language of Equality* (Sardar, 2008), published by the newly formed Equality and Human Rights Commission in the UK.

To presume that if one tweaks the words one uses, then it will lead to a modification in either the structure of power relations or one's experience of reality is to really miss the point about the nature of language and experience. The taken-for-granted is not so easily grasped and addressed; it is much more resilient and ephemeral than that. One reason that the strategy does not really work is that it remains on the surface of things, with what is visible—the word. This way of proceeding fits in well with those who believe in the power of positive thinking; a few self-promoting positive slogans said every morning into a mirror is all it takes to make fundamental change. This way also fits well with early naïve Marxism that conceived of ideology as something *consciously* used by the ruling classes to confound and oppress the working classes. And if it is conscious, then to consciously set about changing words in order to change the experience would make sense. Marxism itself has moved on from that initial simplistic understanding. Cognitive behavioural therapy has not. More convincing are the ideas of Althusser and others, according to whom ideology is unconscious for the rulers as much as the ruled, and, being unconscious, it cannot be directly accessed and worked with. The "problem" is much more problematic and not so easily shifted. To begin the battle for equality with changing the words one uses in everyday life is to get things the wrong way round.

Performance vs. *practice*

To change the words one uses is to shift social "performance" rather than actual "practice". The careful use of language and the following of procedures can tick all the right boxes, but does not necessarily lead to social change. And worse: on occasions, this way of proceeding serves to create the illusion of change while allowing the old ways to flourish and continue as before.

For example, the fascist and racist British National Party (BNP) has become increasingly vigilant about what its members say in public forums. Following Eddy O'Sullivan, a parliamentary candidate for the BNP, writing things such as "Wogs go home" on his Facebook page, "the BNP's national organizer, Eddy Butler, [urged] members to be careful about what they wrote on chat forums" (Williams & Mullholland, 2009). The BNP are learning to *perform* PC-speak, but not because they are interested in putting into *practice* any of its values. The reason they are being careful about what they say is in order not to fall foul of the law found in the *Race Relations Acts*, even while they set about promoting their racist agenda.

Sardar is pleased that "PC language . . . has become the official speak of many administrative agencies" but is disappointed that as "yet it has failed to make a breakthrough into common usage" (Sardar, 2008, p. 20). But has the fact that it has become official speak of some administrative agencies actually improved the situation in those agencies? The short answer is no. Take gender, for example.

Despite a great amount of work having gone into making non-sexist, gender-neutral language the official-speak in the Civil Service, a recent survey of that institution by the Office for National Statistics found that not only does the substantial pay gap between men and women continue, but that it has actually widened over the last years and is over 20%. Further, this is the case at all levels, from that of the boardroom downwards (Hencke, 2009). The same has been found to be true of women in universities.

Russell (2009) tells us that a recent report from The Equality and Human Rights Commission has found that the

> numbers of top female judges, newspaper editors, MPs, public appointees and chief executives have all *fallen* in the past year. David Cameron [then the leader of the Conservative Party and now Prime Minister] is pictured at his spring conference surrounded by his shadow cabinet, and every one of the dozen faces behind him is male.

The rhetoric of each of these organizations is couched in PC-speak, they would all say (and perhaps even truly believe) that they are all for promoting the rights of women; they would be able to demonstrate that their equal opportunity policies are firmly in place; they would all be able to point to numerous procedures and protocols developed to serve these ends. And yet, the actual situation for women is going from bad to worse. The distinction between "performance" and "practice" can hardly be made clearer.

We would all agree (well, perhaps not *all* of us) that women ought not to be unfairly discriminated against by virtue of their being women. Following this line, Sardar says that we all have to guard against our misogynist tendencies, and one way of doing this is by attending to the language we use:

> We need to talk about spouses or partners rather than husbands and wives, acknowledge that housework is something that men do as much as women, and make the case that whatever our gender we should get equal pay for work of equal value. [2008, p. 36]

Buried in this sentence there are two issues of significance that are worth looking at more fully. First, there are questions to be asked about why it is thought wrong to speak of husbands and wives, and why the gender-neutral terms "spouse" and "partner" are thought preferable. Is it to obscure the occasions when the couple is married from when it is not? Or is it because the terms husband and wife cannot be readily applied to same sex couples? Or perhaps it has to do with the fact that in many relationships it is the woman that is the main wage earner, and the concern is that to call her "wife" is confusing because the role she takes is not the traditional one. Whatever the rationale, to my mind this is exactly the kind of inane tweaking of language that creates hostages to fortune for the racists and xenophobes. The issue surely is one of ensuring that women get the same rewards as men for doing the same work. The issue is one of working towards the situation in which same sex couples have the same sorts of rights and status as heterosexual couples (for example, to be able to marry if they so choose). Calling the woman "spouse" or "partner" rather than "wife" does little to change the actual power relations between men and women, or between heterosexuals and homosexuals.

Second, the passage also smacks of wishful thinking. From where did the author get the idea that housework is done *as much* by men as women? It is true that in this day and age more men do housework than was the case before, but it remains true that women do the majority of the housework. And even in the households where the man does contribute to the housework, it is mostly the case that the woman still does much more than the man. The passage reveals how unrealistic fantasy comes to be mistaken for fact. The fantasy is that if husbands and wives were called spouses, then equality will inevitably follow.

The result is that there is an increasingly wide gap between the rhetoric of antidiscriminatory performance and the continuance of racism, with the warm glow from the former obscuring the flourishing of the latter.

The flawed theoretical basis for the suggestion that one should not use certain categories leads into six further conceptual and strategic difficulties. I will take up each of these in turn.

Natural and artificial groups

To get at the first problem, I will summarize the rationale supplied by Sardar for pursuing this kind of strategy: some people have their life opportunities restricted because they are discriminated against. This takes place because there are negative beliefs about the groupings they belong to. These beliefs are reflected in language. If language is changed, then these beliefs become weaker. The result is then that one will come to see individuals on their merits rather than their membership of the groups they belong to. It is on these grounds that it is suggested that certain labels, like "elderly", ought not to be used.

But now, if we were to follow the argument to its logical conclusion we would be bound to say that we ought not also to use any of the categories women, Jews, Blacks, Arabs, Moslems, migrants, and so on, because they, too, are discriminated against. But in fact, we are told that we ought to do the opposite with these categories, *that we should affirm and "respect" them*. Which categories are we to affirm, and which are we to un-see? And why?

In one breath we are told that we ought to un-see the "elderly"; in the next, that we should "*emphasise the differences* between individuals and across groups . . . [because] such differences are best seen as assets to be valued" (Thompson, 2001, pp. 34–35). To comply with both strategies at the same time, of emphasizing differences and simultaneously ignoring them, requires one to first of all unthink and then double-think.

For example, when it comes to the grouping "trans", which refers to people who have gone through a medical procedure that changes their gender, Sardar says, "Trans people should be respected as a discrete group" (p. 33). Why does the argument that applies to the "elderly" not apply to "trans people"? In the literature, there is no explicit answer to be found for this question.

In my view, the reason for this anomaly is the taken for granted belief that some groups are artificial, merely artefacts of ways of thinking, while other groups are real and have an objective existence. In proceeding in this way, they are falling foul of what philosophers call the "naturalistic fallacy", wherein one takes the world as one finds it to be a natural state of affairs and not requiring questioning (deriving "ought" from "is", as it is sometimes put). To question the natural would appear as pointless as Chico Marx asking Groucho in the film *The Cocoanuts*: "Why a duck?" (Chico mishears Groucho's reference to the "viaduct" as "why a duck", and existential mayhem follows.) It is beholden on us to ask not only "why a duck", but "how a duck"? Even a cursory historical analysis shows us how groups and their names come into being through the exercise of power, and then, as context changes, they fade away. As ever, we have to remember the asymmetry: some have the power to name, and others get named, and there is always the struggle between the two.

Anyhow, these "natural" or "real" groups are the usual suspects of race, class, gender, religion, nationality, ethnicity, etc., etc. (It is this same belief system that lies behind the fallacious idea that some differences are primary, deep and do not change, and others are secondary, surface, and do change—see the previous chapter.)

But if we do not follow this essentialist course, then we have to ask, how does a grouping come to achieve the status of being "real"?

The brief answer is that it has to do with power and power relations. Recall the earlier arguments: humanity is riven by an infinite number of differences, each of which creates groupings variously intersecting and overlapping. They are all "real", but not all meaningful. To become a "real" meaningful group, or to designate a group of "others" as "real", requires the power to define, the power to convince others of this definition, and the power to sustain the definition. The grouping called "race", looked at earlier, is a case in point. The Rastafarians, if you recall, failed to claim a "real" identity of ethnicity, in part because they have little power and so were unable to counter the argument that their existence had been of insufficient longevity. However, the group called "trans" has been sufficiently politically powerful to become a "real" grouping.

Removing vs. *transforming words*

The next conceptual confusion is best teased out through the device of testing the strategy advocated for the category "Black" against that advocated for "old". Let me begin, then, by replacing the category "the elderly" with "Black" in the following statements from Thompson (1995, pp. 11–12), which would now read,

> Terms such as ~~the elderly~~ [the Blacks] . . . are commonly used but are . . . very dehumanising—they depersonalize the people to whom they refer.

> We should avoid grouping people together according to ~~age~~ [the category Black] . . . abandon the 'us–them" mentality. [Thompson, 2001, p. 102]

The previous argument would hold that one should, therefore, not use the term Black, as the category is used in the processes of dehumanization and marginalization of persons designated as Blacks. But history did not follow the advice being given by Thompson and Sardar. Instead, the peoples designated as Black came to claim the category as their own. It became the ensign in their battle to rehumanize themselves, in their own eyes as much as in the eyes of their oppressors. Through this process, Black, as the *name* of a kind of people, became progressively (but only partially) cleansed of its toxic connotations. In sum, rather than the category Black as applied to people becoming unthought and unused, it has come to take on the status of a respected social object, and this has occurred through bloodshed and struggle, not through adjustments in the lexicon.

The lesson for "the elderly" to be learnt from the history of "Black struggle" is that they should hold on and make more of their name rather than advocate for its demise. The lesson is that, under the right conditions, the category of marginalization can be transformed into an instrument of emancipation; it can become a category of resistance, and help organize challenges to the status quo. In fact this is exactly what "the elderly" are doing—mobilizing under the term "grey power". Similarly, the gay movement has appropriated the term "queer", mobilizing it for their own emancipatory ends.

It seems to me that if there were any grounds for "banning" the use of a term, it would have to be for "race". This is because "race" is a reification put to insidious ends and because it truly does not exist in the material sense. The lexicon adjusters have not advocated this course of action. And we cannot ban it in the current conditions, for the same reasons as above. Racism cannot be got rid of by not using the term "race".

Do we need "race" in order to talk about racism? Within the equality discourses, we find a range of attitudes towards the notion of race. At one end, it is championed as core identity. At the other end, there is a kind of embarrassed silence in relation to it because the term is awkward and problematic in the following way. Although "race" does not exist in the material sense, it is, nevertheless, brought into psychosocial existence by the processes of racialization, and so it comes to affect lives and interactions; it does not exist, and yet it exists. The way round this conundrum is to attend to the processes of racialization rather than race itself (see Dalal, 2002). Unfortunately, this course of action has not been helped by the legislature instating the term into the statute books, and neither is it helped by its continued use by the groups that have been marginalized on its basis. We can understand why this occurs: the notion of race is used to denigrate and distance a grouping, and, in response, that grouping eventually comes to venerate and champion the difference that has been used to disenfranchise them. What is lost in this turmoil is the fact that the term in itself is meaningless; it is neither good nor bad, because it does not exist. What is important about it is the use it has been put to, to dehumanize and exclude: the racist says, we are of different races, and our race is better/more advanced than yours. The disenfranchised use the same term to try to batter their way back into the mainstream, saying, no, our race is as good as yours and so we deserve the same as you. But, in doing so, the disenfranchised have bought into the myth of the racist that they are indeed a different race with their own ways and values; they accept that they are differentiated on the basis of race, but say that the two races have the same value. The way ahead is unclear, but we can inch our way forward by asking, each time "race" is used, why is it being used and who is using it? What is being described? What is intended? And, in asking these questions, we would have some chance of laying bare the processes of marginalization themselves.

Names and name calling

The third conceptual confusion begins with something sensible, a stand against the use of racial epithets and other kinds of insults against gays, women, and so forth, but ends up somewhere not very sensible.

In recent history in the UK, particularly from the 1950s to the 1970s, gendered insults ("drives like an old woman") and racial epithets (wog, coon, etc.) were commonplaces. Over the decades since, the use of these terms have quite rightly become less acceptable. Now when such epithets are publicly used, there is usually an outcry of some sort. For example, Prince Harry was heard to say of a fellow soldier "our little Paki friend . . ." (August 2008), and Carol Thatcher (daughter of Margaret Thatcher) called the tennis player Tsonga a "golliwog" (February 2009). While the Prince apologized, Thatcher defended herself by saying that it was a "joke".

There is good reason to make a stand against the use of toxic terms in public life, as their use reinforces and legitimates the denigration of those alluded to by them. But to then take the further step of saying that we should not utilize the actual names of those who are unfairly discriminated against (elderly) is a strategy born of confusion.

Ironically, it is a confusion born of an error of categories, between insults and descriptions. Take the publication of the Trade Union Council (TUC) of Great Britain entitled *Diversity in Diction: Equality in Action – A Guide to the Appropriate Use of Language* (TUC, 2005). It is, as its title makes clear, a set of guidelines for good non-discriminatory practice. The line it follows is the norm within the equality discourses.

I cite a section from it in its entirety.

> **Language and its Connotations**
>
> Many words and phrase, while not offensive in themselves, carry heavy negative connotations. It is therefore important to avoid certain terms which use 'black' to portray negativity. Terms such as: Black sheep of the family, blacklist, black mark, black looks, have no direct link to skin colour, but potentially serve to reinforce a negative view of all things black.
>
> Equally certain terms imply a negative image of 'black' by reinforcing the positive aspects of 'white'. For example, in the context of being above suspicion the phrase 'whiter than white' is often used. 'Purer than pure' or 'cleaner than clean' are alternatives which do not infer that anything other than white should be regarded with suspicion. Similarly the term 'play the white man' implies that neither Black people nor women are fair and honest. 'Play the game' or 'be fair' are more neutral alternatives.
>
> However, it is perfectly acceptable to use 'black' to describe colour as in: black bin bag, black shoes, blackboard, there it is in black and white, do you take your tea/coffee black or white? [pp. 26–27]

There are two curiosities to be looked at here. First, the idea that one should not use "black" to signify negativity, and second, that the guidelines feel the need to reassure the reader that they are "allowed" to order black or white coffee. Let me begin with the first of these.

One signifier and three significations

Perhaps controversially for some, in what follows I am going to take issue with the assertion that one ought not to use phrases like "black look" in which "black" works as a signifier of negativity.

Over the last thousand years (in the English language) the word "black" has gained increasingly negative connotations. Over the ages it came to be utilized as a signifier of disapproval when applied to things, thoughts, feelings, actions, and also people. The "people" so designated wrested the term from the denigrators, and turned it into an emblem of liberation. As they claimed it and organized around it, Black as the name of a people began to be somewhat cleansed of the stigma of disapproval, but not entirely, and not for everyone. (A fuller account of the evolving semantic history of "black" and "white" can be found in Dalal, 2002, Chapter Eight.)

At this point in time, the signifier *black* has three possible significations: neutral, bad, and good. When applied to items like "blackbird", then its signification is neutral, when applied to things and events (such as black look and black day), then its signification is mostly bad, and when applied to a people then its connotations are good (to the well-meaning liberal way of thinking) and bad (to the racist way of thinking).

Because the signifier "black" points in three different directions, mainstream equality discourses suggest that we simplify matters by not using "black" to signify negativity *per se* (as in "black day", and instead say "bad day"). The idea is that we limit the use of "black" to the name of a people (with positive connotations), and to instances that are neutral. The concern is that the continuing use of black as a signifier of negativity reinforces the linkage between the two and this makes it harder to keep negative connotations out of one's mind when one uses the phrase "Black people". It is also claimed that the people called Black are offended when they hear phrases such as "black day". No doubt some Blacks as well as Whites *are* offended, but that does not mean that I should therefore unquestioningly follow them, curb my thoughts, and so fall silent. I think their stance mistaken (I might be wrong, of course) and so want to engage in a debate and dialogue on these matters.

The two notions, "Black" and "black", share the same word. This is the situation we find ourselves in. What is so disturbing about it? There are many words that hold several meanings (the word "well" for example), a situation we all seem to manage quite well (no pun intended) without confusion. Are we saying that Black people are not capable of recognizing when the term "black" is being used as a racial slur, or are we saying that every time they hear the term they only hear it as a racial slur? In my opinion, it is perfectly feasible for a person to hold on to a notion of their Black identity, even while they are having a black day. I think Black people are capable of being able to discriminate between the two. I do not think them so fragile.

Of course, a Black or White person might well make it an issue when a colleague uses the phrase "black look", and there might be any number of reasons for making it an issue. The use of the phrase might indeed be a coded provocation. But, on the other hand, the motivation for challenging its use might not be honourable; rather, it might be being opportunistically raised to serve other (hidden) political ends. It seems to me that rather than ban this sort of usage, what is required is that we bring our faculties of analysis, discernment, and discrimination to each situation to work out what is actually going on.

One other reason why some people might find it disturbing when they hear the term black being used with negative connotations is because it strikes a resonance with the repressed, racialized association that resides deep in the mind.

In sum, the benefits to the equalities project of trying to re-engineer language in this way are very questionable, not least because the attempt to banish some terms becomes an opportunity for the mischievous to exaggerate the situation in order to inflame the anxieties of the populace. This then leads neatly into the second of the curiosities above: why the language guide has found it necessary to reassure its readers that they are indeed "allowed" to order a black coffee.

Life savers and coffee drinkers

There are many reports in circulation that tell of local authorities and other "politically correct do-gooders" banning the use of *all* phrases that contain the word black, because it would offend Black people. Thus, we are told that the children's nursery rhyme, "Baa Baa Black Sheep", is being banned in schools by local authorities. There are many reports of the phrases "blackboard" and "black bin bag" being banished from polite speech.

But here is the interesting thing: when one looks for actual evidence for these assertions, there is little or none to be found—they are urban myths perpetuated by gossip. For example, the Media Research Group produced a report in 1987, *Media Coverage of London Councils*, in which they looked for evidence that "Baa Baa Black Sheep" was banned in schools, and found none. (See Petley, 2005 for further argument and evidence.)

The situation has come about in the following way. Guidelines (like the one cited above) have suggested that usages of the terms Black and White when signifying bad and good, should be avoided. This suggestion gets amplified in the racist imagination of the self-proclaimed defenders of liberty and free speech, who maliciously report that *all* usages of black are being banned by the do-gooders.

By dint of repetition, these fictions take on the status of facts in the public imagination, as even a cursory search on the Internet demonstrates.

One such urban myth still doing the rounds on the Internet is that of a White person being chastised for being racist in a coffee shop when asking for a white coffee; they are told that the correct phrase is "coffee with milk". Anthony Browne gives a version of this story in his book. According to him, it was a German student who was recently reprimanded in the canteen of the School of Oriental and Asian Studies (an institution, by the way, that does not exist—he might mean the School of Oriental and African Studies). In another version of the story found on the Internet, it is asserted that it is in Starbucks that one is not allowed to order a white coffee. This claim is found in a posting in response to a mischievous, scaremongering story in the *Daily Telegraph* entitled "Toddlers who dislike spicy food 'racist'" (Prince, 2009).[1] Meanwhile, a female prison officer is cited in the *Independent* as saying "It's gone too far. I have worked in other places where you can't even ask for a black coffee" (Burrell, 2000).

If true, then it is indeed worrying to everyone, Black and White. So it is not surprising that the story also gets lambasted by a Black person, Vicki Washington (2007); we know she is Black as she has put up her photograph. She says, in her version, that the event took place in Glasgow. By the time one comes across the bemused mothers of nursery age children on the Netmums Coffee House website wondering why it is bad to order a black coffee, it is clear that this myth has morphed into fact. The variations in the specific details of each telling—German student, Starbucks, London, Glasgow—are what lend the story the illusion of a real event. But it is precisely the contradictory variation in these details (and there are many more versions circulating on the Internet) that demonstrates that the story is indeed a mischievous urban myth.

Another story circulating on the Internet is that the Royal National Lifeboat Institution (RNLI) was turned down for a grant from the National Lottery for not being "racially inclusive enough". It is cited as another example of politically correct madness. But where did the story originate, and is it actually true? To understand exactly what has taken place, let us carefully take note of the sequence of events:

- The trail begins with a letter written to *The Times* by a reader on the subject of lottery funding. This letter makes no reference to the RNLI, or to the subject of "race".
- The letter is reproduced on the website of the newspaper, *Times Online* (September 26, 2007).
- Next, a member of the general public posts a "response" to the letter on this site, in which he declares that the National Lottery refused to fund the RNLI because it was not racially inclusive enough—more PC madness is the cry.
- The "response" is not a response at all, but a *non sequitur* in that it opportunistically introduces two subjects not previously present in the original letter—race and the RNLI.
- The claim then gets repeated on several other sites and "blogs", circulating with other similar myths purporting to show the insanity of the "politically correct". As one person says on a blog, "yes it is unbelievable, but it must be true because it said so in *The Times*".

But, if true, the news is indeed disturbing. I contacted the RNLI and was told by their press officer that they had *never*, ever approached the National Lottery for funding. The story is a complete fabrication. But despite this, the story continues to live. And with each repetition its presence grows and it comes to look more and more like an undisputable fact.

The visible made invisible

The language police have been somewhat over-zealous in their clean up. Their sweep has taken up the innocent as well as the problematic, and declared them all bad.

To say to a boy "Don't be such a girl" is meant as an insult to both, the particular boy and girls in general. The insult also functions in the service of policing the division of behaviours and attitudes, as some being the property of males and others of females, with the former granted more status than the latter (else the statement would not function as an insult). It is true that established English is formidably masculine in its structures. Many common terms like policeman, manpower, chairman, and headmaster assume that the persons in those roles are necessarily men, and so on. So here, I can stand in agreement with Sardar when he says, "We should make visible what language renders invisible", for example, to avoid the use of man to stand for all of humanity as it renders invisible the existence of women. Attending to language in this way makes sense to me.

But, worryingly, it is also the case that certain streams of equality-speak also work in the direction of rendering invisible what is already visible, the categories "old" and "disabled" being cases in point. But even more is to be rendered invisible. Sardar says,

> We should avoid the use of the word Islam . . . and instead use Muslims. Islamism, often used to describe extreme ideology, is an unclear term with negative connotations, so it is best avoided. Given that "fundamentalist" is always pejorative, frequently offensive and a blanket term, it should also be avoided. The best terms to describe Muslims with literalist or socially conservative views is "pious" "devout" and "politically motivated". [Sardar, 2008, pp. 30–31]

He is saying that we should not use the term fundamentalist, because of its negative connotations. I would agree with Sardar that the notion of fundamentalist is pejorative. But that is exactly why I use it; I use it in the pejorative sense. I would be being disingenuous if instead of fundamentalist I used the terms "pious" or "politically motivated"; this would be PC speak of the dangerous and troubling kind.

The mistaken reasoning employed to control the usages of Black is being replicated in suggesting that because the term "Islam" has taken on negative connotations through becoming linked to an extreme ideology, it should not be used.

I am well able to keep in mind that not all followers of Islam are fundamentalists, and also not all Islamic fundamentalists are believers in violence. I also know that there are many people who, although having an Islamic background, are essentially secular in their attitudes and beliefs. The problem comes about because in the public imagination (and, therefore, mine too) the few come to represent the entirety. Here is a corrective to that tendency: recently, in Luton, an Islamic fundamentalist, Mr Farasat Latif, dressed in the manner prescribed by the ultra conservative Saudi sect, the Salafi school (long beard and white tunic), led a confrontation with members of another fundamentalist group, Al Muhajiroun. The latter group had caused much consternation and outrage when they greeted British soldiers returning from Iraq with insults and placards screaming "Butchers of Basra", "murderers", and "baby killers". Mr Latif told the *Independent* that "The hot-headed young men that belong to Al Muhajiroun promote violence and preach a false version of Islam that reflects badly on ordinary Muslims. That is why we took action" (Taylor, 2009). Note, also, that Mr Latif does not appear to be troubled by the use of the term Islam; ought we to "correct" him?

It is the case that there are a great many important differences between the varieties of Islamic fundamentalists, some of whose beliefs I find entirely repugnant, and others who I am more able to tolerate. But that is the thing—I am tolerating them; that is, I am having to do some emotional work with the negativity that I feel towards fundamentalists generally, be they religious or secular. Fundamentalists are convinced that their version of things is absolutely true; they demand unquestioning acceptance, faith, and belief. I find such attitudes abhorrent. And so, yes, when I use the term fundamentalist, I use it for this very reason—its negative connotations.

Being offensive vs. *causing offence*

To the diversity way of thinking, to offend "ethnic" others, is one of the biggest sins one can commit. We can readily see and understand why this attitude has come about by recalling the not-so-good-old-days of colonialism and imperialist expansion. The colonialist viewed the colonized with contempt. They ran roughshod over their customs and beliefs, wreaking havoc in their path. This attitude was shared by capitalist as well as communist. The liberal attitude acted as a counterbalance to this tendency. The liberal imagination helped re-humanize the dehumanized; "they" became people with sensibilities once more. As soon as "they" became fellow human beings with sensibilities and sensitivities, then they became capable of being offended and the "we" were obliged to take account of their sensibilities. Having invited a religious Jew to dinner, we would take account of the fact that it would be inappropriate to serve them pork, as this would disturb them. This kind of thoughtfulness seems to me to be eminently sensible as well as ethical.

But there is a critical distinction between deliberately *being* offensive and of *causing* offence, a distinction that is often collapsed so that offence itself (like discrimination) becomes the culprit. I might well *cause* offence to this religious Jew because of my way of life and beliefs (say, the championing of the principle that women have the same rights as men), and he might well have been offended, but that does not mean that I have deliberately *been offensive* to him. Neither does it necessarily mean that I should modify my ways in order that he not be offended. If I were to abandon my beliefs in order not to offend, would I not be being unethical?

Things get further complicated by the liberal injunction that one ought not to intrude into the privacy of another, come what may. For example, is one bound to respect and accept the "right" of *some* Black men in the USA to speak of women as bitches? And that one ought to accept and respect it because it is "their culture"? I would say not, and, in this instance, so does Sardar. He draws the line by saying, "Cultural practices that violate the basic principles of human rights, such as female circumcision and forced marriages, cannot be 'respected' or 'valued'" (p. 23). While I agree with his stand, on what grounds is *he* proposing that *some* practices ought not to be respected? To say that they "violate the basic principles of human rights" is to assume that the understanding of those rights, being basic, are *universally* shared by all of humanity.

It would appear that the rules of the game have changed. From it being the case that the particular has been being privileged over the universal (Romantic values), suddenly, now, the universal is being called on to trump the particular (Enlightenment values). Sardar says that rather than subscribing to an idea of culturally sensitive language, he advocates the principle of an "ethically sensitive language". By introducing the word "ethics", he is saying, in effect, do and say what is right. But the way he does this is by assuming that that which is right is self-evident and so agreed by all. What has happened to the concern that we ought not to "impose" our ways on theirs? We can pull the whole argument up short by simply asking "whose ethics?" He gives no answer, and does not even ask the question. The unspoken assumption is that, on the whole, it is "their ethics" that ought to be respected until they cross some taken-for-granted universal baseline standard, after which it is "our ethics" that are to be respected. At this point "ours" becomes "everyones".

Sardar says that the aim of ethically sensitive language is to "promote the use of words that enhance a person's human dignity and value" (p. 23). This boils down to a banal list of correct ways of addressing people: he tells us that instead of saying diabetes sufferer, one ought to say "person with diabetes"; one ought to say "person with arthritis, cerebral palsy and Down's syndrome when talking about a person with more than one impairment" (pp. 34–35); one ought not to say "carer" because it denies the independence of the "cared for" person, and use instead "paid personal assistant"; "person with learning difficulties" is to be used with low-level impairments and "person with learning disability" for higher-level impairments; and so on and on. Not only are these sorts of lists are found in most organizations, they can also be used as the basis of complaints.

This sort of banal list making seems to me to be no more than an exercise in empty etiquette. It is also in danger of obfuscating reality in order to get it to fit into an ideology that idealizes the underdog. For example, some people need "carers" precisely because they cannot live an independent life—because they are disabled. To say otherwise is to be in a state of denial. I do not dispute that on many occasions disabled people are talked down to, patronized, and infantilized (as are the elderly). But that is a very different matter from saying that to name people as disabled and elderly is to patronize and infantilize them.

The arguments tend to run away with themselves. For example, Sardar tells us that disability is understood in one of two ways. There is the medical model, "which sees disabled people as the problem and thus requires them to adjust to the world as it is", and there is the social model, "which focuses on society and the barriers it creates that prevent disabled people participating fully in everyday activities". I would agree with this to some degree: for example, that public transport should find ways to accommodate to the needs of the disabled so that they can travel more freely, and so on. But surely it is a step too far to end up claiming that the difficulties that the disabled have in participating more fully in everyday life are *entirely* due to the barriers put up by society and that "it has little to do with their impairment" (p. 34). With this sort of suggestion we find ourselves once again in 1984 land.

The fallacy of the superior virtue of the oppressed

We have a tendency to idealize victims. The philosopher Bertrand Russell named this tendency "The fallacy of the superior virtue of the oppressed". According to Cohen, in his must-read book *What's Left?*, "Russell said that for too many right-thinking, left-leaning people it wasn't enough to assert that oppression was an evil which destroyed its victims. The oppressed's experience of oppression had to ennoble them" (Cohen, 2007, p. 78).

This fallacy has become absorbed into the equality discourses to take central place as an unquestioned and unquestionable norm. The effects of this norm are pernicious, in that it perverts and inverts the values of liberalism, turning them into instruments of fear and control. The potentially thoughtful principle, to respect the ways of the other, is turned into a monster that is easily mobilized to terrorize the liberal way of thinking. The corrupted principle becomes a draconian directive, that one *must* respect the other, come what may. It is the incorporation of this fallacy that lies at the heart of the thought paralysis that besets the liberal way of thinking.

The acceptance of this fallacy as fact leads to a continuation of black and white thinking and its resultant impasses. For example, in the aforementioned book aimed at educating social workers, *Anti-Discriminatory Practice*, Thompson makes the bold claim: "If you are not part of the solution, you must be part of the problem" (Thompson, 2001, p. 67). While this kind of sloganizing serves the useful purpose of focusing minds, ultimately it is not helpful, as it reinforces the impression of a divide that does not exist in reality—a clean divide between the good guys and the bad guys. The problem is further compounded by the fact that in this strange world, it is the underdog that is *always* the good guy. This is how it is in each and *every* teaching example provided by Thompson for the benefit of social workers: in each it is *always* the social worker that is at fault and in need of adjusting their attitudes and practices; the "user" of the service is always in the right in each and every case.

One teaching example (Practice Focus 7.1, p. 144) informs us of a social worker, Len, coming across a situation in which he discovered that his potential client, an elderly homophobic woman, was estranged from her gay son, Alan. Len finds that he shares his client's homophobic response to the news of Alan's sexuality. The story concludes: "Some days later Len reflected on the situation and his feelings, and felt very guilty about his negative reaction [to Alan]. He began to realise just how deeply ingrained discriminatory feelings and prejudices can be".

All this is fine and dandy. Len has seen the light. But now, what of the mother's continuing homophobic attitude? The teaching example simply avoids mentioning the conflict of values that is now bound to arise between the newly enlightened social worker and the homophobic client. How is Len to deal with this conflict? Should he accept her homophobia? If he does so, he will be going against something in himself. Is that something he ought to do in his role—"get alongside" his client? The social worker cannot be sensitively attuned to the positions of both protagonists, the mother and the son, at the same time. He has to choose sides (i.e., discriminate), or withdraw from the situation entirely.

In another example (Practice Focus 6.1) we are told of a social worker, Mary, trying to arrange appropriate care for a disabled person who was to leave hospital and return to her home. We are then told: "However, Mrs Penhaligon found this intrusive and objected to what she saw as Mary's tendency to patronise her by overemphasising the difficulties she faced and underestimating her strengths and abilities. This situation began to teach Mary that disability was a much more complex issue than she had originally thought".

It is perfectly possible that Mary was indeed patronizing and needed to take more account of her client's strengths. But what of the possibility that Mrs Penhaligon, despite being disabled, was an ungrateful, selfish, difficult, and controlling person? And more, a person who is in denial about the extent of their disabilities. If the teaching example is to be rounded, then surely these other possibilities must also be considered, possibilities that social workers must encounter quite regularly. The teaching example reinforces the myth that the client is always innocent and what they say is always correct, and beware the social worker who dares to think and say otherwise.

In Practice Focus 4.1 we find Jill, a newly qualified social worker, wanting to work with a particular family. "However to her great surprise and consternation, her team leader, Mike, commented that it would be better suited to a more experienced worker 'considering this is a Black family'. When challenged about this, Mike found it very difficult to explain or justify his remarks. He could only reiterate that the case needed a more experienced worker. Jill therefore remained concerned about Mike's apparent negative assumptions about Black families". The moral of this story is that Mike has some issues of racism, and that Jill is rightly concerned about him (and is likely to keep an eye on him and no doubt report him to the authorities if he carries on not seeing the light). What of the possibility that Mike was right in not allowing a novice to work with this family? What if the issue here is one of competence and not racism? And what of the other possibility: that Mike had formed a negative opinion of Jill based on his experience of her (i.e., that she was not up to the job) and that he was speaking in this way in order not to shame her?

I do not want to argue for the reverse situation in each of the above cases, but merely to flag up the fact that life is much more complex than rendered in these exemplars. The situation continually being dealt with by Thompson is of the social worker as oppressor in relation to a hard done by, but righteous, noble, and wise oppressed client. It is always the social worker who must change and adapt. And if they do not, like Mike above, then they are vulnerable to having a complaint made about them on the grounds of being a racist, sexist, or whatever.

If the situation is such that it is always the social worker that is clearly in the wrong, then there is no role for the discriminatory processes, and it is self-evident what needs to be done. You might say that the slant of the teaching examples are to be expected, as it is a book aimed at training social workers, and so the cases are necessarily to do with problems in the ways that social workers interact with their clients. This is indeed the case. But it is surely telling that there is not a single teaching example offered in which the difficulty due to a conflict of values lies with the client rather than with the social worker—a situation that social workers must come across on a regular basis.

What, for example, is the liberal social worker to do when, say, faced with a client in whose view homosexuality is an abhorrent evil, and that homosexuals are to be shunned or locked up, or perhaps attacked, or even deserved to be killed? This view is common to several faiths, as well as to many Black groups. They would defend their right to homophobia, saying that their stance is perfectly legitimate because it is endorsed by their religion or "culture", and so shared by many others. So why has Thompson turned a blind eye towards this kind of situation? We come back to the issue of fear again. The fear is that if a social worker did challenge and confront a Black person about their attitudes, the social worker would be open to being accused of racism, and that a formal complaint would follow. (Of course, atheists and Whites of all "kinds" are also not immune to being homophobic.).

This ostrich mentality, in which one simply does not see or believe that "victims" can also be "bad", is not only blind, but also idiotic. It is as though it were the case that the only way to counter the charge that *all* Black persons are criminals is by the defence that says that *no* Black person is ever a criminal. The defence is as overstated as the charge, a defence (in the guise of antidiscrimination) that is inverted racism and ends up doing more harm than good to the very people that are being defended.

Let me end this chapter with two instances in which the fear of being thought of racist ends up perpetuating racism.

Action paralysis

Recently, in the South West of England, it gradually became clear to the authorities that a more than expected number of people whose roots were in the Asian sub-continent were ending up in hospital with food poisoning of different kinds. An investigation into the matter revealed that although the hygiene inspectorate had concerns about the hygiene standards in the local halal abattoir, they did not pursue the matter in the same manner as they would have with a "normal" abattoir. In proceeding in this way, unbeknown to themselves, they were following Stone and Stone-Romero's line in making allowances for "their ways", accepting and respecting them, and lowering their own standards in the process. This is inverted racism; but no doubt in the mix of things there was also their fear of being accused of being racist, which added to their paralysis.

I was asked to act as a consultant with regard to a difficult situation that a psychotherapy training organization found itself in. It had to do with "Dinshaw", a trainee born and raised in India but practising as a medical doctor in the UK for many years. In a good psychotherapy training (as this one was), there are many aspects and many teachers and supervisors involved. The trainee has to be in therapy themselves, there is the academic side of things (they have to learn theory), and they have to practise under the very close supervision of senior psychotherapists. The whole process is overseen by a training committee that receives reports from the supervisors, academics, and, in this case, also a line from the therapist as to whether, in their opinion, the trainee was able to make use of therapy. The point I want to make is that there are many committed people involved in the training process. As Dinshaw approached the end of an arduous five-year training, the training committee told him that there were serious concerns about his capacity to practise as a psychotherapist. Dinshaw was incensed and made a formal complaint: given that at the end of each year there was a reporting process, why had nothing been flagged up to him before? It turned out that for much of the five years, all the people involved with this trainee had had some concerns, but had "made allowances", and apart from one of the supervisors, none had flagged up their concern to the committee. Of course, there is nothing wrong in "making allowances" in the hope that in time the trainee will improve, and often enough this is the case. But what is wrong is continuing to make allowances when things do not get better. After the concern was flagged up by the supervisor, it emerged that this concern was shared by others. But even when the committee had this information, it procrastinated. Why? It seems to me that the training committee was in the grip of an anxiety not unlike the hygiene inspectorate; they were unable to deal with the student in a straightforward fashion presumably because of a fear of being accused as racist.

Here are two further twists to the story. I found Dinshaw to be an unsympathetic figure, somewhat difficult. My speculation is that the committee members were unable to deal with him in a straightforward manner *because* they had antipathetic feelings towards him. My guess is that the committee were in a state of doubt as to the basis of their negativity towards him: was it born of racist ideations regarding him, or due to his personality? Further, I think that the fact that the trainee was a medical doctor served as an additional inhibition for the committee. Medical doctors carry considerable prestige and status; to some degree, we are all somewhat in awe of those who belong to that category, and so we find it more difficult to challenge them.

Problems abound and contradictions arise. In the case above, the "liberal" institution found itself paralysed in part because of bending over backwards in order to ensure that they were not being racist. In the next case, an institution is outraged at the suggestion that it might be racist. I consulted to a different psychotherapy organization because they wanted to think about the reasons why and how their trainee and patient population was mainly White. I was met with outrage when I suggested that there was perhaps something to be looked at (institutionalized prejudice of some kind) in the fact that out of ten potential trainees that year, of the three that were not selected, two were "ethnics" and one a lesbian. Psychoanalysts pride themselves on being able to look the harsh and disturbing side of human nature unflinchingly in the eye. It is interesting, then, to think about why the idea of institutional racism seems much more disturbing to these psychoanalysts than matricide and patricide. Anyhow, it is exactly this kind of reluctance and affront which has provoked the equality movements into taking some of the stances that they have.

I will have much more to say about why the liberal is so afraid of being thought of as racist in the final chapter.

Note

1. This story was allegedly about a publication from the National Children's Board that allegedly tells the workers to challenge racist behaviour, including the disliking of foods from other cultures. The NCB refutes all the claims made in the article (www.ncb.org.uk/Page.asp?originx_6073ic_23555200356948j64k_2008772856u).

CHAPTER TEN

The vicissitudes of discrimination

The predicament

The intention of the entire equalities enterprise has been to try to create a fairer world. But the task is made difficult because of the predicament that is endemic to the human condition, the condition spelt out in Chapters Four and Five.

First, human beings are social beings. By this I mean that as we grow up, we imbibe the social conventions we are born into with our mother's milk; these conventions become internalized and constitute the Self. But we take in not one set of conventions, but several, some of which are in conflict with each other. Somehow, out of this mix, we cobble together what becomes our habituated ways of being—of seeing, experiencing, and interacting with the world. This happens, not uniformly or universally, but sufficiently broadly for us to be able to speak of "ways of life". In a manner of speaking, we more or less "mindlessly" follow one sort of world view and not another—mindless in the sense that it is the unreflected norm we inhabit and that inhabits us. This taken for granted habituation has variously been called ideology, discourse, and the social unconscious. In this sense, we are cultural sheep.

But it is also the case that humans bring something else to the table. They are thinking beings that are capable of questioning, testing, and enquiring into the conditions of their existence and transforming them. This was exactly Kant's requirement for humanity: that we did not just meekly accept the world we find ourselves in, but test it through the light of human reason. We are not just products of socialization processes, but are active contributors to them. Our existence is dialogical (as Charles Taylor has called it).

Now we come to the following complication: our processes of discernment are never value free; they are deeply patterned by the conventions and norms that we inhabit, and in ways that we are mostly not conscious of. It follows that our processes of discernment cannot ever be objective and neutral; they are forever compromised; the dice are ever loaded. So, as we enquire into the conditions of our existence, the form and manner of the enquiry is already patterned by those conditions, and so the "findings" of that enquiry will not only have a tendency to reinforce the assumptions, they are likely to miss them entirely. As has been sometimes said, discourses are self-validating, or, in the colloquial, to a hammer, everything looks like a nail.

But the situation is not totalitarian and neither is it entirely determined by the mechanisms of cognition. Recall, we are born into multiple conflictual social orders, and so are subject to many different claims on ourselves. In this mix of things, not only are we are pushed and pulled towards and away from particular identities, but we also find ourselves being drawn in one direction and away from other directions. This mix and mix-up is an aspect of the field of power relations that one is born into. One could think of the psycho-social developmental process that we all go through from infancy onwards as a process that irons out this multiplicity, so that we end up more one kind of person than another; in a manner of speaking, we end up with a number of names and think of ourselves and others as residing within certain categories. But this is never fixed and there is always a state of tension, because always, somewhere in the margins, there are other ways, ever ready to subvert the established norms. What is the case is that somehow we end up with certain ways of thinking and feeling that seem natural to us, that form us as well as constrain us.

It is this realization, that there is no pure objectivity, that lies behind the collapse into relativism, where anything and everything goes. And if anything goes, then thinking itself becomes redundant.

Here, then, is the predicament: despite our best efforts, when it comes to the exercise of their faculties of discernment, we humans are intrinsically biased; despite our best rational efforts, we cannot help but take sides. Our minds are partisan. This is the human condition.

All the strategies of the equality movements can be thought of as ways of trying to deal with human bias. This bias is writ large everywhere: in the job market, housing, and so forth, certain "kinds" of people do better than other "kinds". This is a continuing, very real problem, as some of the statistics already mentioned demonstrate. However, elements within the equality movements proceed on the mistaken basis that the bias is due to faulty and erroneous thinking, rather than as the existential predicament I have just outlined above. Faulty thinking leads to faulty feelings (prejudice). If thinking is faulty, then it can be corrected. There are two aspects to this correction process. The first we have already touched on in the previous chapter, training. The second is proceduralization. As was noted earlier, in modern times the favoured means of managing human bias in institutional life has become one of removing humans as much as possible from the decision-making process, and replacing them with procedures and protocols.

The Equal Opportunities interview

Take, for example, the process of appointing a teacher to a school. One's decision should depend on the capacities and talents of the person, regardless of whether they are Black, White, male, female, Jewish, and so on. In this regard, the appointment process is drawing on the values of the Enlightenment—a blindness to differences of "type". But the function of an interview is not to be blind to all differences, because its purpose is actually *to amplify the differences* in ability between the candidates. Obvious as it is, it is worth stating: the interview process is a discriminatory process.

Let us say that, over the years, it becomes apparent that a school has appointed very few Cs (compared to Ps), and the few Cs that have been appointed languish at the bottom of the hierarchy. Having noticed this pattern, what is one to do?

Quotas and targets

One answer is to engage in positive discrimination, to go out of one's way to appoint more Cs until the numbers have equalized somewhat. At this suggestion, Ps are likely to call foul play: "surely", they might say, "this is unfair; the best person should get the job. In fact, this is exactly what has been taking place in each interview over the years. It just so happens that more of the best candidates have been P". Let us assume that the Ps who say this are, in as much as one can be, decent people; that there is no overt conspiracy to keep Cs out; that there is no ring-leader orchestrating the outcomes of interviews (as is mostly—but not always—the case). And so the Ps are genuinely perplexed and wounded at the accusation of unfairness. This is because the bias, the unfairness, is unconscious; it is institutionalized; it is invisible; it is out of sight and out of conscious mind.

But here, despite the bewilderment of the Ps, there is statistical evidence aplenty that Cs are somehow being marginalized. If we do not buy into the myth that Ps are naturally better at teaching than Cs, then we are bound to conclude that something unfair is taking place. When faced with the incalcitrance of Ps to countenance this, one sleeping policeman solution is to enforce a quota system. This is an act of desperation, but desperate situations sometimes call for desperate solutions; its introduction implies that one has given up on addressing the causes of the problem, these being the prejudice of Ps and the bias structured into practices, both of which continue as before. The quota system privileges category of kind over category of merit. Its virtue is that others who were excluded as a matter of course are now able to gain entry; its vice is that those of little or no talent also gain entry simply by virtue of being a C, thereby threatening the well-being of all. The result of this sleeping policeman solution, as usual, is that it will inflame the problem further by fuelling the resentments of Ps towards Cs.

Although organizations in the USA and the UK tend not to pursue a quota system, they are obliged to meet "targets" of all kinds, to meet certain "efficiencies" as they are euphemistically called. In my view, the target is no different from the quota system, and so suffers from exactly the same problems.

How else might one proceed?

Proceduralization: the erosion of responsibility

One answer is to proceduralize all institutional processes, including that of the interview. The intention behind the procedures and protocols is to edit out opportunities for prejudicial bias. The equal opportunities interview is an attempt to ensure that all the candidates will be treated in *exactly* the same way. To this end, it is agreed beforehand what the questions are to be, who will ask them, and what the answers ought to be. In some cases, it is agreed that the interviewers will not ask any follow-up questions for clarification from candidates, because that will advantage those who are asked to elaborate over the other candidates. The equal opportunity interview tries to focus objectively on the competencies of the candidate, and to exclude the interviewer's subjective responses to the candidate-as-person. The answers are "scored" by each interviewer, and the candidate with the highest score is offered the job. As with the ethnic monitoring form, the fact that answers are scored makes the whole process appear more objective than it actually is, because the number is a subjective corollary of a judgement made by the interviewer. But even apart from this, this attempted objectification of the interview process cannot really deliver the desired results, because it attempts to dispense entirely with the humanity of the interviewers as well as that of the applicants. The problem is that it is this very mix of humanities that is key to how well a person will perform in an organization.

Thinking has been replaced with flow-chart following. Responsibility for the appointment is no longer lodged with the individuals conducting the interviews, but in the procedures. The interviewer's responsibility becomes to follow procedure precisely; in effect, the interviewer is the servant of procedure. And in any conflict between the outcome suggested by the procedure and the interviewer's own view, the procedure is trumps. There is less and less possibility of thinking for oneself, and if one goes out on a limb by thinking for oneself, then one is on one's own and exposed. Kant's great cry at the start of the Enlightenment: *Sapere Aude*, think for yourself, is progressively atrophied in this increasingly proceduralized and mechanized world.

Perverting procedures

Procedures which are put in place to help the institution run smoothly are easily perverted and utilized defensively (analogous to the Hawkeye situation). In modern organizational life, the measure of things becomes not a discussion about right and wrong, but whether or not procedures have been followed precisely. A telling illustration is found in a recent event regarding a private hospital. The surgeon cut through a vein and the patient haemorrhaged to death because the hospital did not keep blood on its premises or the equipment to stop haemorrhages. Jeremy Vine, on the television programme *Panorama*, asked of them, "Isn't it just terribly obvious that you need blood in a hospital that is doing operations in case somebody has a haemorrhage?" Astonishingly, the Head of Care Quality, one Tracy McNeill felt able to answer no, because, she said, "we met all of the criteria and all of the regulations. It was not a requirement" (*Panorama*, 2009).

The point of this story is not to have a go at the profiteering motive (well, just a bit), but to show how responsibility is being denied by virtue of the claim that because the institution had met all the criteria and followed the all the rules and requirements laid down by the authorities, it is, therefore, blameless.

The pressure on staff, then, is not to think and not to challenge the status quo. "Whistle blowers" following the dictates of their conscience are cruelly punished by the institutions they expose. But if you follow procedure, then you are blameless whatever the outcome. Recently, a colleague who was part of an equal opportunities interview panel, found herself having serious doubts about the candidate that scored highest. Something she could not precisely articulate did not *feel* right to her. She overrode her doubts and agreed to follow procedure and so the candidate was appointed. In the weeks that followed, he showed himself to be an extremely difficult, demanding, and problematic person, with the result that the well-being of the team he was appointed to was seriously compromised.

So, ought one to allow one's emotional responses to be a legitimate part of the decision-making process?

The rationality of the emotions

One reason that the emotions are viewed as dangerous and tend to get discounted by the positivists is that they are thought of as irrational, and as the opposite of thought. But, in the way that the emotions work, they are, in fact, supremely rational. One's *feeling* is, in a very real sense, a decision. Think about it: our emotional capacities have developed in the ways that they have through the evolutionary process. And they must have done so because the information they give is useful to survival. The emotions are the means by which we orientate ourselves to the world. In fact, one's feeling is a way of registering the conclusion of a decision-making process that is partially conscious and partially unconscious. In saying this, I do not want to make the same mistake as the Romantics and valorize emotions over thought. It is clear that we cannot let emotionality have free rein and to rely entirely on something mysterious called intuition. Just because it feels right does not always mean that it is right.

In fact, this is exactly why the equal opportunities interview was "invented" in the first place, as panellists tend to favour candidates who share similarities of significance with themselves: Oxbridge types favouring Oxbridge types, men favouring men, and then there was Thiederman (who we met earlier), who was naturally drawn towards Whites because of "simple human comfort", and so on. The reality is that our emotions are integral to our thinking processes and *both* are partisan. Proceduralization, then, is the attempt to circumnavigate both the mind and the heart.

Diversity as solution to the individual's partisan mind (and heart)

To compensate for the tendency of individuals to be biased, another solution is to make the interview panel itself "diverse": fill it with lots of different kinds of persons, including "service users". The idea here is that their individual unconscious prejudices and biases will cancel each other out. This does help to some degree, but the situation is more complicated.

Let me start with Elias's profound insight that we have an automatic tendency to read and experience *power superiority* as an indicator of *human superiority*, and vice versa. We tend to attribute more virtues and capabilities to those who belong to groupings with higher status than to those with lower status, and we do this *despite our rational selves*. The phenomenon is well known to social psychologists, who have (unsurprisingly) named it the attribution error (Brown, 1995; Duncan, 1976). Experiments have shown that perceptions of the *same* event will be skewed depending on the social status of the protagonists. When we witness some difficult behaviour (say, anger or anxiety), if the protagonist is of lower status, then we tend to think that they are behaving in this way because it is an expression of their inner (flawed) character, and if it is a higher status person, then we tend to read their behaviour as a reasonable response to the situation they are in. In the first instance, the cause or *blame* is put "inside" the person, and in the other, a *cause* is located "outside" them. Not only are we all prone to the attribution error, we are not even aware that we are always in its grip. But, most importantly, the perceptions of both, the privileged as well as the marginalized, are skewed *in the same direction* by the attribution error. This is one reason why the solution of getting a range of people on the interview panel will not work entirely, because all their perceptions will be skewed similarly; all will tend to read situations in a similarly partisan fashion. For example, the attribution error suggests that the anxiety that a higher status candidate might show in an interview is more likely to be taken to be a very understandable *response* to the interview situation, and in the lower status candidate's case, it is more likely to be taken to be *an expression* of their insecure character. These readings cannot help but influence how the panellists score the interviewees' answers.

But the issue ought not to be overstated; it is not the case that the attribution error is the only process that determines the outcome of an interview. Panellists are also Kantian beings who, despite being fettered with protocols, no doubt call upon their faculties in the decision-making process, which must compensate to some degree for the workings of the attribution error. The point is, however, that the attribution error is always present and cannot help but play a part in the outcome to some degree.

The discussion above has primarily focused on the contribution of individuals to unfair discriminatory processes. What I want to do next is to think about how power relations, institutional procedures, and protocols come to work in the same direction, somehow centrifuging some kinds of human beings to the periphery and pulling in other kinds towards the centre. Of these various sorts of institutional processes of marginalization, the one I will speak more directly of is that of institutional racism.

Processes of institutionalization: the further erosion of responsibility

There are many who dispute the existence of institutional racism precisely because of its invisibility. There is no one to point to, there is no one person to blame. I was recently helped to understand the notion through the story of a schoolteacher. The teacher really struggled to maintain discipline in his first year of teaching. One day, early on in his second year, he was excited to have found a solution for himself. At the very start of the new teaching year with a new class, he presented to the pupils a written set of rules of what was not to be allowed and also a graded set of punishments (detentions and so forth) to do with each infringement. Now, when a student misbehaved, he said to them, I am obliged to punish you in this way for this misdemeanour because it says so in the rules. The teacher was very excited by the outcome. Wonderfully, the students did not complain, but co-operated in the punishment process, because now, whatever was happening, it appeared that it was not the teacher doing it to them. The teacher was only following the same set of rules as the students.

The world is not as simple as this classroom, and even the classroom is not as simple as I have portrayed it. However, the very simplicity of the story allows us to see some of the elements of institutionalization that are normally invisible. Specifically, although it is clear that it is the teacher who has actually created the rules, in day-to-day practice it appears that the teacher is powerless to do otherwise than he does; he is obliged to follow the rules like everyone else. The rules have become "objectified"; the teacher is now merely the helpless instrument through which the rules are expressed.

One can see clearly in the story that the schoolteacher had the power to determine what the rules were. However, we can also see that in the practical situation in the classroom, that fact has become invisible to the schoolchildren. We can intuit that some years later, the way in which these rules came into being will have been completely been forgotten. This would give us the impression of the rules having always been there—from the beginnings of time. This is the process of institutionalization. Further, we can see that the process of institutionalization obscures the workings of power, leaving us with the illusion that the situation we are faced with is natural, self-evident, and eternal. It then appears to us that policemen just are tall, and it does not even occur to us to question the hows, whys, and wherefores of the situation.

This description I have given of the processes of institutionalization is exactly how ideology is usually described. As is well known, the function of ideology is to give particular historical and contingent arrangements of the world the impression of necessity and inevitability. As Roland Barthes put it, ideology transforms history into nature. Thus, I would say that the processes of institutionalization are identical to the workings of ideology, and, indeed, each is an aspect of the other. Institutionalization is ideology made manifest.

The thing about power is that the more one has, the more one is able to keep up the illusion of having clean hands, of being innocent, if you will. For example, the structure of the military is such that the General, having ordered his troops into action, can sit having a quiet evening meal, while the dirty of work of killing is being done by others elsewhere. But even though the soldiers are doing the dirty work, the structure of the situation is such that even they need not feel any personal responsibility for the consequences of their actions. This is possible because a function of bureaucratic structures (and hierarchy in general) is to dissipate responsibilities so that it appears that no actual individuals are responsible for what is taking place. The General has the possibility of sleeping with an easy conscience because (a) he is not doing the actual dirty work, and (b) he has given this order in the service of something greater than him—his country, his people, and so on—and so can actually feel virtuous and noble while other human beings are being slaughtered. Meanwhile, the soldier has the possibility of easing his conscience by virtue of the fact that he is only following orders. He can think that as the intention and decision to propel him into action came from elsewhere, that is where ultimate responsibility must lie. There are two caveats I need to make, however. First, I would like to stress that these are possibilities, not certainties; guilt and responsibility are never machined away in their entirety—many a soldier and even General ends up traumatized. The second caveat is to say that I am not arguing that one should do away with organizational hierarchies, structures, and bureaucracies (which is an impossibility), or that the primary purpose of these systems is to machine away responsibility (and, therefore, guilt). I am suggesting that there is something intrinsic to the nature of hierarchical structures that allows them to be used in this way.

We can also get to see, in this scenario, how rationales are being mobilized to bolster activities. Like the schoolteacher, each can claim that they are only following the rules. It should be stressed, again, that, on the whole, these "rules" are experienced as naturally occurring injunctions: to love one's country, to stand up when the teacher comes into the classroom, to defend one's way of life, and so on.

The analogy of the army also helps us see why it is that the rawest and crudest instances of racism are often seen in the most deprived areas. The captains of industry, or you and me sitting having a cappuccino in Covent Garden, are able, just like the Generals, to make it appear that our hands are cleaner than they actually are.

The analogy of the classroom, although useful, of course seriously misrepresents the ways in which such rules arise. In the classroom, the teacher made a conscious decision to invent the rules in order to manipulate the students. In real life, there is no such Machiavellian figure, or international conspiracy, planning how to benefit certain groupings and disenfranchise others. This is the same as the problem that arises in evolutionary theory: how do we end up with things that look like intricate designs despite there being no designer? And the answer in this sociological and psychological arena is the same as in the biological one. These structures emerge and are thrown up by the processes of interaction that take place in the field of power relations.

In the descriptions I have given so far, I have made things appear more fixed and simple than they actually are. Let me correct that now. Institutions, like cultures, are not homogenous in the sense of sustaining a single ideology. In any one moment there are any number of ideologies, in all sorts of shapes and guises, contesting and struggling against each other. One rule might be, we must make money for our shareholders; another rule might be, we must look after our workers; another might be, we must concern ourselves with the environment, and so on. The conflict between these values and their supporters are what we commonly call politics.

For ideology to function, it must remain invisible; it must be as though it simply was not there. The reasons, the rationales for acting in certain ways, must be given a basis in something else, in something rational. This invisibility is one reason why the issue of institutional racism is so intractable, and allows numerous commentators to say, with equanimity and conviction, that there is no such thing.

Now you see me, now you don't: the vicissitudes of institutional racism

Since institutions (no less than individuals) emerge from and reside within psycho-social discourses, they will, of necessity, come to embody, reproduce, and reinforce the prevailing ideologies and conventions. The denigration of women and the linkage of blackness with badness are two of these. So, all of us, all institutions, must embody and reproduce in some way the discourses that we inhabit and that inhabit us. I want to stress the phrase "in some way": this embodiment and reproduction is not the same everywhere and for all people—it is not hegemonic. To repeat: it is continually contested and modified. So, I am not espousing a crude pessimistic determinism in which things are fixed forever. The point is that something exists (for example, in the British context, the theme of Black and White) that *necessitates* contestation.

Thus, all institutions will come to have structures that somehow work in the direction of privileging males over females, Whites over Blacks, and so on. The evidence for this is found at a statistical level. But because the mechanisms of marginalization are invisible, there exists the possibility of explaining away these facts in a variety of ways, and it is to these I will now turn. (In what follows, I continue to make my points through a discussion on "race" rather than other "differences".)

The denial of the existence of racism is integral to racism itself. It is part of what makes it work. As we saw in the Stephen Lawrence case, if there is no problem in the first place, then nothing needs to be done. Always, another reason—not racism—is put forward to explain what has occurred. Recall Scarman at the start of Chapter Six, claiming that the police's behaviour was due to "errors of judgment, in a lack of imagination and flexibility, but not in deliberate bias or prejudice" (Scarman Report, Par. 4.62, p. 64). And also, Channel 4's claim that the denigration of Shilpa Shetty was not due to racism, but to a culture and class clash.

It is the nature of statistical evidence that some of the data that constitute that evidence will directly contradict the statistical truth. For example, a statistical truth might be "most of the apples in this basket are red". However, it is also true that some of the apples in this same basket are green. What takes place next is that these particular truths are used to deny the reliability of the statistical truth. This is like using the fact that *some* of the apples in the basket are green to deny the statistical truth that *most* of the apples in the basket are red. For example, it is true that some educators have reached the highest echelons of their profession and become university professors. This, then, is used to make the problem one of particular individuals. It is said that if Winston and Satish are able to become professors, then the fact that Delroy, Meena, and Sandra have not been able to must have to do with some difficulty in them. This, then, is one of the main strategies used to render institutional racism invisible. What is being said is that institutional racism does not exist, and that the problem as such is *within* particular individuals.

On some occasions, when it becomes blatantly clear that something racialized has indeed taken place, the individualizing strategy is once again called upon to do its work. Now it is the "bad apple" theory, and it is used to say that it is this or that particular policeman, or social worker, or whoever, who is, unfortunately, racist. And if we cast out these individuals, things will be all right. Recall that Scarman had made recourse to this strategy, too. "Racial prejudice does manifest itself occasionally in the behaviour of a few officers on the street" (Scarman Report, Par. 4.63, p. 64).

The interplay between visibility and invisibility is a complex one. The question one always needs to attend to is: when do people of colour become invisible and when visible? The following story draws out some of the intricacies.

Recently, I was invited to contribute to a training programme to do with leadership which was designed specifically for the so-called ethnic minority members of a number of organizations. By now, it is clear what is meant by ethnic minority—the darkies. Anyway, I arrived at lunchtime and there in the dining room of this conference centre were two groups having lunch, and it was very clear which was the group I was going to be engaging with. One table was entirely White, and the other entirely Black (apart from the two White organizers responsible for them). Recall, this is the same situation that Thiederman found herself faced with in Chapter Six.

I wondered how it was that that such a powerful division had come about in the dining room, given that we were not living under a system of apartheid. I was told that those at the White table were here for stage two of the main training. When the first training had been initiated, it had been noticed that the membership was entirely

White. It had, therefore, been decided to run one specifically for the ethnic minorities, and so here they were, attending stage one of the same training, while the Whites at the other table were there attending stage two of the same training. This is why the tables were colour-coded. So far, so good. What had taken place seemed to me to be a good thing: the trainers had noticed the problem and tried to do something about it.

During the training session, I described the powerful impact the colour-coded dining room had on me when I first entered it. Then one of the Black members told us that, on arriving on this course, he was surprised to see a White colleague from *his* organization in the other training. He was doubly surprised because he did not know (a) that the colleague, whom he thought he knew quite well, was in an ongoing training, and (b) he did not even know about the existence of that training. And then he was further surprised to discover two more White colleagues from his organization also on that training.

How are we to understand what is going on? Clearly something very powerful had gone on in the organization so that the lines of communication had circumnavigated this person, or gone through him as though he were not there. He was invisible to those who had disseminated information regarding the training. We might surmise that unconsciously—or perhaps consciously—the disseminators discounted him as a potential candidate for that training.

We might surmise further that on his return to his organization following this training, if he were to question how and why he was rendered invisible, it is very likely that it would be explained away as a one-off, that it was an oversight of some kind, and that it was not done intentionally by anyone, à la Scarman. And, no doubt, this rendition would at some level be true: no one individual intentionally excluded him. There must have been a chain of communication of A telling B about the training, who made a passing reference about it to C at the photocopying machine, and so on. And somehow, this chain never included the Black person in question. It is really hard to comprehend how this can happen given that (a) there was no conspiracy, and (b) any one of the people who knew could have easily linked him into the information chain. This is exactly what makes the process of institutionalization such a powerful and efficient mechanism in perpetuating ideologies, privileges, and divisions. Its potency lies in its very silence and apparent non-existence.

In my experience, what often happens next is that if the Black person persists and does not buy into the one-off explanation, then they are seen as difficult and as having a chip on their shoulder. It is the case that when one does not feel heard, one either gives up or is compelled to shout louder and louder, until one's voice gets shrill in its insistence, and the Black person gets to sound as if they are whining. The whining does get heard, and is used to condemn the character of the complainer as weak in some way, which in turn distracts from the content of the actual complaint.

Alternatively, the voice might become angry. Now the Black person is experienced as threatening and disruptive. One of the defences put up by the institution (more precisely, people who constitute the institution) is one in which it is said that there is no basis in reality for the complaint; there is no conspiracy to keep Black people down; the event that took place is a one-off and, therefore, meaningless. If this were true, then the conclusion that one is forced to draw is that the difficulties must lie within the Black person. The protestor becomes perceived as the problem. In effect, what has taken place is that the Black person has been diagnosed as being paranoid.

The thing to note in these not improbable scenarios is the fact that what has become visible is the Black person as bad (angry), mad (paranoid), or weak (whining), and what remains invisible is that which has set off the whole situation in the first place.

There is another lesson to be learnt from this scenario. The fact that a "special" training was offered to the ethnic minorities can be construed as positive discrimination. This special training is a compensation for a failure within "the system". However, if this failure is kept invisible, then the only thing that is visible is apparently that "They are getting special treatment! They are being favoured over us!" We can see, then, that if the "compensation" is the only thing that is registered or noticed, it can set off feelings of resentment, jealousy, and envy in the mainstream population. Reports in the mainstream media tend to pick up on and report exactly these sorts of "favours", which, in turn, inflame the populist mind.

This resentment in the mainstream gets further fuelled by a sense of being accused and blamed for being one of the better off; this is particularly galling when it seems that it is "they" that are the better off. To put the privileged mainstream through a training to tell them that they are in the grip of "institutional racism" is no help in a moment like this; it just further fuels the antipathies, and generates an impasse. "What institutional racism?" is the outraged cry. "Just look at the special treatment they are getting—they are jumping housing queues and get all sorts of state benefits, while we have to wait for years".

One last point: curious, is it not, that the organizers thought to invite me to contribute to the "Black" training, and not to the "White" one?

Lineage and typology

I will take up some additional reasons as to why it is so hard to see the workings of institutional racism through another anecdote. An organization convened a workshop to look at and think about the experiences of its Black members in order to reflect on its possible unconscious processes. During this workshop, one of the White participants said, "I am not responsible for what happened in earlier times and places. I did not colonize Africa and have nothing to do with slavery. I am an individual and I treat others as individuals—some people I like more and others less. I am just like everyone else."

This is not an uncommon reaction from those in the mainstream; they feel unfairly criticized and accused of doing something, or feel unfairly blamed and made responsible for the sins of their fathers and their fathers. Now, I have a lot of sympathy for what this person is saying. And yet, something more complicated must be going on. To understand what that might be, we need to recall the fact that racialized discourses conceived the racialized "us" in two sorts of ways—vertically and horizontally.

By vertically, I mean *lineage*, the so-called bloodline that is drawn from one's ancestors to the present day. This "us" stretches back in time, and, indeed, to the beginnings of time. And by horizontally, I mean typology. This "us" is an "us" because all those that belong are of the same "type", Caucasian or Black or Mongoloid, or whatever. In contrast to the first kind of "us" that lives in time, the second kind of "us" spreads across in space (Banton, 1987).

These two versions of "us" are not usually distinguished, and, depending on the rationalization one wants to mobilize, one or other of these will be utilized. In saying that, as an individual living in the year 2004, she really is not responsible for the historical processes of colonization and slavery, this participant is saying that she is not part of the lineage version of "us". While there might be a bloodline between her and her ancestors, she is saying that she is not responsible for their crimes, and should not be held responsible for the actions that they took. To this I say, fair enough, I agree.

However, in the here-and-now she is, in fact, benefiting from privileges accorded to her as a White person by the processes that have become institutionalized. And this occurs without her having to do anything. In other words, while she is personally not responsible through *lineage,* she none the less benefits by virtue of *typology*. This occurs because the actions of the ancestors have prepared the world to be biased towards the Whites. Thus, while this participant's rejection of lineage is understandable and visible, she renders invisible the benefits she derives from typology.

Her cry that she is an individual is an unconscious strategy to avoid countenancing that she does, in fact, get benefits from the way that the system is structured. This helps her to say, truthfully, like the Ps, "But I haven't done anything!" Maybe so, but one is never just an individual. One cannot not belong to groups, and the relations between groupings are always power relations. You can see what is happening here. The Black is systematically marginalized by virtue of the grouping s/he is part of, while the denial of the significance of the groupings by the White person is a means of obscuring the workings of power.

If there is anything at all to the idea of institutional racism, then we would have to admit that those at the centre, those that benefit from the processes of institutionalization, must have a vested interest in not knowing about the conditions that put them there. This is because any change in the situation would necessarily entail a dilution of the privileges that they are currently accorded.

CHAPTER ELEVEN

Islam: the new black

The fear of Islam is burgeoning all over the world. Islam is become the new Black. Is there really something about Islam to be feared, or is the fear born of a kind of racist paranoia, a fantasy? The short answer is that both are true, but in complicated ways.

The first thing to notice is that there is a problem with the question itself. As we have already seen, we cannot speak of Islam as though it were a unity.

Polarizations such as "Islam *vs.* the West" allow us to position Islam outside "the West" and as its opposite. The structure of the polarization is in itself curious, not merely because it suggests two unified ways of thinking, but because of the mix of categories; on one side is a religion and on the other side something more amorphous, but having connotations with modernity. Further, it suggests that there are no disputes within Islam, and all opposition to its ways come from outside it. But this is not the case.

Take the fatwa declared by the National Fatwa Council in Malaysia in 2008, who took it upon themselves to ban the country's Muslim population from practising Yoga, because they feared that yoga practice was the beginnings of the slippery slope to Hinduism. The suggestion was readily lampooned in "the West", but less well publicized was the outrage expressed by Muslims in Malaysia and elsewhere. One voice among a great many was Farish Noor, writing in the *Daily Times* of Lahore:

> I have spent . . . my life trying to convince people that Islam is a moderate religion . . . It has been a hard task in recent years—one needlessly made harder by the narrow cultural dogmatism of some of my fellow Muslims. . . . Malaysian Muslims are more closely policed than ever before, with more and more laws and restrictions on how we dress, eat, speak, interact and even marry. What will these pedants think of next? A fatwa on karate, kung fu, pilates? Nobody voted for them, and they should stay out of our lives. How will we ever build a modern, tolerant Islam if Muslims are not even allowed to exercise in peace? [Noor, 2008, p. 16]

Put under pressure by the protest, the Malaysian Prime Minister, Abdullah Ahmad Badawi, diluted the fatwa, saying that it was permissible for Muslims to do yoga as long as they did not "chant". Idiocies like these are found everywhere, not just in Islam: for example, the Evangelical Christians' insistence regarding the promotion of Creationism in schools as a credible alternative to evolutionary theory.

Neither can we easily divide Muslims into fundamentalists *vs.* moderates, because there are a number of different claims as to who really understands the fundamentals, Sunni, Shia, Wahhabi, leading to many a bloody dispute. The differences in opinion regarding the fundamentals of Islam are readily observable in the following. In Pakistan in 1954, there were riots by Islamic extremists who wanted the government to declare members of the Ahmadiyya sect as non-Muslims. Two justices, Munir and Kayani, were asked to produce a report on the matter. Their report included an investigation into the theology and philosophy of Islam. Shamsie (2011) tells us that they asked

> 10 *ulema* (Islamic scholars) to lay out the minimum conditions a person must satisfy to call themselves a Muslim. After reproducing the wildly divergent answers, the justices write: 'Need we make any comment except that no two learned divines are agreed on the fundamental . . . And if we adopt the definition given by any one of the ulema, we remain Muslims according to the view of that *alim* [scholar] but *kafirs* [infidels] according to the definition of everyone else. [p. 30]

Despite the range of opinion "within" Islam, is there something about it, nevertheless, to be feared?

In Britain, from the sixteenth century on, there has been a law that made blasphemy against the Christian God a crime. Over the centuries, the law had been used to persecute various persons and groups, one of the more recent cases being the prosecution brought by Mary Whitehouse in 1977 against *Gay News* for publishing the poem "The love that dares to speak its name". The Secretary General of the Muslim Council of Britain, Iqbal Sacranie, wanted the same right for those of the Islamic faith. He said that the voicing of any views critical of the ideas put forward in the Koran should be made illegal, because this would be an insult to the Prophet (BBC Radio 4, *The Moral Maze*, broadcast 14 July 2004). He wanted this right because the attempt to charge Rushdie under the law of blasphemy had failed, as the law only applied to Christianity.

Rather than remove the suffocating and antiquated notion of blasphemy entirely from the statute books, the self-declared Christian Prime Minister, Tony Blair, saw a religious ally in Sacranie, and granted him his wish by pushing through the *Racial and Religious Hatred Act* in 2006 (against the wishes of a great many others). Now consider this: according to Sharia law, death is the only fit punishment for not only the crime of heresy, but also apostasy. In Pakistan, for example, there are approximately 700 to 1000 executions a year for the charge of insulting the Prophet. Leaving aside whether or not people should be killed for insulting the Prophet, the issue turns on what one considers an insult. For example, scepticism in itself is not an incitement to hate. But the zealot would consider a sceptical attitude towards the mythology and content of the Koran as an insult to the Prophet and, so, punishable by law. Sacranie wants the state to legitimate and support *a very particular reading of Islam*, a very particular fundamentalist voice, and, in the process, silence other dissenting democratic Islamic voices. While there are indeed some Moslems who hold these kinds of extreme beliefs, there are also untold others to whom such ideas are anathema, for example the newspaper columnist Yasmin Alibhai-Brown. Then there is Salman Rushdie. His blasphemy consisted of the temerity to feature a character in a story that was reminiscent of the prophet (although the fatwa was on the basis that he was an apostate). And if you were to discount Rushdie's stance on grounds of his being an apostate, then you need go no further than reading Ziauddin Sardar's powerful volume called *Desperately Seeking Paradise*. He is a true believer in the Prophet, who nevertheless finds it possible to subtitle his book: *Journeys of a* Sceptical *Muslim*. For the likes of Sacranie, there would be no possibility of an Islamic version of Monty Python's film, *The Life of Brian*.

If Iqbal Sacranie is the moderate voice of Islam, then to my mind there is indeed something to fear. What is frightening to me is not just the world vision of the fundamentalists, but the fact that politicians of all persuasions seem keen to help them do their repressive work. For example, Canada has been considering allowing the setting up of Sharia courts to allow the so-called Islamic community *to see to their own*. I say so-called community because, as I have repeatedly been saying, it does not speak with one voice. There is ample protest and dissent from the Moslem population, particularly from women (for example Homa Arjomand), who fear and resist being delivered into the hands of the Imams.

We have other examples here in the UK: the Court of Appeal ruled in March 2005 that the sixteen-year-old Shabina Begum was to be allowed to wear full jilbab instead of the school uniform: shalwar, khameez, and headscarf. The ruling was driven by a reading of the Human Rights Convention, which grants persons a right to express their religious stance in public. However, this ruling was not universally welcomed by followers of the Prophet in this country: Dr Ghayasuddin Siddiqui, Chairman of the Muslim Institute, said, "This may be a victory for human rights but it is also a victory for fundamentalism" (Rosenberg, 2005). A year later, the Law Lords overturned the verdict, and found in favour of the school (Rosenberg, 2006).

Kenan Malik gives another example:

> In 2005, the Australasian Police Multicultural Advisory Bureau published a 'religious diversity handbook' which advised that 'In incidents such as domestic violence, police need to have an understanding of the traditions, ways of life and habits of Muslims' . . . The implication, as Jourmanah El Matrah of the Islamic Women's Welfare Council observed, is that 'one needs to be more tolerant of violence against Muslim women' rather than Muslim women 'should be entitled to the same protection as everyone else'. [Malik, 2008, p. 203]

Peculiarly, the Imam is granted the status of spokesperson for Muslims of all kinds everywhere; this has come about because, when it comes to Islam, religion is conflated with community and culture. This would be like presuming that the views of the Bishops of the Anglican Church are representative of the range of views of ordinary folk in the UK. And, on occasions when the Bishops have had the temerity to voice criticism of some government policy, they have been met by howls of outrage from the politicians who feel encroached upon. In this instance, what is good for the goose is clearly not good for the gander. Anyhow, the error of conflating religion with community and culture is compounded further by the assumption that they all think with one mind. The result is that liberal society delivers the Muslims that are its potential allies in the project of "live and let live" into the hands of their enemy—those who would suffocate thought. The situation is too tragic to be called an irony.

The main point of the above discussion is worth underlining again. It is not possible to simply respect "their" differences from "us", because there are many differences of opinion *within* "them". In respecting and validating one "cultural" view, one is inevitably taking a moral stand against the other "cultural" views among "them". Non-interference is an impossibility. The act of non-interference, "our" silence, is an act, an act that effectively ends up supporting the more powerful grouping within the "them".

So, to now directly answer the question: is there something about Islam to be feared? My answer is that it is not Islam *per se* that is to be feared, but the way that it has been appropriated by some believers, and what they seek to do with it. But what of the riposte that the Islamists are merely using passages found in the Koran, and so the problem is with Islam *per se* and not just with interpretation and appropriation? If Islam is to be feared on this basis, then so are most other religions. Christianity in itself does not stir up any fear in me, but in the hands of Mary Whitehouse or the right-wing evangelicals in the USA, it certainly does. Hinduism in the hands of the Hindutva terrifies me, as does the Zionist version of Judaism, and on and on. There are problematic passages to be found in the holy books of most faiths. For example, in the Judaeo-Christian tradition: the Book of Leviticus (particularly chapter 20, verses 9–21) enjoins one *to put to death* those who have committed acts of adultery, incest, bestiality, and homosexuality. The same fate is also to be meted out to those who curse their parents. While some Jews and Christians take these passages unquestioningly as *instructions* from God, happily, others do not.

Projection

But it is also the case that some of the fear of the Muslim is a paranoid fear born of projection. My thoughts about that are as follows. Although there are several million Moslems in this country, they remain mysterious; they remain othered. Their mysterious otherness is an empty space ready to be filled with all kinds of projections and fantasies. Through these mechanisms Moslems become both lascivious sensualists, and, simultaneously, fierce puritans. As Freud has pointed out, the unconscious knows no contradiction (Freud, 1915, pp. 186–187). In these kinds of emotional and thought processes, parts easily come to stand for wholes—but not in any which way. In their book, *The Established and the Outsiders*, Elias and Scotson show us that these associations are ideologically driven, the image of the outsiders being modelled on a "minority of the worst" of them, while the image of the established is modelled on a "minority of the best" of them. Elias and Scotson call this mechanism "an emotional generalization from the few to the whole" (Elias & Scotson, 1994, p. 159).

It is through this sort of process that the Jihadists (who are few in comparison) come to stand for all followers of Islam. Any criticism and dissenting opinion regarding the world view of the Jihadist activates the liberal taboo against racism (because to criticize one is to criticize all), and silence follows. Let me underline this point: it is because we are unable or unwilling to discriminate between varieties of Islamic belief and practice that we end up by homogenizing them, and so either idealizing them all, or damning them all.

Further consequences follow out of the fact that in the Western imagination, the Moslem is located outside Europe, and is made container of all that is opposite of the sensibilities that are attributed to the European (recall Stone and Stone-Romero's descriptions from Chapter Seven). On this basis, there are multiple unconscious and conscious denigrations and vilifications continually in play in regard to the idea of the Moslem. The Moslem has been made the opposite of the European "us". Recall also the advice given by the Home Office when collecting "ethnic" data: that Greek Cypriots were to be thought of as a part of the White category, and, by implication, the (Moslem) Turkish Cypriots were not.

What can take place now, in Freud's language, is a reaction formation (Freud, 1905). A reaction formation is a mechanism that is used in the service of obscuring something by emphasizing its opposite.

Vertigo might be obscured by a love of sky-diving, greed by anorexia, and so on. The mechanism is only partly successful, in that it does not resolve the issue, only represses and subjugates it. The subjugated remains somewhere in the wings, leaving us ever haunted by a discomfort that is hard to name. What must not become visible, to oneself as much as others, are one's real feelings of antipathy about *some* Moslems because of what they say or do. In other words, the feelings of antipathy are rendered unconscious. And, in order to keep them there, they are buffered by their opposites—a fierce non-judgemental acceptance of "them" come what may, mixed in with manic admiration. Moslems are now fetishized. The strategy can be described as one of trying to ensure that any feelings of antipathy are completely covered up so that no one can say that "your racism is showing".

There is another, much referred to, component of this mechanism—liberal guilt. A certain kind of guilt has arisen in some who are of a liberal persuasion, to do with the excesses of colonization, imperialism, and modern consumerism. While there might be grounds for this guilt, in excessive amounts it adds to the paralysis and leads to the Manichaeism that "we" are bad and "they" are good. To think that some of them might be "bad" is difficult to countenance, because, in doing so, the liberal fears that they are allying themselves with the forces of oppression. According to this position, they are not allowed to conceive of the possibility that some of "them" might be in the wrong; we are back with Russell's "fallacy of the superior virtue of the oppressed".

To repeat once again, what is needed is more discrimination, not less. Quite simply, "they" are not all the same, and neither are "we". I need to work hard to continually resist the collapse of categories. I need to be able to discriminate between the murderous Islamo-fascist and Mr Khan, the shopkeeper down the road.

Riding the tiger

More troubling than silence is the fact that, bizarrely, when faced with the excesses of the Shariat, some sections of the revolutionary left support it, and have gone so far as to develop a deliberate strategy of overtly siding with fundamentalist Islamists. One reason they have followed this course is that some of them have fallen for the

Manichaean fallacy and think that my enemy's enemy is bound to be my friend. According to this simplistic logic, Al Qaeda is on the same side as the Green Party and the radical Left because they all variously take a stance against the usual suspects, George Bush, Imperialism, large corporations, and so on (Cohen, 2007). Even Foucault became intoxicated by Khomeini and the Iranian fundamentalists; he defended them, saying, "They don't have the same regime of truth as ours ... [in their regime] not only is saying one thing that means another not a condemnable ambiguity, it is, on the contrary, a necessary and highly prized additional level of meaning" (Foucault, 1988, quoted in Wheen, 2004, p. 84). Foucault seems to share the same view as Stone and Stone-Romero's cross-cultural "psychology" that we came across in Chapter Seven; both agree that lying is part of their culture, and so to be respected and tolerated. I have to say that this is not my experience of Iranians, or other exotics.

Even so, the alliance is perplexing, given that the left-wing revolutionary aspires to a very different kind of Utopia from that of the religious fundamentalist. However, both are in agreement about the "means" to each of their different "ends": the current world order needs to be overturned—violently if necessary. As late as 2000, the left-wing intellectuals Hardt and Negri were still besotted by the Iranian revolution, despite all the horrors that had been perpetuated in its name. They said in their book, *Empire* (2001), that the Iranian revolution was to be celebrated because not only had it rejected Western hegemony, it was also "the first post-modernist revolution". These elements from the left believe that they can appropriate the vitriol of the fundamentalist to help kick-start *their* left-wing revolution. In Britain, Chris Harman of the Socialist Worker's Party has said that the revolutionary capacity of the Islamists "could be tapped for progressive purposes" (Harman, 1994, quoted in Phillips, 2006, p. 187). He, too, thinks that he can ride the tiger for his own purposes.

It is not just the so-called "revolutionaries" that have fêted reactionary Islamists, but also the establishment. British and American governments have a long and disreputable history of trying to use militant Islamists to achieve foreign policy objectives in the service of empire and capitalism (Curtis, 2010a). In 1953, the British plotted with the militant Devotees of Islam to overthrow the democratically elected Mossadeq government in Iran. The British also funded the Muslim Brotherhood in Egypt to undermine Nasser. In 1970, "British officials were still describing the Brotherhood as 'a potentially handy weapon'" (Curtis, 2010b, p. 27). This was exactly the kind of arrogant thinking that later led the governments of the USA and the UK to support the Ayatollah Khomeni in Iran, then, when that particular tiger turned, to support the dictator Saddam Hussein in his illegal war against the Iranian Ayatollahs, and then the Muhajaddin against the Russians.

Curtis tells us,

> the attacks of 9/11 and 7/7 have made Britain revise but not end its secret affair with radical Islam. In the occupation of southern Iraq Britain ... [connived] with Shia militias. Liberal, secular forces were bypassed after the invasion, and when Britain withdrew ... in effect it handed responsibility for 'security' to these militias. [*ibid.*]

Similarly, as "the West" withdraws from Afghanistan, it is negotiating a way of handing power back to the Taliban, who, it will be remembered, are the villains that the West rode in to free Afghanis from in the first place: it was asserted that the war was a moral crusade, in particular to free Afghani women from the bondage of Taliban ideology.

Each time the tiger has turned and savaged the rider. It is embarrassing to realize what a significant role our meddling has played, how complicit we have been in the creation of these monsters that terrorize us. So, this is another reason that we avert our gaze, we do not want to see how we have contributed to our own misfortunes, and, in order not to see, we blind ourselves.

The fact that the left and liberals in general are struck dumb means that questions being raised are primarily by those on the right of the political spectrum. And they are having a field day, with so much ammunition for their xenophobic agenda. For example, in her book *Londonistan*, Phillips (2006) raises a number of very valid points, but she places them in the midst of her beleaguered world view in which the English are being swamped by inferior others, and in the process are losing their values, identity, and culture, and so on.

Then there are other reasons that are to do with fear as to why we mute and blind ourselves. We do not want to look at what is frightening, quite simply because it is frightening. The frightening reality is that there are an increasing number of Jihadists whose wish is to destabilize the world, Islamacize it, and compel everyone to live according to the tenets of Sharia Law. This is no secret and it is no exaggeration. Having said that, I need to keep repeating the caveat, for myself as much as anyone else, that not every Moslem is a Jihadist. It is as well to remember that the Jihadists are not just targeting the West, they are also attempting to radicalize the other 99% of the Islamic world that are reluctant to join this nihilistic dash to Paradise.

My speculation is that it is fear as much as Machiavellian motivation that drove the likes of Tony Blair to write legislation that supports the radical 1% in their efforts to dominate the other 99%. It is much less frightening to disagree with Salman Rushdie than with a fanatical Islamist, because the latter has not only threatened violent retribution, he has carried it out on a number of occasions. As far as I know, Rushdie did not send any death threats to Germaine Greer when she declared him to be stupid and should have jolly well known better than write *The Satanic Verses*.

The spiritual is political

The mistaken belief that it is possible to separate out the internal world from the external has led the equality discourses into many a cul-de-sac. What we have seen is that the private cannot help but be public. Nevertheless, we continue to be bewildered by the mythology that the external social world is distinct from the internal psychological world. For decades, the feminists have been challenging this dichotomy with the adage, the personal is political. The Jihadists have gone one step further to say that the spiritual is political. Here, I think that they are right. The practical and the ethical cannot be differentiated. My ethics, my ideas about what constitutes a moral life, of necessity involves ideas and practices about how I am to live with others. The fact that the liberal conscience operates as though the (private) ethical is distinct from the (public) practical allows the Jihadist a powerful strategy. They use the language of faith and spirituality to paralyse the liberal, and then walk in and take over. Through this device, the liberal is made fodder.

But, as we have seen, these very same Western liberal democracies have not been shy of suspending the liberal taboos of respect and non-interference as and when it has suited their commercial and political agenda, rudely intruding and interfering in the "private" matters of other nations and territories.

CHAPTER TWELVE

Tolerating discrimination: discriminatory tolerance

Chapter Ten attended to the processes unfair discrimination and marginalization that have been institutionalized and so are invisible as well as unconscious. I now want to turn to the more conscious realm in order to think about the notion of tolerance. I will do this through the problem that is called "cultural difference", which is said to occur when one is faced with a way of life or a belief system that is at odds with one's own. The diversity promulgator's solution to this problem is celebration; they reframe the difference from problem to asset. In their view, there is no necessity to give an account or explanation for the differences, they just "are": this is our way and that is their way and both are valid. Neither is there any necessity for the celebrator to engage their mental faculties, because if they just celebrate and party hard enough then they will somehow find themselves in equality heaven. As we have seen, there is no place for politics in the diversity movement, and so they are easily led to the presumption that "they" (the exotic others) think with one mind. To the diversity way of thinking, *they* really are "all the same" and not the problematic, politicized, and conflicted complex multiplicity that they actually are.

Rather than follow the diversity advocates into their default stance of automatic acceptance and celebration, I want to engage more fully with the questions already asked: should one always and necessarily accept and tolerate every way of life simply because it is "their" way? What is the ethical course of action? Ought I to try to tolerate that which I find intolerable? And ought I to try to tolerate the intolerant? These questions pose another: what does the activity of tolerance actually consist of?

The politics of tolerance

In what follows, keep in mind the dual fallacies: the fallacy of the superior virtue of the oppressed, as well as the fallacy of the intrinsic wickedness of the oppressors. A person is never fully *either* an oppressor *or* one of the oppressed; recall the jazz-playing, wife-beating, beleaguered factory worker in Chapter Two. Keep in mind also the insights of Hegel, who remind us with the master–slave analogy that power is never absolute. Elias builds on this to say that power is not an amulet which one is either in the possession of or not; no one has complete absolute power and no one is entirely powerless; rather, there are degrees of power between protagonists. So, rather than think of people having or not having power (power as a noun, a thing, and, therefore, a possession), better to think of power relations and power differentials between protagonists. In other words, the picture is never as black and white as it often might seem.

Tolerance is often spoken of in the abstract, as an ideal. When spoken of in the abstract, tolerance has the appearance not only of being a universal ethical ideal, but also apolitical. However, it is always the case that it is some who are doing the tolerating and others who are the tolerated; the situation is never symmetric. The activity of tolerance is taking place in a power-relational field, and so the meaning and experience of the more powerful tolerating something about the less powerful is going to be different from when the less powerful tolerate something about the more powerful.

In actual fact, the less powerful are likely to be in situations in which they are *continually* obliged to tolerate (that is, put up with) the attitudes, requirements, expectations, and ways of the more powerful. Their options in the matter are heavily constrained, and so they have very limited choices available to them (but they are never entirely powerless). When the master of the house humiliates the servant and treats them with blatant contempt, the servant swallows hard, subjugates their rage, and endures the insult in order to keep their job and feed their family. In this sort of case, tolerance stands for helpless compliance. So, rather than tolerance, perhaps the better term here is endurance. Moreover, this kind of "tolerance", that of the underdog, although it is going on all the time, is not noticed or recognized as the activity of tolerance; it is taken for granted and so remains unnoticed.

Meanwhile, the more powerful have more possibility to choose what they will or will not tolerate. For example, think of what takes place between parents and their children. The parent decides whether or not, and how much, they will tolerate a number of difficult behaviours from their child. Here, tolerance can sometimes become indulgence. But, more generally, when the more powerful tolerate something about the less powerful, then it is an act of patronage; a gift that can be retracted at any time. Now, because the activity of tolerance from the more powerful is an act of choice, it is more likely to be noticed, to be visible, and so be recognized as a generous and noble act.

We can now see more clearly the irony and the asymmetry. On the one hand, the "underdog" is the one who continually has to tolerate things, but this activity is not noticed, and neither is it named as tolerance; on the other hand, the occasional acts of tolerance and kindness dispensed by the more powerful, *because* they are choices, are noticed and come to be lauded and applauded. To anticipate a term not yet formally used in this work, the underdog gains no "recognition" for their ongoing tolerance, while the more powerful are granted this privilege for their acts of tolerance. Of these two versions of tolerance, the one alluded to by the equalities agenda is the latter, and embedded in this ideal of tolerance is the assumption of autonomy, of being able to choose.

Degrees of tolerance

Not all differences require the activity of tolerance. When the other and what they bring is appealing or interesting, then there is nothing *to tolerate*. We can easily celebrate, appreciate, and enjoy the differences and similarities between samosas and pies, between tortillas and chapattis. Tolerance is only required when faced with a difference that is problematic, and not all differences are problematic. For example, despite being an atheist, I am well able to tolerate those of my friends who believe in deities; as a meat eater and a consumer of alcohol, I am well able to tolerate vegetarians and teetotallers. But consider: in what I have just said I have not been required *to tolerate* anything. But if I am sitting with a smoker at a dinner table, then I do find that disagreeable. To continue to sit and converse with the smoker, I do have to tolerate discomfort. The point being that I am only required to exercise my capacity for tolerance when I am impinged upon by something that I find disagreeable.

And even then there are degrees of tolerance. At its mildest, in my day-to-day life I am continually called upon to tolerate little things that annoy me: the train is late again, the coffee is too weak, the shop assistant is unhelpful, and so on. More difficult to bear is the person at a dinner table who monologues, or the person on the train who talks incessantly and loudly on their mobile phone.

The psychology of tolerance

But what is it that is taking place when I say that I am tolerating something? It seems to me that what I am tolerating is not so much about what the other person is saying or doing *but my response to it*. Tolerance consists of the management of responses of discomfort or affront *arising in me*. Tolerance, then, is the containment of this internal response; it is an activity in which one is subjugating of a part of the self.

Consider the very young infant who is hungry or distressed and wants her mummy "NOW!" and nothing else will do; gratification has to be instantaneous or there is uproar. And then, slowly, over many months, with repeated experiences the infant comes to be able to tolerate, that is, hold on for longer and longer periods while her mummy warms the food, or washes her hands. With the help of the parents, the infant comes to develop a capacity for deferring gratification, of being able to tolerate the discomfort of hunger, until eventually the hunger pangs are tolerated for one whole minute; what an achievement that is. I think that for all of us, this is our first encounter with the capacity for tolerance through which we learn to tolerate feelings of discomfort *within* us. This is a lesson learnt with immense difficulty, with enormous protest, and great reluctance. It seems to me that these sorts of experiences are the precursor for the adult activity of tolerance born of ethical reasoning, which is what I turn to next.

What am I to do when faced with another who is saying or doing something that I strongly disapprove of: say I witness an act of bullying. What is the decent thing to do? Ought I to subjugate (tolerate) my disapproval and so allow things to continue? Ought I to breach the liberal taboo, to say something and "interfere"? And on what basis do I make that decision? Notice, we are *deciding* what to tolerate and what not to tolerate. In other words, the exercise of tolerance requires the engagement of one's discriminatory process; *tolerance is not the opposite of discrimination.*

Indiscriminate tolerance, of the kind that the diversity enthusiasts seem to advocate, to accept everything and all things, is dangerous nonsense as it leads to the annihilation of all internal responses and so a complete annihilation of the self. But the decision as to what we will or will not tolerate is not by any means solely rational, and neither is it fully ethical. I am much more likely to tolerate the rude behaviour of a large frightening man and much less likely to tolerate the same behaviour from someone I am not so intimidated by; I am much more likely to tolerate obnoxious behaviour from someone more powerful than me, say, my boss, than from my subordinate. There are two interlinked themes to be underlined here: first, self-interest (including self-preservation) is always in play in these discriminatory processes; in other words, fear and power relations come to play a critical role in what one ends up tolerating or not. But, as the saying goes, there is no such thing as a free lunch. On the occasions that I silence myself when *I think* something wrong is taking place, then the costs paid by me are feelings of shame and guilt. If it is also the case that I have remained silent because the other is much more powerful than me, then feelings of humiliation are added to the mix of emotions. These emotions can be experienced as "attacks" on the self, in the sense that I feel bad when I am subject to these sorts of emotions.

We can see that what tolerance really means is "to endure" and "to put up with". There might well be acceptance of a situation, and if that acceptance is genuine, then one could say that one is at peace with the situation. But being at peace is not the same as being peaceful. One might be at peace with the situation that one has resolved to put up with, but that state of mind is not peaceful. It is likely to contain turbulence, and what one is tolerating is the turbulence. To put it more strongly, to tolerate is to suffer. If one finds oneself in a state of pure acceptance without any disturbance, then the activity of tolerance is unnecessary as there is nothing *to tolerate*. Tolerance is the activity of *continuing* to put up with a state of discomfort due to something that *continues* to disturb one's equilibrium in some way. To be tolerating something is to be in a state of tension, a tension born of the demands of two conflicting sets of values, those of fairness and authenticity. The issue then becomes one of how to manage this tension.

Three (unhelpful) ways of dissolving the tension between authenticity and fairness

The values of liberalism point in two different directions. First is the duty to be true to oneself, of authenticity. Second is the duty to others, of non-interference and fairness. Not only are these two values always in a state of tension with each other, they need to remain so if one is to abide by the principle of "live and let live".

The imperialists and some kinds of fundamentalists collapse the tension by doing away with the duty to others; their principle is not "live and let live", but "*my way or no way*". As the imperialist is mostly convinced that their way is the right way, then they need feel no guilt nor shame at riding roughshod over the other.

Meanwhile, the diversity enthusiasts collapse the tension by ignoring the injunction to be true to oneself, and so end up practising a version of "*I defer to your way, and celebrate it*". Any doubts about whether "their" way is the right way would bring up feelings of guilt. The guilt is mobilized to crush one's own sense of right and wrong. But as they crush and abandon their own sensibilities, there must arise in them feelings of shame at negating and abdicating their ethical selves. My guess is that what happens now is that these feelings of shame are defended against by generating a state of manic positivity, admiring the other come what may. Any let-up on the activity of manically admiring the other would be dangerous, as it would allow in the possibility of thought and reflection, and this would rejuvenate the tension that has just been collapsed with so much effort. In this group, we find those who fetishize otherness.

And, finally, a certain kind of liberal does manage the feat of abiding by both duties, but only by the device of not having anything to do with "them". Through this means, it is easy enough to remain true to oneself, as well as not interfere with "them" and allow them the freedom to live according to their ways, as neither impinges on the other. But this strategy creates ghettos, and what they are actually practising is not "live and let live", but "*live and leave well alone*". This stance can breed a kind of superior complacency, born of the fact that as one is not doing down the other or oneself, there is no necessity to feel guilt or shame.

What alternatives are there? How is one to live with others while holding on to the tension between authenticity and fairness, without collapsing on one or other side of the fence? The situation is made complicated by the fact that I am unable to trust my response. How do I find out whether my antipathy is a racist response or whether it is an ethical one? (Recall the training committee in Chapter Eleven.) There are two different kinds of situations to be thought about here, one in which "they" and I are able and willing to have some conversation regarding the difficulties, and one in which "they" are not. I will begin with the former.

Live and leave well alone: the unwashed

Let us imagine an unlikely culture, members of which believe that it is not only bad to wash themselves, but also that it is morally wrong to do so. They have their rationales, having to do with a science of bacteriology (washing removes good bacteria from the body), allowing the body to find its "natural" bacterial balance, living as God intended, and so on. And let us say that in all other ways, they are perfectly reasonable human beings trying to lead normal lives, attending to their gardens, shopping, and so on. Unfortunately, they do rather smell. They themselves, being used to the odour, do not register it. When we speak to them about it, they are very reasonable, they listen, they explain, they engage in argument, but remain unconvinced; they think that this way of living would actually be good for us, too, but they are happy to let us follow our mistaken ways; they "live and let live".

The diversity enthusiast would have me somehow celebrate this difference, but, not being of a saintly disposition, I cannot imagine how I would do it. What would the multi-culturalists have me do in such a situation? How could I practise "equal but different"? The multi-culturalist would remind me that despite washing regularly, I, too, have a smell; so the situation is not that they smell and I do not, we all smell (and so are equal in this sense). It is just that their smell is different to mine. Equal but different: QED.

Despite being convinced of this argument intellectually, I would, nevertheless, have to draw heavily on my capacities for tolerance because I would have to find a way to endure, that is, tolerate, the discomfort set off in me by their odour. I imagine that their powerful odour would actually offend my sensibilities, and so I would have to put up with quite a lot of discomfort. According to the multi-culturalist paradigm, I should accept their ways and be careful not to offend them by making reference to the nature of their smell. Perhaps the term "smell" itself would become so charged that it would become unacceptable to use it in polite company. For me to continue to live in such a situation, it would require me to somehow distance myself from my olfactory mechanisms; in other words, I would have to find some way of cutting off from an aspect of my body.

But I imagine that what is also quite likely to occur in actual practice is that I will find myself tending to avoid being in their proximity, and, over time, this will lead to less and less intersection between my life and theirs. I will, of course, continue to speak of them respectfully, but will not actually have much to do with them in my day-to-day life. It is in this way, little step by unconscious step, that I will find myself inhabiting the familiar liberal solution of "live and leave well alone".

And if it turned out that the Unwashed were being unfairly discriminated against by mainstream society, then the lexicon adjusters would be telling us not to use the term "smell", because it was this category that was utilized to marginalize them. As we have already seen, this would do little to remedy the situation.

A corrective: from cultural difference to racism

In the above, I have vastly simplified the situation. I have created an extreme scenario in order to throw the predicaments into sharp relief. I have not, for example, taken account of the fact that not all of "them" will be sold on the practice of not washing, and many of "us" might wash so infrequently that one would be hard put to say where they belonged. Divisions would no doubt arise within them (as well as within the "us") around any number of matters concerning ritual, belief, and so forth. But, most importantly, the way I have constructed this scenario, there exists a material reality, an objective concrete reason for the difficulties arising in me (i.e., they really do smell); in other words, I have not had to consider the possibility that my negative response towards them is an outcome of my racist sensibilities.

And although this scenario captures mostly how we think of the predicaments created by "cultural differences", this is not actually how things are. When we look at ordinary life, we are hardly ever confronted by such cultural differences that literally nauseate us. In fact, as I think about it, I find it hard to come up with any "cultural differences" that are worthy of creating such a strong response of revulsion or nausea in me as might well be the case with "the Unwashed". In reality, it is mostly the case that whatever one's "culture", we all want similar things to each other: to be happy, to live in decent conditions, to work, to prosper. Although to the racialized imagination the psychological experience of repulsion might be as though one's sensibilities were being assaulted by something repugnant, mostly this is not what is actually happening.

For example, it is not unusual for a neighbour to be troubled by the noise emanating from next door, and bad feelings are bound to follow. If the neighbours are both "White", say, then the other is just a bad neighbour. However, if Mr Smith is being troubled by the noise is emanating from Mr Singh's residence, then the disturbance becomes racialized. The disturbance becomes reframed and what is said now is that problems are bound to arise because this is how "they" are—noisy and uncaring. No doubt the smell emanating from Mrs Singh's kitchen also comes to be experienced as an assault on the senses. It is in this sense that I mean that the disturbance has been racialized. And it will not be all one way. The Singhs might also say that the cooking smells emanating from the Smith kitchen are particularly unpleasant, and that "White people" do not wash properly in running water, instead they lie in dirty water in a bath, and so on. In saying that the Singhs, too, are well able to employ mechanisms of contempt, and that they are not just victims, I do not want to suggest that the situation is the same for each party. They are differently positioned in the power relational field, and so their activities will have different significations.

In sum, although these "differences" can trigger violent antipathies and even disgust, they have little real substance in themselves. *The cultural differences are vehicles, not causes.* Mostly, the "cultural differences" we come across are mundane and not particularly provocative in themselves. But then, these ordinary enough differences become cathected with hatreds and amplified into something repugnant by the activities of the racialized imagination.

It seems to me that this is one of the key flaws in the reasoning of the equalities projects generally (anti-racism, it should be said, did not fall into this error). They have mistaken "differences" to be the cause of the iniquities, and so have put all of their resources into solving this false problem. In sum, in the main, the problem is not cultural difference, but racism. As is mostly the case, I use the term racism as a shorthand, in the loosest of senses, to mean the disparagement of one grouping of people by another.

On (not) tolerating the intolerant

I had begun the previous section by considering the situation in which, whatever the differences between "us" and the Unwashed, the parties were at least willing and able to talk with each other. But even here, in this more hopeful scenario, we see that one can easily end up in a "live and leave well alone" arrangement. So, what of the situation in which "they" are unwilling to even try to abide by the principle of "live and let live" when the "we" are trying to live by it?

We are now faced with extreme kinds of proselytizers and fundamentalists who are found in all places and all walks of life. They would live and only let you live if you live according to their ways. They have no truck with the liberal principle of "live and let live" and instead follow that of "my way or no way". They demand that you do your liberal duty by them and not interfere in their ways. They use the liberal principles of ownership and authenticity to legitimate and sequester their own ways, making them unavailable to be questioned. This tactic is used to fend off outsiders, even while the notion of authenticity is used to cover up unfair practices *within* the "culture". We can see, then, that one set of rules apply in the space outside the culture, and another set of rules applies inside them. The move, it has to be said, is a clever one.

To this sort of situation, the diversity advocates and multi-culturalists have given no answer. They have avoided thinking about it by the tactic of simply ignoring it. And it is ignored because it is embarrassing to the liberal sensibility. Even as I write this, I can hear the diversity advocate say "but that is just your judgement about them—saying that their beliefs are obnoxious. And it is a judgement that only makes sense from within your belief system, and so is not a valid criticism". But this is exactly what I want to hold on to—my right, no, my duty, to hold on to my partisan ethical values, to speak and not be rendered silent.

When confronted by the intolerant, it behoves us not to meekly roll over. To utilize the principles of live and let live in such a scenario is to commit suicide; it would be akin to playing chess with an opponent who has no intention of engaging through the rules of the game, but instead comes at you with a hatchet. As the philosopher Charles Taylor has said: "liberalism is a fighting creed" (Taylor, 1994, p. 62).

On (not) tolerating the intolerable

There are still many questions that I am left with, questions that the multi-culturalist and diversity agendas do not address. The primary one is that there are some differences that I find that *I* am unwilling to tolerate, respect, or celebrate, because they go against my ethical values and deeply affront me. For example, the world view of the pederast, or that of the racial supremacist, or that which promotes the mutilation of female genitalia, or the belief that promotes the practice of child marriage, or the killing of whales, or that of the misogynist, or of the views of libertarian capitalists who deify the profit motive, to name but a few. Here, *I am the intolerant one* because some things are, indeed, intolerable to me. They are intolerable because they go against my deeply held beliefs; I think them wrong. In these cases, it seems to me that *the ethical response is that of intolerance*; what would be unethical is if I tolerated, say, the burning to death of those decreed to be heretics.

Am I wrong in this? And if not, then what is the difference between the intolerant me and the fundamentalist? My intolerance, driven by my ethics, feels to me to be virtuous and a good thing, since I am standing up for truth and justice. But, no doubt, the fundamentalist would say the same thing about their intolerance of those who do not sign up to their belief system (what ever it may be, culinary, ecological, psychoanalytic, theistic, etc.). Once again we are at the danger point where we could collapse into relativism, in which case I would be left with no leg to stand on. Recall, in Chapter Eight, when Sardar was faced with this very dilemma, he capitulated on the Romantic ideology he had been championing. Up to that point, he had been saying that we ought to respect "their ways" simply because they were "their ways", and he had also been cautioning against taking Eurocentric beliefs to be universal norms. But then, when faced with "ways" that he found abhorrent, he suddenly gave himself permission to *not accept* them, because they went against his ethics, which were now suddenly deemed universal: "Cultural practices that violate *the basic principles of human rights* . . . cannot be 'respected'" (Sardar, 2008, p. 23, my italics).

I have no problem standing with him shoulder to shoulder against practices that mutilate female genitalia, but neither he nor I are able to take this stand on the grounds that what we take to be right is a universally held view. For one thing, this attitude is clearly not shared by those who promote the practices that Sardar finds abhorrent; they think it their "right" to continue mutilating genitalia, because it is their way. Sardar's solution—a sudden recourse to universality—is a fudge; he has shifted from cultural relativism to a universal absolute without giving any grounds for doing so apart from the fact that his sensibilities have been disturbed. He is saying, in effect, "it is obvious that this is wrong". No, it is not obvious, even though both he and I might think it wrong.

And that is exactly the point. What do we do when "our" sensibilities are disturbed by "them"? The reality is more complex: my ethical stance (as well as Sardar's) *is* "centric", born of and located within a particular tradition and world view and is not universal. My ethical stance is without doubt "mine" and perhaps also "ours", but, most certainly, it is not "everyone's". What is one to do *in this situation*? The alternatives we have already met are the annihilation of the self, or the annihilation of the other; meanwhile, the relativists, refusing both, collapse into a kind of paralysis because they believe that a person inhabiting one world view has no grounds for making comments or judgements on the ways of another world view.

Grasping the nettle: validity despite relativity

To repeat how things stand: my stance against female genital mutilation is born of a *particular* set of values; it is "centric", born of a particular sort of liberal sensibility. I cannot get away from that, and neither ought I to try to do so. How am I to go forward even as I grasp this particular nettle? To the charge that my reaction is invalid because it is spoken from a particular vantage point, I say, no, the reaction is valid, but in a particular way. Here, then, is my attempt at grasping this nettle.

The fact that the judgement is "centric" does not mean that the content of the judgement is rendered invalid. However, what the fact that the judgement is "centric" does mean is that the judgement ought to remain open to interrogation. I think that it is this that rescues me from the charge of being fundamentalist in my convictions: however strong my convictions, I need to remain open them being challenged and questioned. But, of course, this openness is never infinite; eventually lines will be crossed (say, by the pederast) and dialogue will end. And this is the nettle that the diversity promulgators and multiculturalists will not grasp: the line that will be crossed will be "centric"; it is *my* line that is being crossed, not a universal one, and I should stand by it until convinced otherwise. Charles Taylor is called for again: liberalism is a fighting creed—fighting for what it believes to be right and wrong. Through the fight, I might well change my mind about what is right and wrong, but what must not be allowed to take place is for the liberal sensibility itself to be defeated and silenced by the fundamentalist. But, often enough, the liberal sensibility is defeated and silenced—and this occurs because it does not discriminate enough.

In speaking of "me and mine" *vs*. "theirs" in the discussion above, there is the danger that my viewpoint is misunderstood as another version of Romantic individualism in which it is presumed that what is "mine" is the opposite of the social and has nothing to do with it. This is not what I intend. To use Charles Taylor's language, the self is dialogically generated through engagement with others. To put it another way, the personal is the communal personalized. So, although these are *my* views, they did not spring up fully formed in me, with no recourse to the external social world. Further, the personal is not a precise replica of the communal, it is the communal personal-*ized*; that is, I have made it my own in my own way and so it will be unique and different in detail from how another has personalized the same communal.

Engagement vs. *recognition: the exchange of ideological fluids*

Let me return one last time to the troubling issue that I cannot truly trust the basis of my negative response to this other. How do I find out whether my antipathy is a racist response or whether it is an ethical one? Just because my response really, truly *feels* right does not make it so, as the Romantics would have it. And just because my response seems rational, that does not make it fully objective, as the Enlightenment would have it, because, as we have seen, rationales are always to some degree rationalizations. How do I test the ethic of my response?

That in itself is the first clue—the response has to be "tested". Testing takes place in the territory between deification and denigration. It is through dialogue and engagement with the other that testing occurs. Although the idea of dialogue and engagement sounds banal, it is far from it. True engagement is terrifying. Engagement requires me to allow your world view into me, so that I may cognitively and empathically come to know (if only momentarily) where you are coming from. It also requires you to genuinely countenance my world view. This kind of engagement is more than a debate and more than an exchange of rhetoric. This kind of intimate engagement consists of the exchange of ideological fluids. The danger, of course, is that as I let your view *into* me, then there is a real possibility that I will be changed, I will become something that I did not recognize a moment ago. My identity shifts, I will have become Other to myself.

This is why true engagement is not only profound, it is terrifying. But this is also the hope, that the engagement will be a mutually transformational process. This picture, although terrifying, is still relatively benign. What makes it less benign is the fact that the "engagement" does not take place on a level playing field. This is what the whole equalities project is about, after all. The protagonists are positioned in a field of power relations, and one will have more opportunities and status than the other. The struggle, the engagement, is mostly initiated (to use Norbert Elias's terms), by the "outsider" who demands to be recognized by the "established"; it is this outsider who demands recognition as a full human being, of equal status to the established, and so deserving of the same opportunities. There is no symmetry between the parties regarding their motivation to participate in this struggle; in actual fact, the established are likely to be extremely reluctant to participate at all.

Another name for this kind of engagement is recognition. But this notion, too, is sometimes too simplistic, especially when it is rendered sterile by equating it with the demand for an undiscriminating compulsory respect. Faced with the dehumanizing gaze of the imperialist, the dehumanized demand that they be recognized not only as humans, but as particular kinds of humans. It is through the act of recognition that one becomes human. This is true. But then we have to ask, what is it that is being recognized and by whom? Recognition, too, has its costs; in gaining recognition from one quarter, one necessarily loses it from another.

Let me approach these questions via the treatment of women. Is gender destiny? Well, let us place a woman in a certain kind of setting where there are rigid expectations of the role and place of women in society. For example, in the Orthodox Jewish community, in Saudi Arabia, in the Mormon community, or in a traditional Indian family. The list is endless, and there is no place where there are no expectations, even in the secular metropolis. Say the woman wishes to (a) follow a vocation as a modern dancer, and (b) wants to marry someone who is from another background. She insists that it is her fundamental human right to be able to choose how she lives her life. In her eyes, what is fundamental about her is her humanity, and that this category trumps every other. Meanwhile, her father asserts that what is fundamental is her duty to the family's honour with regard to the community, and the course she wishes to follow is anathema to their way of life and so she will bring shame on them. The father might say that what is most fundamental to her is the fact that she is a woman, and what it means to be a woman is "written" in the holy books and legitimated by the conventions and convictions that he and others like him live by; in brief, that this is the way of their "culture". What are at stake here are different ideologies, different ways of organizing and thinking about the world; ideologies determine which categories are presumed fundamental and which secondary.

So, which should be privileged—the fact that she is a woman, or the fact that she is a woman of a certain caste, culture, and class? The woman defends her position by drawing on Enlightenment values of universality, and the father defends his position by drawing on Romantic values of particularity. The father requires his daughter to recognize him and the authority vested in him by a particular tradition. The daughter requires the father to recognize her as a woman and a creature of the modern world. Instead, the daughter "recognizes" the father as a controlling tyrant that would squash her authenticity, and the father thinks his daughter a slut who has lost her way. So, although some kind of process of recognition is taking place, neither party likes what is being reflected back to them. Quite literally, neither recognizes themselves in the image of themselves given back to them by the other. Each of the protagonist's experience is that of being subject to mis-recognition, although each would say that they have recognized the other in their true colours.

It is exactly here that the liberal stumbles. And s/he stumbles on several counts. First and foremost, the liberal is gripped by doubt: should he or she say anything at all? Is the difficulty something that "belongs" to them, an "internal" matter, and so is it for them to sort out? If this were the case, then anything the liberal did or said would be construed as interference. This is the line sometimes taken by governments (when it suits them) in international relations. Despots attacking and murdering their populations (for example, in Zimbabwe, and Burma at present) are ignored, or, even worse, tolerated.

But what this story also shows is the link between recognition and belonging. (We have previously looked at the Foulkesian idea that belonging is necessary to psychological well-being, and that we cannot not belong.) One has to be recognized as belonging in order to belong. If the woman gains the recognition of the liberal—her rights as a woman—then she will lose the recognition of her father. If this happens, then she will become an outcast, losing the recognition (and therefore respect) of her family and community, and this loss, it has to be said, is not a light one. For her to gain the respect of her father, she has to recognize a particular version of him, one deserving of respect. To follow this course, she will have to give up her own particular desires, in a sense, to give up her authenticity. If she follows this course, she will perhaps lose the respect of her "modern friends", who might think that she has capitulated and "sold out".

But if our liberal does nothing, then in practice they would, in effect, be supporting the status quo—that is, the more powerful protagonist, the father. But say our liberal declines the option of doing nothing; the next difficulty he or she has to contend with is the issue of neutrality. However, as we have just seen, one cannot be neutral. If s/he actively sides with the father and supports his right to "his" culture, then, of necessity, s/he acts against the freedoms of the daughter. And if s/he supports the daughter over the father, then s/he falls foul of the injunction not to violate the integrity of a culture. We are ever obliged to choose who and what we respect.

CHAPTER THIRTEEN

The road to nowhere: conceptual cul-de-sacs

In this final chapter, I reprise, deepen, and further contextualize some of the key contradictions within the discourse of the diversity celebrators. I begin with the error in which respect comes to be promoted as the antidote to racism, as it is this that has led us towards the sterile philosophy of culture preservation.

Celebrating diversity: apartheid by another route

Culturalism: respect no antidote to racism

There are two interlinked issues, one of which is used to undermine the other.

- The first has to do with the processes of marginalization (which include racism, sexism, etc.) that benefit the "established".
- The second issue has to do with rights and recognition—the demands of the groups that are marginalized, the "outsiders".

Racism is a dehumanizing process through which others are made other and turned into commodities, in order to be used and abused at will. To counter this, the dehumanized demand to be recognized as human and valued for the *kind* of human they are. They want to be respected for who they are, and so they emphasize what they are. The "progressives" support this stand by the marginalized because it is a stand against the powers of oppression.

Faced by the imposition of the ways of the imperialist, the marginalized counter by asserting their own ways. They fear that any change to "our ways" is a capitulation to the ideology of the imperialist (who says our ways are better than your ways). This fear generates a rigidity regarding the "us". The intention of this gesture of the dehumanized is to enable entry into the discourse of full humans, but the fear and rigidity born of that turns the gesture towards life into a conservative, regressive impulse. Their focus becomes the *preservation* of their culture. In effect, the imperialist's gesture that would annihilate them is countered by a gesture that rigidifies them. While one can well understand the reasons behind this rigidity, it is not a particularly helpful solution. This is the benign explanation for this regressive conservative attitude. There is also another, more insidious, reason.

The conservative elite among the marginalized cultural groups, the so-called traditional authorities (primarily bearded men, it has to be said), hijack the very real problem of racism to silence the liberal, and in its stead perpetuate something one might call "culturalism", and they do this *in order to bolster their positions of privilege within "their" communities.* They demand that the liberal grant unconditional and unquestioning respect for the oppressions they inflict on members of their own community. Any liberal who dares to question "their" ways is swiftly silenced by the charge of "racism" being levied against them. The silencing is made possible by the liberal falling for the story that any questioning of "their ways" is necessarily oppressive. If the liberal also buys into the private/public split, then cultural practices are rendered untouchable because they are the *property* of that culture. And if these practices are granted the status of religious practices, then they are made even more unquestionable, since they are deemed sacred.

This sleight of hand is aided and abetted by the other split gifted by the diversity movements—that between politics and culture. This split allows these elites to pretend that their political actions are not political at all, but cultural actions. The split allows them to use "culture" for political ends, and, at the same time, render their political activities invisible in the guise of culture.

It seems to me that while racism is the tool of the more powerful, culturalism (although also used by the more powerful), is primarily the weapon of the elite within the less powerful. Bewildered by the fallacy of the superior virtue of the oppressed, the liberal does not see the contradictions that are endemic in the culturalist's position and so happily goes along with it.

The celebrators of diversity have founded this myth: that the way of countering racism is by preserving, respecting, and valuing cultures. Leaving aside whether or not cultures ought to be preserved, the strategy of being respectful does not work, because respect does not actually address the structures and practices of racism, respect does not necessarily make for a shift in the material conditions in the power relational field. And without any material change, respect is but another term for patronage. Further, when respect is delivered blindly, indiscriminately, and without taking account of the fact that the cultures that are being respected are political and politicized entities, then one does not notice that in respecting some of them, one is necessarily disrespecting others of them. In sum, respect is no antidote to racism.

But this does not mean that the activities of respect and acceptance are now redundant and ought to be discarded. What is rendered redundant, however, is the idea of indiscriminate respect for "them" as a homogeneity. What is required is a discerning respect, an ethically driven respect (even while keeping in mind that these ethics are not universal and neither are they unassailable). We cannot just respect them, we have to take sides with some of them and so, inevitably, against others of them (for Sacranie and against Alibhai-Brown, for instance, or vice versa). And if we shirk this responsibility, then all we can do is fall silent and abandon them all together.

We have just seen why the conservative elites within the "outsiders" and the progressives within the "established" both come to be in support of a conservative agenda of the preservation of cultures. The reactionaries do so to retain the alleged purity of their culture, and the progressives do so to help them make a stand against the imperial juggernaut. What we have also seen is that the motive for each is political; culture is a pawn in power struggles taking place between the various protagonists; the battle for the "soul" of a culture is a means to a (political) end.

All of this fits well with the apolitical ethos of the diversity celebrators, and so they, too, join in the rush to preserve cultures. Their apolitical ethos connives with the status quo; it says don't worry about politics and power because that just creates conflict, instead let's just look at each other, let us celebrate our differences and respect each other. It is a great trick. It seems to me that the ethos of "celebrating diversity" is, in fact, the institutionalization of culturalism in the equalities project, *from whence it undermines it.* Recall the analogy I drew with parasites early in the first chapter.

Devaluing the values of diversity

The use of diversity in the cause of preserving cultures is curious, because what diversity stands for is actually in conflict with the conservative project of preservation. Consider: nature is in a constant state of change, of evolution. Through the accidental mixing of things, events, and processes of mutation, new species are thrown up and others cease to be. This, then, is the point of diversity—it facilitates the emergence of something novel from the mix of things and events. The virtue of diversity is its fecundity, from which emerges the unpredictable novel. In the state of nature, species and their varieties never remain static, they are constantly mutating and evolving, albeit so slowly that we are not readily able to perceive it, and not always in directions that enhance their chances of survival. In this realm, diversity is said to be a good thing precisely because, from the mix of things, it continually produces something new that challenge the established status quo.

The diversity experts and organizational consultants accept this viewpoint when it comes to the generation of ideas in organizational life. When speaking to the boardrooms of the multi-national corporation, diversity consultants (rightly) make much of the fact that innovative and novel ideas are more likely to emerge when the discussion group contains a wide range of diverse viewpoints and perspectives (although, in their version of things, these discussions are conflict free). The exchange within the diverse conversational group, if real, is *fertile,* and so new ideas are born. They fully expect that the emerging novel will challenge the already established, the taken for granted norm, and here, too, they take the challenge of the new to be a good thing. In the realm of the natural world, diversity (the mixing of things) is the basis of *creation* itself; meanwhile, in the human world, diversity is the source of *creativity*.

But when it comes to cultures, then the celebrators of diversity change their tune. Now, suddenly, fertility, change, and interaction are a bad thing. The diversity agenda portrays the situation in the following way. To begin with, it requires the presence on stage of a number of diverse and different cultures, and the more the better. But now, having coaxed the range of different cultures on to the stage, the injunction is that *they must not interact*. Because if they interact, they will influence and be influenced, and so, change. What cultures ought to do is to be respectful of each other, but they must ensure that they preserve themselves in their "authentic" form.

We have to ask, why is it that what is good for the generation of ideas and for "nature" is not so when it comes to culture? And, in fact, is this not what has actually been taking place ever since the beginnings of human social life: cultures evolving, morphing, begging, borrowing, and stealing from each other? It is their "nature" to mutate, to change; cultures are in a constant state of flux. How can it be otherwise? And why should they not change? I can see no ethical imperative or rationale for the preservation of cultures in a "pure" form, in part because they never were pure; they have always been amalgams of bastardized attributes drawn from here, there, and everywhere. Cultures never sprang forth fully formed on to the earth (as Athena did from the head of Zeus); instead, they take form over time, they evolve, they change, they split off, they amalgamate, and they die off.

The discussion is now made more complex by taking account of the field of power relations that pattern how cultures interact with each other. For example, it was mostly the case that imperial powers deliberately set out to destroy the ways of life of those that they vanquished. Even within its own islands in the past, the English establishment had cultivated a strategy of not allowing the Irish, Scottish, and Welsh to speak or teach their native tongues. The strategy sought to deliberately "cultivate" a new generation, to mould them, so that they fit better into the ideals of the imperial vision. We can see why, in such a situation, local forces would be marshalled to preserve languages and ways of life that were being deliberately extinguished by the imperialist. This kind of resistance makes political, rational, and ethical sense. Franz Fanon was well aware of this regressive movement in the struggle for liberation, but he saw it for what it was—a transient moment in a longer emancipatory process.

When it comes to the modern metropolis, the situation is very different from that of the colonial context. Of course, power relations also pattern the interactions in the modern metropolis, but not in the same way as in the colonial context.

In the modern metropolis, the mixing of (diverse) peoples and their ways will inevitably throw up new and different ways that necessarily challenge the old ways. But now, when a person *deemed* to be of one culture takes on something *deemed* to be of another culture, it is decried as betrayal, as it threatens the existence and continuation of a particular identity. The key word in this passage is "deemed". Who deems what belongs where, who owns what? And yes, it does make for a shift in identity, but only a particular version of that identity. For example, it is a well-known phenomenon that when migrants (or their children) who have kept diligently to the old ways return to the mother country, they can find that the attitudes there have changed considerably and become much more liberal (and sometimes much less liberal). The culture has mutated, it has moved on (not always for the better, of course). Where does authenticity lie in such a situation? Who are the true guardians of authenticity?

Change is not necessarily betrayal, and often enough it is, in fact, liberational. For example, listen here to the Indian micro-biologist, Meera Nanda, telling us about herself:

> Natural science . . . had given me a whole different perspective on the underlying cosmology of the religious and cultural traditions I was raised in. Science gave me a good reason to say 'No!' to many of my inherited beliefs about God, nature, women, duties and rights . . . Without knowing it then, I was speaking the language of the Enlightenment. [Nanda, 2003, p. xii, quoted in Malik, 2008, p. 196]

But then, when she came to study in the USA, she found that

> Enlightenment was seen as the agent of colonialism, and modern science as a discourse of patriarchy and other dominant Western interests . . . Someone like me could only be *pitied*—which I often was—as a "colonised" mind, dazzled by the superficial charms of the West. [*ibid.*, my italics]

Those that pity Nanda are in the grip of an inverted version of Russell's fallacy: The fallacy of the inferior virtue of the oppressor—nothing good can ever come of them. Would the celebrators of diversity join forces with patriarchal elements within Hindu elites to push Meera Nanda back into her "original" cultural box, to know the place allocated to her as a woman and become a good, chapatti-making wife? The logic of their reasoning would suggest that yes, they would.

So, when it comes to culture, the version of diversity that is being promoted by the celebrators of diversity is a sterile and contradictory one. On the one hand, they require the presence of a multitude of diverse cultures, but then insist that they do not interact and exchange ideological fluids in order that they retain their authenticity and "essence". And even if some form of contact is to be allowed, it is a very cautious form of contact, because of the fear that one will make a mistake and so offend the other. This, too, works against creativity, because, as the educationalist Ken Robinson (2006) points out, our institutions are increasingly run according the mythical belief that it is possible *not to make mistakes*. The "mistake" of interest to our discussions is that of "cultural offence". Mistakes might be due to incompetence, or a lack of motivation, or clumsiness, or indifference, and so forth. Mistakes are punished. In our increasingly punitive culture, there is no difference between *causing* offence and *being* offensive. And although we all constantly make mistakes in our day-to-day lives, our institutions continue to be run according to the myth that it is possible, with sufficient engineering, procedure, and training, to do away with mistakes entirely.

But, as Robinson argues, mistakes are necessary to creativity. He says that creativity "comes about through the interaction of different disciplinary ways of seeing things"; in other words, through diversity. But in order to be creative, we have to risk being wrong. He says that although "being wrong is not the same as being creative . . . if you are not prepared to be wrong you will never come up with anything original". The general intolerance of "mistakes" in organizational life come to interlock with the diversity insistence that one ought to avoid anything that could lead to a cross-cultural "mistake" and cause cultural offence. This results in creativity being stifled and thought being suffocated. A world run according to this sort of conservative version of "diversity" ends up barren and sterile.

In my view, the deification of culture in the way that has been promoted by *some streams* within multi-culturalism and the celebrating diversity movements is another form of racism. Culturalists draw on the same sorts of argument as the racists—of purity, of essence, of incommensurability and lineage—to fix people into one or other "cultural" grouping; a scenario in which movement comes to equal betrayal. Racism uses "race" to divide humanity into different kinds, and then says that there are irreconcilable differences between them and so it is best that they do not intermingle; for one thing, they would say, miscegenation dilutes the purity of the races. Meanwhile, culturalists use a notion of essentialized, homogenized, differentiated cultures to arrive at the same position regarding irreconcilable differences. Like the racists, culturalists make much of lineage to determine someone's allegedly "true cultural heritage", a heritage (in the singular, notice) which can be lost, taken away, given away, and neglected, but can also be found and restored. (Sometimes, they do grant that a person can have "dual" heritages.) Both, the racists and culturalists seek to preserve their purity and resist being contaminated by the impure. In this way, the celebrators of diversity and some versions of multi-culturalism come to support a particular and peculiar form of apartheid.

Rationality: the villain of the piece?

This is the predicament regarding the human condition as discussed variously through the book: that our thoughts and feelings are structured by particular histories, that we are necessarily "centric", that we inhabit and are inhabited by particular ways of thinking and particular ideologies, that we are born into multiple discourses that become an intrinsic part of our sense of our conflicted selves, our moralities, and our sensibilities. We are partisan, ambivalent, and our ways are "local".

This realization has led to a double disaster. First, it has led to an extreme relativism in which anything goes, because those belonging to one "system" are not allowed a view on another "system". Moral compasses" are thought only to work within the particular contexts that they arise in, and if used in contexts they were not designed for, they are said to give false information. Second, it has led to an attack on rationality itself, so that thinking itself has become equated with oppression. All thought processes are suspect because they have been formed in the crucible of particular histories and communities and, therefore, they cannot be objective and universally applicable. In this process, the Enlightenment in its entirety has become completely trashed and portrayed as villainous. True, the Enlightenment erred by presuming the existence of universal values and thought processes; it also gave succour to individualism and fed the fantasy that individuals exist as entities prior to participation in societies. But the Enlightenment also promoted egalitarianism, it stood up for the ordinary person against popes and princes, and, most crucially, it encouraged people to think for themselves. Yes, it is Eurocentric, in that it arose within a certain milieu. But the principles it promotes are not unfamiliar in other quarters of the world, in other milieus. Many of its values are found in other parts of the world, and other "systems" of thought and belief. Foucault was so very wrong when he said that "They [the Iranians] don't have the same regime of truth as ours". It has been repeatedly claimed that democracy, autonomy, freedom, etc., are Western concepts that do not sit easily and do not suit the mentality of other peoples in other places. There is not just irony, but also great injustice in claims like these.

Almost every time one of those "other" people actually set up a genuine democracy, every time they use their autonomy to choose destinies that are for their own interests rather than the interests of the old imperial and colonial masters, then it is has been destroyed and replaced with a dictator favourable to the interests of the old masters. One such instance is the home of the Ayatollahs. In the early 1950s, Iran was a fledgling democracy—chosen by the people for the people. The Prime Minister, Mossadegh, proposed that Iran should nationalize its oil resources. For many decades, the Anglo-Iranian Petroleum Company (later called British Petroleum and now BP) had a monopoly over this oil. From the 1920s onwards, the entire British industrial system as well as its armed forces relied completely on this oil. However, the Iranians did not profit from it. So, Mossadegh thought it in the interests of the country to nationalize it. In 1953, a coup was successfully engineered by the Near East Director of the CIA, Kermit Roosevelt (grandson of Teddy), with the connivance of the British. Mossadegh was replaced with the puppet dictator, the infamous Shah and his entourage. So, it is somewhat outrageous to claim that democracy is alien to the Iranian way of thinking, given that it was the champions of freedom that deliberately destroyed the newly burgeoning democracy and then set up the conditions for autocracies and theocracies to thrive. Untold tens of thousands of Iranians were murdered first by the Shah and his secret police, Savak, and then by the Ayatollahs, all because they did not subscribe to the same "regime of truth" as decreed by their oppressive rulers (Kinzer, 2008).

Neither was it the case that all Europeans were "on message" when it came to the agenda of the Enlightenment. Many within Europe thought its proposals dangerous, heinous, and against the natural order of things.

It is truly ironic that the diversity enthusiasts dismiss the values of the Enlightenment on the grounds that it is Eurocentric, but then valorize and venerate the values of the Romantics, which are no less Eurocentric.

Pity the difference

At times, one unfortunate consequence for those recognized as "socially disadvantaged" is that they can all be thought of and treated in the same kind of way. Lists of the socially disadvantaged are to be found in equal opportunity statements, and consist of categories such as race, gender, colour, disability, etc. The irony is that having differentiated, "recognized", and listed each category of the socially disadvantaged, they are then put back together as *the* socially disadvantaged. True, what is common to them is that they are all stigmatized in some way and subject to denigratory attitudes. All of them suffer from unfair discrimination, and in this sense they are all "disabled" in some way or another. But what can now occur in the guilt-ridden liberal mind is a slippage, this being, because those on the list are unfortunate, they come to be thought of as unfortunates, and unfortunates in need of help. In some circumstances, the fact that they are all *less able* to prosper comes to mean that they *are disabled* in some way. Being disabled, allowances ought to be made for them; being disabled, they are to be pitied.

This kind of experience is not unfamiliar to me. In certain contexts, when I have been looked upon in a kindly way, when I have been treated particularly carefully as something fragile and vulnerable, when what I say is listened to as one might listen to a child, when I am given undue deference, when concern is shown for me particularly and not for others; in effect, when I am treated as a guest. It is an attitude that implies people feel sorry for me, as though I was not really capable of looking after myself and needed help to do so. None of these gestures has been unpleasant, and are quite the opposite of the explicit hatred of the racists. Surely I should be grateful for these kindnesses? I am, but it is mixed. For example, on joining a discussion group a few years ago, the first thing said to me was what good English I spoke. The statement is simultaneously both a gesture of welcome and a gesture of exclusion.

Anyhow, at this point the person who *is* disabled is likely to take umbrage, and rightly so. The last thing that the disabled want is pity, because pity makes them other. What they want is certain kinds of extra help to enable them to have more equality of opportunity with the able-bodied. And then what they want is to be treated like everyone else. They do not want to stand out, they do not want to be pointed out, in a sense they want to disappear into the mass of humanity. In the extraordinarily moving film, *I Have Tourette's but Tourette's Doesn't Have Me* (Kent, 2005), the final evocative sentence spoken by a child is: "I am just like you."

Next to this wish, "treat me like everyone else because I am like everyone else", is the other, "treat me in a special / different way because I am special / different". These apparently conflicting desires are both present at the same time, for each and every human being; it is part of the existential human condition. We need to belong (same), but also need to be recognized in and for our uniqueness (different). The fact that we need both these to be true simultaneously is what makes the situation a paradox rather than a contradiction. This paradox is writ large during the time of adolescence. Adolescents find it excruciatingly painful to stand out from their crowd of friends, and so they tend to closely follow the uniform of their peer group. But within that grouping, each takes pride on tweaking the uniform to individualize it.

Anyhow, the point is that there is this double existential call from each of us, as individuals and as social groups: *never forget that I am the same as you, and never forget that I am different from you.* The first of these is backed by the Enlightenment, and the second by the Romantics. But it can be forgotten that both are true and necessary at the same. What is more, in order to increase equality of opportunity, some categories might need more of "difference" to balance things out for them, while other categories might need more of "sameness".

The Black person is not disabled *per se*. Their difficulties are in part (the part that is of interest to the themes of this book) caused by something outside them, this being racism, which construes them as different and inferior, and treats them as such. Racism makes them *too* different. But by thinking of them (in some subliminal way) as being disabled (which I am arguing is the case at times), the problem is construed as being *within them*. No change is required in the structures and arrangements of the world; rather, what is required is that they be helped to become a part of it. And so it comes to be thought that they are deserving of charity, of a kindly helping hand, of pity. These sorts of acts of kindness are deeply corrosive, as they accept that Blacks are different and inferior, and so one ought to make allowances for them and their inadequacies. Clearly, this is still racism, but in a more kindly guise.

This tendency to pity is exacerbated by power differentials. We saw earlier in the discussions around tolerance that it was the more powerful that had the option whether or not to tolerate something. When they opt to tolerate, then it is, in some sense, an act of kindness. It is in this way that this capacity of the more powerful comes to fit so well and reinforce the tendency to pity in the guilt-ridden liberal.

Meanwhile, activism and identity politics counter the denigration by *agreeing* that Black people *are* different, but not *that* different to other human beings, and that there is something to be valued in that difference. Now the demand becomes, respect me for my difference, for what I am. As I argued earlier, in my view, the assertion of this kind of identity might well be necessary as a tactic in the struggle for equality, but if it gets stuck there, if it becomes an end in itself, then this is ultimately counterproductive, because it perpetuates a racialized world view which decrees that Black and White *are* different. But, as we are still living in a racialized world, one can understand the reason for the assertion of a Black identity, an identity to be respected rather than denigrated. We can see in this whole ongoing process the tension between both assertions constantly in play: remember I am the same, remember that I am different.

Let me now come back to disability and speak about it through the experiences of the children featured in the film on Tourette's Syndrome. In the first instance, these children suffered because their peers' expectation was to think of them *being like everyone else*. But because some of the behaviours of the children suffering from Tourette's were well outside expected social norms (various tics), they were judged by their peers and some teachers as inferior retards, and, consequently, mocked and shunned. To underline the point: their difficulties in the first instance were due to their difference *not being recognized*. Paradoxically, the deepest wish of these children was to be accepted by their peers and be just one of the crowd and not stand out. We see in the film how, over time, some of their peers come to gain an understanding of the condition, come to see the humanity behind the condition, and come to see that indeed "you are just like me". The children with Tourette's become accepted to some degree into a peer group. We can put it like this: their peers have come to *recognize* and accept the victims of Tourette's in their difference. What these children manage to do is to allow their friend with Tourette's the possibility of regaining and retaining their dignity.

Although one of the crowd, it is not the case that now the children with Tourette's are treated the same as everyone else, because they are not. They continue to fall outside social norms. And to treat them the same as everyone else is to do them a grave disservice. What we see is that their peers come to accept them and make allowances for their symptoms. They tolerate them, in the best sense of the word. But this tolerance is not infinite, and neither can it be. To be accepted as one of the crowd means that, just like everyone else, one is part of the whole range of human interaction. All children get irritated with each other, they get annoyed with each other, they fall out of friendships and in again, and so on. The children suffering with Tourette's will be a part of this mix of things—the politics of friendship. And so children will also at times get irritated with the children with Tourette's as and when their symptoms become too intrusive, and vice versa. Being one of the crowd means being a part of the rough and tumble of life. What would become a problem is if it were decreed that one ought compulsorily to respect the person who has Tourette's *because they have Tourette's*. This last step is the step too far, the step into thought paralysis. What this scenario shows is that both extremes are problematic. If we think of Tourette's sufferers as the same as everyone else, then we find them wanting and annoying. And if we think of them as especially different, then here, too, we end up distancing them, either through pity or through idealization. Which brings to mind Russell's fallacy, and we have to remember that not all sufferers of Tourette's will be equally likeable. The paradox is that, initially, allowances have to be made for their differences; this then allows them to be (more or less) accepted to become (more or less) like everyone else, there being no absolutes.

Three points still remain to be drawn out of the above scenario, the first of which, to some degree, rehabilitates the multi-culturalist solution of education and familiarization. Some of the "ordinary" children did move from intolerance born of irritation and ignorance to a place of more tolerance born of understanding and familiarity. However, this change did not come about through them going through "training", or the ubiquitous e-training. The changes happened over time, through struggle and conflict, through hurts delivered and felt, and, yes, also through education, information, and knowledge. Trainings of the kind I have already touched on cannot get anywhere near the kinds of deep ethical change these children went through. The change did not come about through the imposition of rules; rather, they came about through engagement. But also, and most important, as the scenario shows, the struggle to live and let live is ongoing for all parties; there is no end; we are bound to fail and fall short of our ethical aspirations, to say something cruel, and then, one hopes, sometimes reparation follows.

The second point takes us back to Sardar's perspective on disability, touched on in Chapter Nine. He told us of two models of disability, the medical model, "which sees disabled people as the problem and thus requires them to adjust to the world as it is", and the social model, "which focuses on society and the barriers it creates that prevent disabled people participating fully in everyday activities". It seems obvious enough that both are true; it is overly excessive to say that the difficulties that the disabled face in living their lives have "little to do with their impairment" (p. 34). To this way of thinking, there is no problem whatsoever with the Tourette's sufferer, the problems all reside in the minds of their classmates and teachers and in the ways that the classroom functions and teaching takes place. The reality that is being avoided is as follows: there is a medical problem in "them", which gives rise to a problem in "us" (the able-bodied) and for our ways. This is "our" difficulty, "our" difficulty with "them", and remains with "us" for all time. We cannot do away with it, neither can we cognitively train ourselves out of it, because it is an ongoing part of the existential situation. The way being proposed by Sardar for sorting this intractable problem in "us" is to pretend that there is no problem in "them", and the problem, as such, comes to be lodged in social arrangements. And, of course, to adjust the social world to accommodate the disabled is helpful, and is a course that ought to be pursued, but not at the cost of obfuscating reality.

The last point takes us back to the start of the section: having had this brief discussion on Tourette's, the danger is that the same thinking gets transposed to all the other categories that feature on equal opportunity lists. While some on the list need to be helped and "held", the problem for others on the list is not that they require holding, but that they are being "held back". But what neither of them needs is tolerance *per se,* because that suggests that there is some difficulty in them that needs tolerating.

In conclusion

Having argued that, in my opinion, there is no virtue in respecting someone merely *because* of their difference *per se,* I want to make it clear that I am not proposing that we should find a way of *not seeing differences* between people because we are all the same and if only we learnt to see the world right, then all this nasty stuff would disappear. I am not arguing for such a simplification. My position is that we cannot *not divide,* cognitively, emotionally, or in any other way. The divisions I make are what make me an ethical being; without these divisions I would not be human: I divide, therefore I am an ethical being. The places we find ourselves "naturally" dividing are aspects of the ideologies we have imbibed that lead us to experience and see the world in particular ways. And even as we try to address one set of iniquities born of one set of ideologies, we will find ourselves manufacturing others despite ourselves, and all because we cannot not divide.

This leads directly to two of the key difference between the arguments I have been putting forward and the view taken in the mainstream of the equality movements. First, to my mind, they have mistaken "differences" to be the cause of the iniquities, and so have put all of their resources into solving this false problem. Second, they think that unfair divisions are born of faulty thinking and feeling processes, which can be corrected. Their solution is cognitivist and two-pronged: to educate people by providing them with "training" in the right ways of thinking, and to proceduralize the decision-making processes. And if all of this is done with sufficient commitment, will, and passion, then we will arrive in equality heaven. In contrast, the view I am putting forward is that the unfair decisions we arrive at are only in part due to "mistakes" in our thinking processes; I think the mind is intrinsically partisan. So, even while I try to correct one kind of us–them dynamic (as I ought to try to do), I will inevitably create another kind of us–them dynamic with its own set of difficulties and problems. This, however, is not a cause for pessimism, and neither do I think that this makes education, training, and proceduralization redundant. But I think that there will never be a point of arrival in equality heaven, because even as we address one inequality, we will create another. When we do not keep in mind that the whole equalities enterprise is a continual work in progress and there is no point of arrival, then it becomes an instrument of fear and control. Having said that, I do not want to replace one set of idealizations with another. The idea of "engagement", as I have spoken of it, is also a continual work in progress. For one thing, it presupposes a willingness to participate in the activity of engagement, and mostly we (I include myself in this "we") are very reluctant to do so, precisely because we would be engaging with something that we find problematic.

Racism, sexism, and the other forms of disparagement continue to flourish. The work against these processes is intrinsically and intensely political. I have been arguing that the celebrators of diversity, with their apolitical emphasis on respect and their apolitical reframing of difference from difficulty to asset, have done the battle against the processes of marginalization no favours; in fact, they have seriously undermined it.

But having said that, I also need to stress that I am not against the principles of respect, acceptance, and tolerance. What I am against is an indiscriminate respect and tolerance that requires the tolerator to disengage from their own discriminatory processes. In doing so, they would be abandoning their own humanity as they suspended living according to the claims of their own ethics. On this basis, the price for allowing the other their "authenticity" is being paid by abandoning one's own "authenticity". My argument is that in order to exercise the faculty of respect (which I am keen to do) I have *to discriminate*. My argument is that we need more discrimination, not less. If I cease discriminating, then I cease to be human. To call on Descartes one last time: I discriminate, therefore I am.

REFERENCES

Apperly, E. (2009). On another planet: how Italy's women saw Colonel Gaddafi. *Guardian*, 13 June. www.guardian.co.uk/world/2009/jun/12/colonel-gaddafi-italy-women-speech

Appiah, K. A. (2005). *The Ethics of Identity*. Princeton, NJ: Princeton University Press.

Arendt, H. (1998). *The Human Condition*. Chicago, IL: Chicago University Press.

Banton, M. (1987). *Racial Theories*. Cambridge: Cambridge University Press.

Barnett, H. (2004). *Constitutional & Administrative Law*. London: Cavendish.

BBC News (2007). news.bbc.co.uk/1/hi/magazine/6275363.stm

Benhabib, S. (2002). *The Claims of Culture*. Princeton, NJ: Princeton University Press.

Bennett, R. (2011). Adoption couples blocked by race barrier. *The Times*, 24 January, 2011.

Branden, N. (1994). *The Six Pillars of Self Esteem*. New York: Bantam.

Brittain, V., & Begg, M. (2006). *Enemy Combatant*. London: The Free Press.

Brown, R. (1995). *Prejudice*. Oxford: Blackwell.

Browne, A. (2006). *The Retreat of Reason: Political Correctness and the Corruption of Public Debate in Modern Britain*. London: Civitas.

Burkitt, I. (1999). *Bodies of Thought*. London: Sage.

Burrell, I. (2000). Prison service admits it is 'institutionally racist'. *Independent*, 21 August. Available at www.independent.co.uk/news/uk/this-britain/prison-service-admits-it-is-institutionally-racist-710902.html

Business in the Community www.bitc.org.uk/workplace/diversity_and_inclusion/race/hesa_report.html

Clements, P., & Spinks, T. (2006). *The Equal Opportunities Handbook*. London: Kogan Page.

Cohen, N. (2005). Ken has a lot to be sorry for. *The Observer*, 20 February. www.guardian.co.uk/politics/2005/feb/20/london.politicalcolumnists

Cohen, N. (2007). *What's Left: How the Left Lost its Way*. London: Harper Perennial.

Commission for Racial Equality (2002). *Ethnic Monitoring: A Guide For Public Authorities*. London: Commission for Racial Equality.

Curtis, M. (2010a). *Secret Affairs: Britain's Collusion with Radical Islam*. London: Serpent's Tail.

Curtis, M. (2010b). Bin Laden, the Taliban, Zawahiri: Britain's done business with them all. *The Guardian*, 6 July, p. 27.

Dalal, F. (1998). *Taking the Group Seriously: Towards a Post-Foulkesian Group Analytic Theory*. London: Jessica Kingsley.

Dalal, F. (2002). *Race, Colour and the Processes of Racialization: New Perspectives from Group Analysis, Psychoanalysis, and Sociology*. Hove: Brunner-Routledge.

Davies, H. (2011). Focus on horrific reality of child sex grooming. *Chroniclelive.co.uk*, 17 January. www.chroniclelive.co.uk/north-east-news/evening-chronicle-news/2011/01/17/focus-on-horrific-reality-of-child-sex-grooming-72703–28000420/

Denning, A. T. (1979). *Science Research Council v. Nassé: Leyland Cars Ltd. v. Vyas*, Court of Appeal.

Denning, A. T. (1983). Court of Appeal, QB 1.

Department of Health and the Health and Social Care Information Centre/NHS Employers (2005). *A Practical Guide To Ethnic Monitoring In The NHS And Social Care*. London: Department of Health.

De Saussure, F. (1959). *Course in General Linguistics*, C. Bally & A. Sechehaye (Eds.). New York: The Philosophical Library.

Devon Partnership Trust. Equality and diversity training. www.devon-learning.net/jointlearningprogramme/view_course.php?c_id=175

Dunbar, R. (1997). *Grooming, Gossip and the Evolution of Language*. London: Faber and Faber.

Duncan, B. L. (1976). Differential social perception and attribution of intergroup violence: testing the lower limits of stereotyping Blacks. *Journal of Personality and Social Psychology, 34*: 590–598.

Dyer, C. (2008a). Briton sues over deportation as failed asylum seeker. *Guardian,* 7 June. www.guardian.co.uk/world/2008/jun/07/humanrights.pakistan

Dyer, C. (2008b). Man deported by mistake wins home office payout. *Guardian,* 10 June, 2008. www.guardian.co.uk/uk/2008/jun/10/law

Elias, N. (1976). Introduction. In: N. Elias & J. Scotson (Eds.), *The Established and the Outsiders*. London: Sage, 1994.

Elias, N. (1991). *The Symbol Theory*. London: Sage.

Elias, N. (1994). *The Civilizing Process*. Oxford: Blackwell.

Elias, N., & Scotson, J. (1994). *The Established and the Outsiders*. London: Sage.

Ethnic Monitoring: A Guide For Public Authorities (2002). Commission for Racial Equality, p. 14.

Eusebius (AD 263–339). *The Life of Constantine*. www.fordham.edu/halsall/basis/vita-constantine.html

Foucault, M. (1988). Iran: the spirit of a world without spirit. In: *Politics Philosophy, Culture: Interviews and Other Writings 1977–84*. New York: Routledge.

Fox, K. (2005). *Watching the English: The Hidden Rules of English Behaviour*. London: Hodder and Stoughton.

Freud, S. (1905). *Three Essays on Sexuality. S.E., 7*: 125–245. London: Hogarth Press.

Freud, S. (1915). *The Unconscious. S.E., 14*: 161–215. London: Hogarth Press.

Freud, S. (1921c). *Group Psychology and the Analysis of the Ego. S.E., 18*: 69–144. London: Hogarth.

Freud, S. (1933). *New Introductory Lectures on Psychoanalysis. S.E., 22*: 5–184. London: Hogarth.

Fromm, E. (2010). *The Sane Society*. London: Routledge.

GAP. www.gapinc.com/public/Careers/car_diversity.shtml

Gold, T. (2011). The battle for equal opportunities still needs fighting. *Guardian,* 8 January. www.guardian.co.uk/commentisfree/2011/jan/08/tanya-gold-equality-legislation

Gould, S. J. (1984). *The Mismeasure of Man*. London: Pelican.

Grayling, A. C. (2007). *Towards the Light*. London: Bloomsbury.

Guigon, C. (2004). *On Being Authentic*. Oxford: Routledge.

Hakim, C. (2010). *Feminist Myths and Magic Medicine: The Flawed Thinking Behind Calls for Further Equality Legislation*. London: The Centre for Policy Studies.

Haq, R. (2004). International perspectives on workplace diversity. In: M. Stockdale & F. Crosby (Eds.), *The Psychology and Management of Workplace Diversity*. Malden, MA: Blackwell.

Hardt, M., & Negri, A. (2001). *Empire*. Harvard: Harvard University Press.

Harman, C. (1994). The prophet and the proletariat. *Marxism Online*. http://www.marxists.de/religion/harman/

Harvard Business Review on Managing Diversity (2001). Boston, MA: Harvard Business School Press.

Hays-Thomas, R. (2004). Why now? The contemporary focus on managing diversity. In: M. Stocksdale & F. Crosby (Eds.), *The Psychology and Management of Workplace Diversity* (pp. 3–30). Malden, MA: Blackwell.

Hencke, D. (2009). Gender pay gap rises in Whitehall's top ranks. *Guardian*, 9 May, 2009.

Henry, P. K. (2003). *Diversity and the Bottom Line*. Austin, TX: Turn Key Press.

Herder, J. G. (1968). *Reflections on the Philosophy of the History of Mankind*. Chicago, IL: University of Chicago Press.

Indiadivine.org. www.indiadivine.org/audarya/hinduism-forum/215579-cow-slaughter-banned-all-over-india-except-kerala-w-bengal.html

Institute of Race Relations (a). www.irr.org.uk/statistics/housing.html

Institute of Race Relations (b). www.irr.org.uk/statistics/employment.html

Jha, D. N. (2004). *The Myth of the Holy Cow*. London: Verso.

Kent, H. G. (2005). *I Have Tourette's but Tourette's Doesn't Have Me*. Film, HBO.

Kinzer, S. (2008). *All the Shah's Men: An American Coup and the Roots of Middle East Terror*. New Jersey: John Wiley.

Kochman, T. (1974). Orality and literacy as factors of 'Black" and 'White" communicative behaviour. *International Journal of the Sociology of Language*, *3*: 91–115.

Kochman, T. (1981). *Black and White Styles in Conflict*. Chicago, IL: University of Chicago Press.

Lelyveld, J. (2010). Did Churchill let them starve? *New York Review of Books*, 23 December.

Lewis, P., & Taylor, M. (2009). Culture of impunity at police unit. *Guardian*, 7 November.

Lincoln, J. (1951). *Incentive Management*. Cleveland, OH: Lincoln Electric.

Loden, M. (1996). *Implementing Diversity*. Boston, MA: McGraw-Hill.

Loden, M., & Rosener, J. (1991). *Workforce America: Managing Employee Diversity as Vital Resource*. Homewood, IL: Business One Irwin.

Lubensky, M., Holland, S., Wiethof, C., & Crosby, F. (2004). Diversity and sexual orientation: including and valuing diversity in the workplace, In: M. Stocksdale & F. Crosby (Eds.), *The Psychology and Management of Workplace Diversity*. Malden, MA: Blackwell.

MacAskill, E. (2011). Freedom Riders hit the road again, 50 years after ending segregation at bus and railway stations. *Guardian*, 28 May, p. 23.

MacPherson, W. (1999). *The Stephen Lawrence Inquiry*. London: Stationary Office Books.

Malik, K. (2008). *Strange Fruit*. Oxford: Oneworld.

McDougall, D. (2007). Child sweatshop shame threatens GAP's ethical image. *Observer*, Sunday 28 October.

MIND www.mind.org.uk/help/people_groups_and_communities/statistics_3_race_culture_and_ mental_health#psychosis

Nanda, M. (2003). *Prophets Facing Backwards: Postmodern Critiques of Science and Hindu Nationalism in India*. New Brunswick, NJ: Rutgers University Press.

Narayan, U. (1997). *Dislocating Cultures: Identities, Traditions, and Third World Feminism*. New York: Routledge.

Netmums www.netmums.com/coffeehouse/coffeehouse-chat-460/coffeehouse-chat-514/news-current-affairs-topical-discussion-12/245512-words-still-considered-racist-2.html

Noor, A. F. (2008). Let Muslims do their yoga in peace. *The Week*, 6 December, p. 16.

Nussbaum, M. (2001). *Women and Human Development*. Cambridge: Cambridge University Press.

Panorama (2009). John Hubley's Faith in the NHS. BBC1, 30 September, news.bbc.co.uk/panorama/hi/front_page/newsid_8212000/8212960.stm

Parveen, N. (2011). Jack Straw sex grooming comments: the reaction. *Lancashire Telegraph*, 10 January. www.lancashiretelegraph.co.uk/news/blackburn/8780436.Jack_Straw_sex_grooming_comments__the_reaction/

Petley, J. (2005). *Culture Wars: The Media and the British Left*. Edinburgh: Edinburgh University Press.

Phillips, M. (2006). *Londonistan*. London: Gibson Square.

Ponterotti, J., & Pedersen, P. (1993). *Preventing Prejudice*. Newbury Park, CA: Sage.

Prince, R. (2009). Toddlers who dislike spicy food 'racist'. *Daily Telegraph*, 15 January.

Puniyani, R. (2001). Beef eating: strangulating history. *The Hindu*, 14 August. www.hinduonnet.com/2001/08/14/stories/13140833.htm

Race Relations Act (1976). London: HMSO.

Robinson, K. (2006). Ken Robinson says schools kill creativity. www.ted.com/talks/ken_robinson_says_schools_kill_creativity.html

Rosenberg, J. (2005). Schoolgirl wins right to wear Muslim gown. *Daily Telegraph*, 3 March, 2005. www.telegraph.co.uk/news/uknews/1484810/Schoolgirl-wins-right-to-wear-Muslim-gown.html

Rosenberg, J. (2006). Law Lords back school over ban on Islamic gown. *Daily Telegraph*, 23 March, www.telegraph.co.uk/news/uknews/1513730/Law-lords-back-school-over-ban-on-Islamic-gown.html

Russell, J. (2009). Women can't depend on liberals for equality. We need radical action now. *Guardian*, 11 May, p. 29.

Sardar, Z. (2008). *The Language of Equality*. Manchester: The Equality and Human Rights Commission.

Scarman, L. G. (1981). *The Scarman Report: The Brixton Disorders, April 10–12, 1981*. London: Stationery Office Books.

Shamsie, K. (2011). If it takes up the extremists' baton, liberal Pakistan is lost. *Guardian*, 8 January, p. 30.

Shepherd, J. (2011). 14,000 British professors – but only 50 are black. *Guardian*, 28 May, p. 6.

Sivanandan, A. (1983). *A Different Hunger: Writings on Black Resistance*. London: Pluto Press.

Smith, H. (2011). Inquiry into grooming of girls for sex. *Metro*, 10 January.

Stockdale, M. S., & Cao, F. (2004). Looking back and heading forward. In: M. Stockdale & F. Crosby (Eds.), *The Psychology and Management of Workplace Diversity* (pp. 299–316). Malden, MA: Blackwell.

Stockdale, M. S., & Crosby, F. (Eds) (2004). *The Psychology and Management of Workplace Diversity*. Malden, MA: Blackwell.

Stone, D., & Stone-Romero, E. (2004). The influence of culture on role-taking in culturally diverse organizations. In: M. Stockdale & F. Crosby (Eds.), *The Psychology and Management of Workplace Diversity* (pp. 78–99). Malden, MA: Blackwell.

Tajfel, H. (1981). Social stereotypes and social groups. In: J. C. Turner & H. Giles (Eds.), *Intergroup Behaviour*. Oxford: Blackwell.

Taylor, C. (1989). *Sources of the Self*. Cambridge: Cambridge University Press.

Taylor, C. (1994). *Multiculturalism*, A. Gutman (Ed.). Princeton, NJ: Princeton University Press.

Taylor, F. (1911). *Scientific Management*. New York: Harper Brothers.

Taylor, J. (2009). Luton fights back against right-wing extremists. *The Independent*, 3 June, pp. 16–17.

Thiederman, S. (2003). *Making Diversity Work - Seven Steps for Defeating Bias in the Workplace*. Chicago, IL: Dearborn Trade.

Thomas, K., Mack, D., & Montagliani, A. (2004). The arguments against diversity: are they valid? In: M. Stockdale & F. Crosby (Eds.), *The Psychology and Management of Workplace Diversity*. Malden, MA: Blackwell.

Thompson, N. (1995). *Age and Dignity: Working with Older People*. Aldershot: Arena.

Thompson, N. (2001). *Anti-Discriminatory Practice*. Basingstoke: Palgrave Macmillan.

Thorpe, V. (2010). Proms draw flak from equality groups over scarcity of women. *Independent*, 18 July, p. 15.

Times Online (2007). Lottery Funding. www.timesonline.co.uk/tol/comment/letters/article2532033.ece

Timmons, H. (2010). India claims a stake in world drug market. *The New York Times*, Sunday 18 July.

Travis, A. (2009). Police increasing searches to 'balance race data". *Guardian*, 8 July, p. 9. www.guardian.co.uk/uk/2009/jun/17/stop-search-terror-law-met

Travis, A. (2010). Black and Asian stop and search is up 70%. *Guardian*, 18 June, p. 16.

TUC (2005). *Diversity in Diction: Equality in Action – A Guide to the Appropriate Use of Language*. TUC/Unison www.tuc.org.uk/extras/Diversityindiction.pdf

Twitchett, D. (1974). *The Birth of the Chinese Meritocracy*. London: China Society.

Washington, V. (2007). When PC goes too far. www.deafdc.com/blog/vikki-washington/2007–01–22/when-pc-goes-too-far/

Wheen, F. (2004). *How Mumbo Jumbo Conquered the World*. London: Harper Perennial.

Williams, R., & Mulholland, H. (2009). Mayor intervenes in BNP Palace party row. *Guardian*, 22 May, p. 5.

Winnicott, D. W. (1965). *The Family and Individual Development*. London: Tavistock.

INDEX